Teaching Preschoolers in the Christian Community

Teaching Preschoolers in the Christian Community

Phoebe M. Anderson

Revised and updated by John M. Barrett

A revised and updated edition of the classic *3's in the Christian Community*

UNITED CHURCH PRESS
Cleveland, Ohio

United Church Press, Cleveland, Ohio 44115

"Helpful Rules of Thumb" on page 104 adapted with permission from Katherine H. Read, *The Nursery School* (rev. ed.; Philadelphia: W. B. Saunders, 1960), 72ff.

Biblical quotations are from the New Revised Standard Version of the Bible, © 1989 by the Division of Christian Education of the National Council of the Churches of Christ in the U.S.A., and are used by permission

Printed in the United States of America on acid-free paper

99 98 97 96 95 94 5 4 3 2 1

Library of Congress Cataloging-in-Publication Data

Anderson, Phoebe M.
Teaching preschoolers in the Christian community / Phoebe M. Anderson ; revised and updated by John M. Barrett.
p. cm.
Rev. and updated ed. of : 3's in the Christian community. c 1960.
Includes bibliographical references.
ISBN 0-8298-0922-8 (alk. paper)
1. Christian education of preschool children. I. Barrett, John M. II. Anderson, Phoebe M. 3's in the Christian community. III. Title.
BV1475.7.A53 1994
268'.432—dc20 94-6910
CIP

Contents

	Preface	vii
	Introduction	ix
Part I	Welcoming the Children	1
Letter 1	Meeting Charles	3
Letter 2	Company's Coming!	7
Letter 3	Doing Big Things in Little Space	11
Letter 4	How to Avoid Being in Three Places at Once	17
Letter 5	How to Plan Your Program	21
Letter 6	The First Sunday	23
Letter 7	The Second Sunday	31
Letter 8	Love and Understanding	35
Letter 9	Teachers Are Dependable: All Children Have Rights	39
Letter 10	A Change of Session Plans	47
An Extra Letter	How to Use the Resource Sections	51
	Resource Section I	55
Part II	Hearing the Children	101
Letter 11	How to Teach When You're Not Talking—and When You Are	103
Letter 12	Every Child Asks: "Who Am I?"	107
Letter 13	And "Who Are You?"	113
Letter 14	And "What Is the World Like?"	117
Letter 15	Listen: What Are They *Really* Saying?	119
Letter 16	Dealing with Fears and Feelings	123
	Resource Section II	129

Part III Guiding the Children 169

Letter 17 Lynn's Father Asks: "Is This *Christian* Education?" 171
Letter 18 The Use of the Bible with Preschool Children 175
Letter 19 What Kind of Prayer for Preschoolers? 179
Letter 20 Art Is Not for Art's Sake in the Preschool 183
Letter 21 Discipline, Hurtful or Helpful? 187
Letter 22 Summertime 191
Letter 23 They Are All Growing Older 195

Resource Section III 197

Appendix 221
Art Activities 221
Making Equipment 224
Supplies 231
Room Designs 233

Bibliography 235
Books for Teachers 235
Books for Children 236
Addresses 238

Preface

This updated edition of *3's in the Christian Community* is, like the first edition of 1960, very much focused on the child's needs and life. Every child, like the rest of us who are not children, needs love and care and support—all the time. Some days are bad days. We all have them whether we are three or thirty-three or seventy-three.

The changes that have been made in this edition are mostly editorial. First, the continuing drive for the equality of women has affected the English language. Not every child or student is a *he* nor every teacher of preschoolers a *she*. Nor is God always *He*. We have eliminated that language bias. Men are now recognized caregivers, and women have a variety of talents and occupations as well.

Second, reflecting the changing population, the children's and teachers' names have been made more inclusive.

Third, marital and family structures have changed dramatically since 1960. "My little brother," referred to by one of your preschoolers, may actually be the child's half-brother. Many children have only one parent, or a new parent and older or younger siblings. Changes in family life require getting used to just as all changes do. You may experience many situations that reflect this.

Fourth, the texts of five of my original storybooks, which had been published separately, are now incorporated within the resource sections.

Fifth, substitutions have been made for a few of the original finger plays, music, and poems. (Some permissions could not be renewed.) Additional selections have also been included.

Sixth, the bibliography, which lists books for children and for teachers and parents, has been updated by the consulting editor. Some of the books that were listed in the first edition are classics and will be so for a long time. We repeated them and added many current books which may also become classics in another thirty years.

Yet, the basic understanding of and attitude toward children expressed in the first edition is unchanged. In today's world your preschooler may be able to read, to print her or his name, or even use a computer. Nonetheless, that child—indeed, every child—needs love and care and understanding. You, the teacher (who is the church that the child knows), can and will provide that.

I am pleased and honored to be able to present this new edition of *3's*. Many teachers from many denominations, from Friends (Quakers) to Episcopalians, have written to me reporting successful experiences that have occurred in their Sunday church schools. I hope and pray that this edition will also be useful.

Phoebe M. Anderson

Introduction

Teaching Preschoolers in the Christian Community is concerned with the nature of preschool children and how they grow toward Christian maturity. It seeks to answer such questions as: Where and how does Christian growth occur? What are some of the steps along the way? How do Christian teachers help this growth take place?

The best way for teachers to learn the answers to these questions is to observe experienced, Christian teachers working, playing, and living with young children. Since this is not always possible, Phoebe Anderson, an experienced teacher, has written a series of letters to you describing actual incidents from her own experiences and observations to illustrate what young children are like and how they grow as Christians.

As Phoebe Anderson wrote these letters, she had in mind the questions and concerns you have: how to get ready for the children, how to help them feel at home in the church school, how to guide them in Christian growth, and how to work through problems that arise. Through firsthand reports of real teachers and children, you will be helped to think about yourself, your methods, and your understanding of the children whom you teach.

To teach, you also need resources of songs, stories, poems, and activities that will provide and enrich experiences for the children. These resources, together with suggestions for using them in your sessions, whether Sunday morning church school or weekday programs, are gathered in three sections.

The materials in Resource Section I are related to the child's first experiences in the church, the child and the family, fall time experiences, and Christmas. Resource Section II contains suggestions for developing the themes of wintertime, animals and pets, springtime and Easter, and friends. Resource Section III focuses on personal growth and summertime activities.

The Appendix contains art activities, directions for making equipment, a list of supplies, room designs, a bibliography of books for teachers and for children, addresses for materials, and acknowledgments and sources.

HOW TO USE THIS COURSE

Glance through the whole course: letters, resources, and appendix. Take the time to read all the letters. Give yourself a chance to respond to the whole picture of what preschool children are like and how they begin to develop their own faith. Know that you will be helping children ask and answer the following questions: Who am I? Who are you? What is the world like? Think about your own answers to these questions and your role as a teacher in the community of faith.

"An Extra Letter: How to Use the Resource Sections" (page 51) provides some guidelines for using resource material. Become thoroughly acquainted with the three resource sections. (Many of the separate picture books that accompanied the first edition of this book have been incorporated into the resource sections. Look for *Mr. Red Ears* and *The First Christmas*, two favorites.) Learn your way around the resource sections so that you will be able to use the story or song or activity that will stimulate new experiences or contribute to the experiences the children are having. Try out some of the activities, stories, songs, and finger plays. Jot down notes on where to find what you will need. Make this whole book *your* resource book.

Keep your own situation in mind as you use the materials. Build your sessions to fit *your* children and to deal with *their* needs and questions. Feel free to be flexible, to adapt, to change, and to create your own materials as you and the children become a Christian community.

Our task as Christian teachers is to surround our children with the reality of the Christian fellowship, past and present, so that they will respond to God in a free and responsible relationship, becoming active participants in the Christian community. In the preschool group we are building the foundation, helping children feel at home with the church, as they experience the love of God.

John M. Barrett

Part I

Welcome the Children

"Whoever welcomes one such child in my name welcomes me."
—Mark 9:37a

Photo © Kathryn Abbe

Letter I

Meeting Charles

So you are going to teach in the church preschool. Congratulations! I have taught preschool children for several years and have been asked to send you some ideas and materials to help you. I shall be glad to do that, for I am convinced that the help of an experienced teacher working alongside you is invaluable.

WHO IS COMING TO YOUR PRESCHOOL?

You will want to know who is coming as definitely as you can because it makes the beginning of your relationship with the children more confident and relaxed. I have often thought that the usual experience of being a teacher in church school is something like being a host to a dozen or so strangers invited into your home as they were passing down the street. You would not know whether they were hungry or thirsty or, if they were, what kinds of food or drink would best satisfy them. You would not know whether they needed entertainment, help, or earnest discussion. Worst of all, you could not so much as greet them by name. Even after being introduced, you can be sure that after the eighth or tenth guest had arrived you would probably have forgotten at least one name and confused several others. What an unthinkable way to treat guests!

But more often than not we treat children this way in our church schools. We know nothing about them, not even their names, but they have been invited to come to church. We, as teachers, are their hosts. In the eyes and experience of the children, their teacher represents the church. Their feelings about the kind of place the church is and the people who are the church depends largely on the kind of relationship they develop with you. If their teacher cannot even call them by name, how can they be sure that God knows and cares about them?

THERE'S SOMETHING MAGIC ABOUT A NAME

The ancients felt so and took care not to disclose their names to their enemies, lest the enemies work a hex or curse upon them. To know a child's name is the first step in knowing the child. This name will always be the symbol by which you think about that child as you plan for and pray for that child. To be able to address each child in the preschool group by her or his name is like saying to the child, "You belong here. You are important here. I know you, and you are significant to me." It is the first means you have for extending your warm feelings and friendship to a child. Most children are pleased by such a gesture—although you often would not guess that it mattered at all. We all like to have people remember our names. I am always pleased when someone whom I would not expect to know or remember me calls me by name. It makes me feel that

I am a little bit important, to that "someone" at least.

Try to get a list of names, addresses, telephone numbers, and birthdays of the children who might attend the preschool. You may not be able to obtain a complete list, but it will be a good start.

VISIT IN THE HOMES

One year I visited each child on my list before church school began, and I had the best year in the preschool in my five years. True, each year's experience helps, but when it comes to knowing a child, nothing takes the place of spending time with that child. The time I spent with each child and his or her family in their own home was worth six months of Sundays in the groups. If it is not possible to visit each home before church school begins, try to visit during the year if you can.

You may never have called on a family as a church school teacher. If you haven't, you may feel hesitant about it. You may feel unsure about what to do or say or how you will be received. I understand that, for I felt that way too; but after a few calls you will be more at ease and probably will find home visiting interesting and enjoyable.

Start with a family whom you know to have an active relationship in the church. Telephone ahead of time to make an appointment for the visit. For instance, Bobby Ames is a child on your list. You might say: "Mrs. Ames, I am the preschool teacher at (give her the name of your church and your name). According to our records, Bobby is old enough to enter the preschool class this September. Is that right? I would like to drop in for a short visit this week or next so that Bobby and I might become acquainted with each other. Would Saturday afternoon be convenient, or would some other time be better?"

I am sure you will find that a parent appreciates your interest in the child and your service to the church and that you will be cordially received. Most pleased of all will be Bobby, because his teacher came to see him. You may find that it quickly breaks the ice between you and Bobby to ask him if he would like to show you his toys.

During your visits you should tell the parents something about the preschool program—the free play; the rug time when the children rest, eat a cookie, listen to a story, sing, talk. The parents will want to know about the program both for themselves and in order to answer the child's questions. But guard against letting this visit be all conversation between you and the parent. The purpose of calls is to get to know the children as well as the parents and to let the children get to know you.

Telephone calls to other families on your list will bring different responses. One family may have moved away, another may be attending a different church, another may have lost interest. These things are good to know ahead of time, for they will help you determine who church preschool children are likely to be.

Even if you know every child on your list, try to make a call in each home especially to meet the children and to invite them to come to the church preschool.

WHEN I CALLED ON CHARLES

I remember well one of the first home visits I made. Charles thoroughly enjoyed my coming. He showed me everything he had and everything he could do, watched to see if I split my sandwich cookie to get the icing out the way he did, and was genuinely sorry to see me go. As I was leaving, he came running out of the house calling at the top of his voice: "I want to give you a kiss! I want to give you a kiss!" I submitted—that is the way I felt—to the expression of affection. I was highly amused and, of course, gratified.

From that call on I was set up. After Charles, it did not matter that there were some children who did not warm up to me, who did not show me anything they could do, who stood beside their mothers, speechless, and watched me and watched me and watched me. "Some children grow fast and some children grow slowly," I said to myself. "And some children like their teachers right away and a whole lot, and other children like their teachers not quite so quickly and not quite so much."

One complete acceptance sealed with a warm, wet kiss equipped me to handle many slow and timid relationships without feeling inadequate. I think it works this way with children too. Children who feel completely accepted by their teacher, even when they are not at their best, are better able to accept and get along with other persons, even when those other persons are not at their best. I hope you will find a Charles.

Letter 2 Company's Coming!

I just realized that the first session of your new church school year is not far off and I promised to write you some details about setting up the room and the equipment. Over the year things seem to become misplaced, so it is not too soon to take stock. (While I am thinking of things that become misplaced, I might mention that lost puzzle pieces can frequently be found under the radiators or the piano. Preschool teachers have to be flexible, the books tell us. It's true—especially in the back and leg muscles!)

A preschool room in a church reflects to a high degree the understanding of children and the idea of Christian education which the church holds. Our church believes that young children are active, moving persons rather than sitting-down persons and that play is the "work" of their lives. Through play they learn about things—what they are for and how to use them—and about people—what *they* are for and how *not* to use them. Through play, children dramatize, organize, digest their partial understandings and their bits of experience; through play they reveal what they do not understand, what they are anxious about or dislike. Through play—by watching, helping, listening, explaining—you may be able to establish a relationship with each child and to begin to understand what help the child needs to grow in the Christian community.

THE IMPORTANCE OF NUMBERS

I think the biggest factor in the excellence of a preschool program is the number of children you try to accommodate in a room. Nothing can handicap a teaching relationship so much as having too many children to relate to. Here are a few standards—established by educators of preschool children—which may help.

1. Every group, no matter how small, should have two teachers. You never can tell when an emergency may arise that will take the total attention of one teacher while the other teacher carries on with the rest of the group.
2. Five or six children to one teacher is a good ratio to follow. Two teachers can work with a group of six to twelve children. Three teachers are needed for a group of thirteen to eighteen children.
3. No group of preschool children should number more than fifteen to twenty children. Eighteen is usually considered the maximum.
4. Space requirements for preschool children are a minimum of thirty-five square feet per child, fifty square feet being preferred. For instance, the top enrollment for a room twenty by thirty feet is seventeen children. Why not take a pencil and figure how many children can be enrolled in your preschool room or space?

It may be that new housing developments around your community will bring a large number of young children to church. If that happens, be firm about not overcrowding your room. Other space can be found, somewhere. Having found some, you may discover that the best use of it requires that all the departments of the church school be relocated. Meet together with all the teachers and work out the necessary arrangements. Here is a hint: In general, preschool children should have the best space in the church. Often they have the worst.

SETTING UP THE PRESCHOOL ROOM

There are no hard and fast rules about how to arrange a preschool room any more than there are for a living room. Do it in any way that seems best for you and for the children. After you have lived with your arrangement for a while, you will begin to see how it can be improved; so change it, just as you do your living room.

Before you start moving furniture, sit down and draw a plan of your room. (You will find sample room layouts on pages 233 and 234.) You can rearrange interest centers on this paper plan until you have a likely-looking arrangement. Then tackle the room itself. I shall write about preschool rooms in small or shared space in my next letter, but here are a few suggestions to start your planning, no matter what size your room or space is:

1. Separate the lively, noisy activity from the more quiet activity. The play with blocks, cars, trucks, toy people and animals, as well as the riding toys, needs space and some separation.

A housekeeping center with dolls; doll beds; cupboard; stove; dishes; a small, low table; and chairs does not require a large space, but it should also have some separation. Place it in a corner if you can. I made a third wall one year with a row of preschool chairs with the seats facing in. The children often used the chairs as "the parent's bed" when they were dressing the dolls. The trouble was that the chairs did not stay in line. Perhaps you can find someone to build you a low, moveable screen. The screen has the advantage of providing a place for you to display pictures.

2. Have a rug that is large enough for *all* the children to sit on—although they may never all sit at once. A good rug that is vacuumed each week is best. Have the rug cleaned before the opening of the fall term and just before Christmas and Easter. The use of a rug eliminates the confusion of moving chairs and gives you more space.

3. Place one or two small tables, the size that four chairs can go around, next to the rug. The tables will be used for looking at books and working puzzles. The rug could also be used for these activities if the places at the tables are all taken. These are quiet activities and might well be next to the housekeeping center.

4. Place a low table with the offering basket, a Bible, and a bowl of flowers or a plant or something beautiful or interesting at the edge of the rug. I call this table the "special table," for it is just that in the minds of the children. Here is the special book, the Bible, and the offering basket for the children's special money, their church school money. (As children grow older, they begin to associate this special table and the special symbols of our faith with worship, and the table is called a worship center. Candles and the cross are added, usually in the upper elementary grades, as children begin to develop an understanding of these symbols. For junior and senior high and adults, the communion table or altar becomes a center for worship.)

5. Place a piano, if you have one, at the edge of the rug for singing time. A piano is not at all necessary, however, for singing in the preschool. A two-octave xylophone, a guitar, a keyboard, an omnichord, or an Autoharp is very satisfactory; so is your singing voice or a recording.

6. Art activity tables and easels should be as close to a source of water as is feasible. However, if the water is some distance away, ten steps more or less make no difference, so place the tables and easels where they have good light and can be a little apart from the other interest centers. It may be helpful to bring a pail of water, a stack of paper towels, and a few sponges into the room before your session begins. This will minimize the necessity of the children leaving the room for the purpose of washing their hands.

7. Devise some place for your own supplies, such as rubber bands, paper clips, pencils, pens, markers, paper, records or cassettes, string, tape, and other items. I have used an old roll-top writing desk and stored the children's books and puzzles in the space below. I have also used a tall, metal, kitchen cabinet, keeping the top shelves for my supplies and storing crayons, paste, construction paper, and the like on the lower shelves, where the children could get them. You might be able to use a hanging wall shelf for your supplies.

8. Hooks or lockers or cubbyholes for children's coats should be in place and at a height that children can use easily. These may be in a corridor adjoining the preschool room, in a small room that opens off the preschool room, or in the room itself, if you have enough space.

IS EVERYTHING READY?

Having everything in the preschool room ready to go is one of the biggest helps there is for having a happy, productive time. If the clay is hard, the paste dried out, the dolls still undressed from the last session, and the puzzle pieces all mixed up, you will spend your mornings housekeeping instead of living with and responding to children. The housekeeping need not be burdensome if you and the other teachers come half an hour before the children arrive each day and stay ten or fifteen minutes after the close of the session. Beyond that, occasionally laundering the doll clothes, washing up the doll dishes, cleaning the stuffed animals, and repairing equipment now and then is about all you need to do during the regular church school year.

Here is a checklist I developed for myself. You might use it until you think up one that is more exact for your purposes.

1. Is the room clean?
   - floor
   - rug
   - curtains
   - windows
   - furnishings

2. Are the toys clean, in good repair, in place, and easily available to the children?
   - cars, trucks, trains, tools
   - unit blocks, large hollow wooden blocks
   - dolls, doll clothes
   - soft cuddly dolls or animals
   - dress-up clothes
   - play dishes
   - table and chairs
   - books
   - puzzles
   - easels, brushes, smocks or aprons

3. Are there enough supplies for the first month?
   - tempera paint
   - large crayons (several boxes of eight colors each)
   - skin-tone crayons
   - paste
   - clay or dough clay
   - newsprint for painting
   - manila construction paper for crayoning, pasting
   - colored construction paper

4. Is there a pretty cloth for the special table? a vase or bowl to hold flowers, cattails, pussy willows, or whatever is in season? a stand to hold a picture from time to time? a Bible?

5. Are there a few mounted pictures which can be used to make the room more attractive, to illustrate a story, to depict diversity, or just for looking at and talking about?

A picture file is an excellent asset. You can get one together surprisingly quickly, by saving pictures from old calendars, magazines, and newspapers and by mounting them as you use them.

Now make two name cards for each child. One should be small enough to be taped to the wall beside each coat hook. Each child should have a place for coats and sweaters. Tape the name cards in place, alphabetically, before the first session. You can identify the child's place by the name card. Children can identify their own places by small pictures or stickers beside their coat hooks. Each child may choose a picture the first session from some you have prepared ahead of time. You can often secure suitable small pictures by cutting up worn-out children's picture books or toy catalogs. Or you can buy stickers. Help each child put the picture or sticker in place.

The second card should be larger, or a size that you can read a few feet away. The children will wear these with their names on them. Make one for yourself, too, so you will each know who the other is. For these cards you might use colored construction paper cut in various shapes, such as gingerbread persons, squirrels, and leaves. Use a small safety pin, not a straight pin, for pinning on the name cards. Get some plain cookies or those delectable cinnamon graham crackers. One way you can help children rest a bit at the close of a stimulating or long morning is to have them sit down and eat a snack. The parents will be glad their children are not cross and ravenously hungry the minute they get home from church. You can change the character of this snack and have fruit or vegetables too. Try not to make the snack too sweet or too much.

TWO MORE THINGS

Now you are almost ready for the first session. What yet remains to be done? Two things:

Stand at the door of the room and imagine how Miriam, the lively one; Hiro, the cautious one; and Ralph, the fearful one, will feel as they enter the room. (It even helps to crouch down and look around the room from the children's eye level.) If you are feeling a little uncertain about what may happen, think how much more uncertain the children must be feeling! They do not know what it is like to go to church, who will be there, how anyone will act, who will take care of them if their parents leave, or what they will be allowed to do with all those interesting playthings.

They may come to the preschool not knowing anyone they can depend on or trust and not feeling at all sure they belong there or will want to stay. Your job, then, during that first session—in fact the whole year—is to become the children's grown-up friend whom they can trust and, at the same time, to provide for them the kinds of experiences that assure them that they belong.

How you will do this will be different for each child. In general you will welcome the children by using their names and telling them yours. You may help each choose a coat hook and tape his or her name beside the picture. Perhaps you will tell the children that they can play with whatever they like while parents are in their adult class or in worship, and that you will be in the room with them all morning if they need anything. In general, you will stoop down when you speak to children so you can look in their faces. You will be relaxed, unhurried, genuine, and warm. You will welcome each child as you would a guest in your home, as an interesting delightful person with whom it will be your pleasure to live for a brief hour or two each visit.

And even if you were once accustomed to wearing nice or dressy clothes to church, rethink this! I learned this years ago from Ramone, who asked me halfway through the first Sunday morning, "Teacher, why are you so dressed up? Are you going someplace?" That was the beginning of my dressing down for preschool teaching on Sundays, from graceful high heels to comfortable walking shoes; from slim sheath to full skirt or slacks. Now I can sit on the floor, hold two children at once, or play "High Stepping Horses." Thanks to my pretty, printed smock that the children love to study, I can mix finger paint or wet down the clay with vigor.

The second thing that yet remains to be done? Get a colorful smock or a brightly colored washable shirt for yourself.

Letter 3 Doing Big Things in Little Space

If you are meeting with the children in some kind of space that is less than perfect, this letter is particularly for you. I cannot really solve your space problems, but I will try to help you work at them. Any situation can be improved if someone wants badly enough to see it improved. I hope that someone is you.

CONSIDER THE SPACE

If your space is large and cheerless and barnlike—this is not the usual complaint, but there are some teachers who face that problem—rejoice at the largeness and begin thinking in terms of paint, curtains or draperies, and a rug for part of the room. Curtains can be made quite inexpensively from unbleached muslin trimmed with rickrack or varied bindings.

But if the space is small, crowded, or shared with different age groups, you may have to begin shifting and rearranging, knocking down partitions or making new ones in order to make an attractive and valuable church home for the preschool.

You know the standards for preschool children: at least thirty-five square feet of floor space per child, good light, good heat, near bathroom facilities, furnishings scaled to size, sturdy equipment that can be used creatively, room clean and attractive.

Where should the preschool be in a room that has to be shared by other age groups? Wherever the children will be least disturbed and disturbing to the other groups. If that place could also have outside light and be close to the bathroom facilities, that would be good. Or if the preschool could be placed close to where the equipment, furniture, rug, and materials are stored during the week (I am assuming that you cannot leave your space set up), it will be easier for you, your coteachers, and the custodian to set up the equipment and put it away again. Do not let the preschool space become the traffic lane for other groups. It must "feel" separated, or the children will be constantly distracted.

THERE ARE MANY WAYS TO SEPARATE SPACE

Three-panel screens, five and a half feet high, can be used for hanging pictures at the children's eye level; and grownups and big children will not be tempted to look over the top at the young children. Tall screens knock over easily, however, and children like to crawl or reach under them. Lower, rectangular, one-panel screens do not knock over. They are often used for one wall of the housekeeping center and might prove useful to separate the entire preschool area.

An upright piano, its back toward you, might offer a partial solution to the preschool's need for separation. Cover the back with burlap and you will be able to use it as a picture board.

Curtains strung on wires divide space visually but not audibly. They are easier to handle than screens,

Photo from Sunrise/Trinity Photos, © Robert Meier

but preschoolers love to play and hide in the curtains.

Two or three open shelves, three feet high, twenty inches deep, and four feet long, mounted on casters, can be built to house blocks, cars, other small equipment, and the art supplies available to the children. They may be placed in the room to form a partial wall. (See diagrams on page 230.)

IF YOU HAVE TOO MANY CHILDREN

If you have too many children in your group, none of these ideas about rearranging and separating space may be helpful. Look first for any unused space in the church and see if it could be made usable. Even kitchens and balconies have, with some work and ingenuity, been transformed into pleasant and possible, if not ideal, space for children. A second solution is to divide the group and have two sessions at different times.

If you have used all the space and doubled your sessions and still need space, obviously some group has to move out. I knew a wonderful fifth- and sixth-grade group that met in the basement of a nearby home. The children loved it. It was their room, and they painted the walls and fixed it up. In other communities the village hall, a neighboring public school, or nearby homes of church members have provided space for different age groups; or older children might have their church school classes on a weekday afternoon or evening, releasing space for the younger children on Sunday. The younger children need their parents close at hand, and they need to begin their church relationship in the church building.

Once you have the best space you can possibly get, make it clean and attractive. Dirty windows do not give very clear pictures of God's world, and dirty walls and floors do not speak to the child of thought and concern for God. Coming to church is a strange experience for preschoolers at best. If the place to which they come is dull, dirty, and unattractive, the experience is even more uninviting. "Cleanliness is next to godliness," my grandmother used to tell me. I have discovered that there is more to it than rhythmic words: a feeling of peace and quiet and harmony comes over me when I am in a clean, light room. I never feel the same way in a soiled, careless, down-at-the-heels-looking room. I feel like staying in the pleasant room; I feel like leaving the dirty, dull one. You know how good you feel in your own living room after a good job of housecleaning. Children respond to order, color, cleanliness, light, just as we do.

Paint is not too expensive or difficult to put on, and it can make more difference in the attractiveness of your space than anything else I can think of. Light greens or blues are good colors for warm, sunny rooms. Light yellows or ivory will warm and brighten a room that has less light and heat. If you can add some bright contrasting colors in the print of the curtains or on an occasional piece of painted furniture, all the better. If you paint tables and chairs for the children, keep the table surfaces a color that is easy on children's eyes and that does not intrude itself into the creative art activities. In other words, keep the color neutral—not cherry red or deep aquamarine, as I have seen in some places. If you have chairs of different heights, you might use different colors of paint to help the children distinguish them, as well as to lend contrast to the room. Parents can do this painting at an evening work party. Such a party is usually fun for the parents and a great improvement for the preschool.

THE FURNISHINGS AND EQUIPMENT

You can get along with a minimum of furnishings if necessary. In fact, if your space is limited, you can do almost entirely without tables and chairs. Children can sit on a rug for nearly everything they can do in limited space. Instead of tables use 16-inch-square plywood boards for working with clay or crayons. Cover the boards with heavy plastic when you use clay.

A child-sized table and two chairs for playing house with dolls and dishes in one corner, a low chair for you to sit on at story time (the children can hear and see you better if you are sitting a little above them), and the special table may well be all the tables and chairs you require. Some churches have found that a table, hinged to the wall, which can be dropped out of the way provides a good work surface for children and does not take up space when not needed.

As I mentioned before, open shelves for the children's toys and supplies and some kind of cupboard space for your supplies are necessities. Fortunately, they are not difficult to construct. (See pages 229–32.) Open shelves can be built into unused space alongside heating units, fireplaces, or chimney walls. Old bookcases can be made into good open shelves by cutting off the legs and removing any doors.

You do not need a piano. Children can learn a song from hearing you sing it or by listening to a record or tape. The songs included in the resources are not difficult; some of them may be familiar to you. I have known several preschool teachers who have used guitars, keyboards, Autoharps, or small xylophones to accompany the children's singing. These instruments are fine for little space because they are small and easily portable.

The only other item you need is a rug—a clean one. Preschoolers spend much time playing on the floor, and a rug is desirable especially if the floor is cold. A rug for the children to sit on during story time is more valuable than chairs.

Equipment, too, should be determined by your space. Try, if you can possibly manage it, to have at least three interest centers: one for blocks and cars; one for dolls, beds, and dishes; and one for clay or crayons or pasting, books, and puzzles.

Inexpensive materials can be used to make most of this equipment. I have seen child-size stoves, cupboards, refrigerators, sinks, even chairs, made from crates or scrap lumber. (See page 226.) Doll beds and cradles can be made, too. Doll clothes made by hand are better than the ready-made ones. The doll clothes should have large snap fasteners and good seams and openings.

The blocks are unit dimensional. This means that the large ones are two or four times the size of the smallest one. (They are described on page 225.) Blocks made by a group of parents cost much less than commercial ones. If you have to improvise until the blocks are finished, perhaps you can secure a large bag of mill ends from a local lumber company. They have to be sanded and are not as stimulating to build with because the children cannot match sizes and shapes, but they are better than the two-inch-square blocks every toy store sells for children. If you have some small blocks on hand, keep them for loading into dump trucks or trains, but provide bigger blocks for building.

WHAT NOT TO HAVE

Do away with the battery and windup toys, the stuffed ones that are beyond cleaning, the broken ones that cannot be repaired, and the doll house with furniture that is just dandy for seven and eight year olds but not for preschool children. Cut out pictures from the torn and backless books and save for another use. Discard all cardboard puzzles. Put aside the coffee can of dirty, broken crayons and everything else that looks like a discard. If you have nothing left, obviously there is work to be done.

In many churches parents have developed a good relationship with one another and an understanding of the needs of preschool children in the church by spending three or four work nights at the church doing over the preschool room and equipment. Some parents may paint, sand, or sew curtains and doll clothes. Others repair, tighten up, paint, and construct. They have refreshments at the end of the evening. Perhaps you could start some work parties rather than trying to do everything yourself. Just be sure you have everything ready for such an evening. Have three or four people cut out doll clothes and set up the paint work and the repair section ahead of time. Two or three projects that can be finished are better than half a dozen just started. Some parents may offer to take items home. Be sure to record who has what and note when it will be returned.

THE PROGRAM

With small or shared space, your program will have to be adapted to fit, just as the furnishings and equipment have been. Choose activities from the resource sections that are suitable for your situation. You may know of others equally good that are not in this book. It does not matter where the idea comes from, but it does matter that the *children can do it* (not you do it for them) to *their* own satisfaction (not to your standards).

In general, your program—no matter how much or how little equipment you have or what kinds of creative art activities you can provide—should develop from the interests and abilities and concerns of the children. They will grow in their personal relationships with one another and with you, and in their feelings of worth and belonging, more quickly and surely if they are given considerable freedom in what they do and how they do it for a good part of each session.

Teaching a few children in a small space can be fun and has many assets. The biggest advantage you have is the opportunity to know your children and their parents well, to call on them before church school starts, and to visit them during the year. The second advantage is your mobility. With four or five children you can be outdoors in a few minutes to plant bulbs, play shadows, gather leaves, or take a treasure walk.

But, as I said before, small space and hordes of children must not be tolerated. A child's relationship to the church can be affected for all his childhood years by his feeling alone, not cared about, and nameless in a room full of too many children.

Look once more at your space. Use your own critical eye and your children's feelings and point of view. Does the space show your concern for children, your understanding of the kind of persons they are and the needs they have? Will your children be enticed to enter this room because it beckons them? Will they feel expected and wanted here? Will they be eager to return for the next session?

If the answer is no or maybe, do not feel discouraged. Even lethargic and tradition-bound churches have been known to make radical—well, no, but pretty thorough—changes in their church schools. Surely your situation can be improved. The change must start with a person who has both zeal and understanding. The next move is yours!

Letter 4 How to Avoid Being in Three Places at Once

Some time ago I saw three teachers arrive at the preschool room. They took off their coats and mingled with the children. Within fifteen minutes, two of them had turned into spectators. It was a subtle transformation; even the third teacher did not realize what had happened at first. The two teachers sat in small chairs. Sometimes they talked with each other, but mostly they smiled benignly at the children. Only when the noise of falling block towers or the clatter of tin dishes became worrisome did either of them go to the place of discord. They restored order, spoke briefly to whichever child was at hand, and quickly relaxed into their half-bored, half-amused postures.

They did nothing wrong, mind you. They also did nothing good and valuable other than protect children and preserve the furnishings. It could almost be said they did nothing. Only one teacher of the three kept a lively mind; awareness and understanding of the children were apparent in responses to them. But the teacher could not do the kind of teaching that is desirable because of being needed in three places at once.

No one can do that, of course. Every preschool group of fifteen to eighteen children needs three *teachers*. Small groups need two teachers. Why? In every group there should be a teacher free to go for a parent when needed, to take a child to the bathroom, or to go for help in an emergency without creating another emergency by leaving children without adequate care.

EACH TEACHER PLAYS A POSITION

Teaching preschool children is something like playing baseball. You must be alert to a whole field of activity and, at the same time, play your own position. If you make the mistake of trying to play the field, you may miss an important opportunity at your own position. On the other hand, if you become so single-minded about your own position that you do not hear or see what is happening in the rest of the field, you are very likely to make the wrong play, although you have been faithful to your appointed place.

LET US TAKE AN EXAMPLE

Suppose each teacher in the preschool room assumes responsibility for part of the room. Perhaps you have the art activity table. The children are pasting colored shapes on sheets of construction paper. To an observer you may not seem to be doing very much. The paste and paper are at hand, and the children are proceeding on their own.

You look around the room and see Keisha carefully building a tower of blocks. This also may mean nothing to the observer. But it means a great deal to you and, you know, to Keisha. For three sessions Keisha has painstakingly laid block on block only to have the whole structure fall down just short of the last block which she had chosen for the top. Today she is trying again, patiently, completely absorbed. The tower goes higher and higher, until it is nearly as tall as she is. Almost breathlessly she puts on the last block. She slowly takes her hand away, but she hardly dares to move her eyes lest the whole structure fall. Finally, she looks up, triumphant. This is a moment of high achievement for her. It is even more joyous because you are celebrating it with her. A nod and an approving smile from you across the room tell Keisha that you know and you understand what an important, exciting thing she has done. Without saying a word, you are helping her rejoice in her new accomplishment. You are her teacher, in deed. (I really intend that space in the two words "in deed.")

Had you been giving every bit of your attention to the children who were pasting at a time when no child needed or wanted you particularly, you would have missed Keisha's triumph. Had you crossed the room to rejoice with Keisha, you would not have been on hand to hear Billy say to Carmen, "I have lots of smelly, squishy 'grunt' on my fingers. Do you want some?" Carmen titters and looks up at you, wondering what you will say or do. "Billy isn't talking nice," she tells you.

"Paste feels smooth and slippery," you say, responding more to Billy's experience than Carmen's report. "That's one reason it is fun to play with paste. It feels like soft mud. Did you ever make mud pies?"

Then Keisha is at your side at the pasting table, flushed with excitement, her eyes dancing. Now you have three children to teach.

Carmen and Billy say that they have never made mud pies. "I'm sure someday you'll have the chance to," you reply. "It's fun to do things you haven't done before. Keisha just did something she has never done before. She built a big high tower that didn't fall down."

While Carmen and Billy agree that *they* have built towers many times, you give Carmen a large sheet of paper and a pile of brightly colored paper shapes. She begins spreading paste with gusto.

Carmen and Billy say together, "We're through, Teacher. Where's the sponge for our fingers? We want to build with the blocks."

HOW THREE TEACHERS WORK TOGETHER

Here is an outline that will give you an idea of what I mean by working together. Actually, you may work out your responsibilities in a much different way. Let us say that you and Mary and Tim are the teachers. Your church preschool runs for an hour each Sunday.

10:30 *All* teachers arrive—not just one! Tim sets out manila paper and fat crayons, colored paper cut out in geometric shapes, and paste on one table. He puts dough clay on another table. On some days he may have easel painting or finger painting materials to get ready, and, of course, aprons. The art activity is a big responsibility. Mary puts finishing touches on the housekeeping center and checks on the dress-up clothes. She places a few books and a few puzzles on their respective tables. She also puts a pan on the stove.

You check on the block center and the cars and trucks. You also put the cloth on the special table and place a picture, a Bible, the offering basket, and a bowl of flowers on it. Note that any music books you need are in place. Be sure name tags and pins, pictures for coat hooks, and registration cards are ready. Check condition and temperature of room and bathroom. Your responsibilities are the block center and the general direction.

10:45–11:05 Tim and you welcome children and their parents, take care of name tags and cards, and help children begin to feel at home. The program begins when the first child arrives. At 10:55 Tim may have to become the responsible teacher in the room while you greet the rest of the children. It all depends on how many children you have and where Tim is most needed at the moment. Mary, who is taking care of the housekeeping, dress-up, and the books and puzzles, can seldom leave her post to help a child who may be across the room.

11:05–11:35 Each child plays freely. During this time each teacher is at their post, helping when needed. The teacher may converse with the children if doing so does not intrude on their play. Each teacher listens to the children's conversation and questions, observes what they play and how, and thoughtfully tries to assess the quality of the experience each child is having, *but does not intrude.*

From time to time any teacher may read a child a story, but two teachers should not get tied down with books at the same time. It is very hard to watch and listen to all parts of the room when you are reading.

About 11:35—or before, if the children seem to be played out—each teacher tells each child in their area, personally and individually, that it is time to come to the rug for a snack.

11:35–11:50 **(about)** Serve your guests cookies. If the cookies are in a basket, the children can help pass them to one another. You sit on the low chair beside the special table. The children sit on the rug, facing you. Mary and Tim help pass cookies and show children how and where to sit. After the children have finished their snacks, invite them to participate in the songs or finger plays. You direct the group time.

1. Start the conversation or finger plays
2. Tell a story about the picture on the special table or read from a picture book. (You may wish to start with a story some sessions.)
3. Say a sentence prayer related to the story or conversation.
4. Sing with actions:

This is the way we wash our hands,
. . . .
So early Sunday morning.
Tune: "Here We Go Round the Mulberry Bush"

Sing another song if you wish.

Not all children will stay on the rug for the story and singing. Some will go back to their unfinished play or find something else. We expect this. Few preschoolers are group-minded. As they approach four, they will nearly all stay through the group time. Mary or Tim will need to help the children who leave the group to play quietly so that they do not disturb those listening on the rug.

11:50–12:05 **(or until the parents come)** Children may continue free play or help put away toys. Tim will probably be putting away the paint and clay. He might leave the crayons out during these last few minutes. You might work with children picking up in the other corners of the room. Mary may stay on the rug reading, singing, helping children work puzzles, doing finger plays, or whatever is suitable.

12:05–12:20 All teachers finish picking up, cleaning up, putting away:

Remove torn or broken equipment until it can be repaired
Wash paintbrushes
Tightly wrap and cover modeling clay
Put all puzzles together

POINTS TO REMEMBER

The points to remember about this schedule are that the timing must be flexible and that *any* of the activities are dispensable—on any one day, not for always. There is no part of this program that is of superior value to the other parts. What you plan to tell or sing or talk about on a given morning is one means by which Carlos or Liu, Daiki or Sue may grow toward Christian maturity. This talking part of the program should be thought of as part of the environment, like the toy iron and ironing board, fascinating and meaningful to some, mildly interesting to a few, holding no attraction at all for others. Use whatever song, story, finger play, conversation, or activity that serves your emphasis for the session and is valuable and interesting to the children.

Growth toward Christian maturity takes place through the *experiences* the child has with the teachers and the other children in the preschool room. The songs and prayers and stories are part of the total experience, as are the toys and interest centers. From the child's point of view, the talking is not always the important part. You can check this with the children themselves. They can often tell you what they did on a morning. Rarely can they tell you what they heard.

If you are feeling a little unsure of your ability to tell stories, sing songs, and pray prayers with children, it may help you to know that your teaching goes far beyond the materials you prepare ahead of time. The words are important, but they are not all-important. Your willingness to try new things and to love the children and share your faith with them are what matter the most.

Letter 5 How to Plan Your Program

To plan a session successfully, all the preschool teachers need to sit down and work it out together. The planning is a group process. Teaching young children should be a shared responsibility. One teacher cannot do the job that should be done if the other teachers confine their activities to tying shoes, wiping noses, or reading books.

If you who are reading this letter are a couple, you are a team right from the beginning. The children in your care are especially fortunate. Whether you are a man or woman teacher, that is wonderful. Most children enjoy having a "father" or "uncle" teacher as well as a "mother" or "aunt" teacher.

Whoever you are, set up some good teachers' meetings. Until you really get under way, you may want to hold a meeting every week. After you have learned to work together and the children are feeling happy and secure in the room, try meeting every two weeks. You may want to continue meeting every two weeks throughout the year. Or you may feel that meeting once a month is enough. But do not meet less often than that. If you do, your teaching will be less and less sensitive (and less exciting to you); your program will find itself settling into a great big rut.

PLANNING YOUR PROGRAM

These four steps will help you plan and evaluate your program. At your first meeting begin with step one. At all other meetings, begin with step four, the evaluation. On the basis of what happened the previous session, plan the program for the following session or sessions.

1. Consider the interest centers. Plan as many as your space will permit. The more restricted your space, the more important it is to do away with tables and chairs. Get a good clean rug. Save one low chair and a small table, as suggested in the letter "Doing Big Things in Little Space." Use small boards for work surfaces.

From time to time, change one of the interest centers entirely. With few children and little space, you may have to choose between the creative art activity table and the block center. After a few sessions of one, change to the other. This way you can provide good experiences for all the children.

Whether your space is large or small, plan to introduce some new equipment now and then to add variety and interest. You might bring in several large cardboard cartons (see page 147) or some new (to the children) things for the dress-up box.

2. Decide on an art activity. Change it at least every other session. Avoid the "dog-eared coloring book, broken dirty crayon" activity at all costs. Every church can invest in a few large crayons and twelve-by-eighteen-inch sheets of plain paper, at the very least. The church that does not make an effort on behalf of its children does not really care about them, in spite of what it professes.

Do not feel that each child must take something home every session. If some children do not enjoy the art activity, there is no reason why they should be expected to engage in it. If they wish to, let them take home whatever they create.

If materials and equipment for art activities are not available in your community, write for one of the catalogs listed on page 239.

3. Work out a time schedule and an area of responsibility schedule for each teacher. These should change from time to time to accommodate the teachers' skills and interests and the children's growth. For example, in the spring of the year the group time can be longer than in the fall. The children will have longer attention spans; will enjoy longer, more complex stories; can carry on conversation better; and can participate in music and rhythms more enjoyably.

Decide together on the group time material that will fit the theme or the unit with which you are concerned. If you hold your meetings early in the week, the teachers who are responsible for this part of the program (one teacher may do the music, another the story-conversation) will have ample time to get the material well in hand the night before class.

4. Evaluate the session at each of the following points:

A. Interest Centers: Are they in the best place in the room? Are they adequately equipped? Is it time for something new? Have the children made suggestions or indicated interests?

B. Art Activity: Was it one the children could do with satisfaction and without the teachers' help at every turn? Was it creative rather than copy work? Did we encourage the children to express their own ideas and feelings? Did it provide a stimulation to conversation? For example, cutting Halloween pumpkins leads to talk of seeds and falltime and God's "plan" and to singing "This Is the Fall-time." Did it bring forth an expression of feelings and imagination, as painting and clay work usually do?

C. Time and Responsibility Schedules: Did these schedules work easily and satisfactorily for both teachers and children? Do the children need more free play time or a longer group time on the rug? Are there some children—or some teachers—who are overstimulated? Do we need more teachers to help? Do the teachers need to exchange or enlarge their individual responsibilities?

D. Group Time on the Rug: Did each teacher have a part in making this a good experience for the children? (Helping the children who are not on the rug to play quietly where they are, sitting beside a child who is restless or between two with the giggles, and holding one who is tired are all ways of making the group time experience a good one for the children.) Was the story too long, too short, understandable, important to the children?

E. The Children: This is the most important point. Is each child happy? Does each child feel secure? Is there something appealing for each child to do? Which child needs particular help? What kind of help might we provide? Are there ways in which each child is growing toward Christian maturity?

F. Ourselves: What are we doing well? What should we be doing better? How are we growing in our understanding of each child, in our ability to love and to respect each one? (Go down the roll, one by one.) What person-to-person relationships are being developed with each child?

Are you tired of reading and thinking and planning for your first session? If you are, stop working for a while and practice making one of the recipes in the Appendix (see pages 221–24). If you can get a young child to join you, that's fine. But, if not, play with whatever you make yourself and find out what it's like. The chances are that when you were three or four your parent or your teacher did not have these wonderful recipes for fun. You probably have some catching up to do. Wish I could join you. I like to finger paint my own Christmas wrapping paper. Maybe you would like to try it too.

Letter 6 The First Sunday

The preschool teachers in a church near me let me observe the first Sunday with a new group of children. It was a good session, and I asked their permission to write to you about what I saw. I have added notes of explanation and interpretation at the end of each section.

GETTING READY

Mrs. Kaufman, Mrs. Furushima, and Mr. Greene had obviously worked hard to be ready for this first Sunday. They had determined to change their drab half of the church basement into, if not a place of beauty, at least a place with color and charm for preschoolers. It was not quite finished, but the transformation was thrilling to everyone. The teachers and parents had held two work parties with great success. The concrete block walls and pillars had been painted light green. The high windows had been curtained with thin white sheeting so as not to cut down the light. The custodian had put brighter bulbs in the ceiling fixtures. The room looked bright and clean and cheerful.

One parent, who was a carpenter, had built two open shelves on casters to house blocks and cars. These shelves were lined up next to an old cabinet, which was the teachers' supply cupboard, to form part of a wall. Screens from the church's storeroom completed the separation.

Unfortunately, good blocks were part of the unfinished business. For this Sunday, well-sanded lumber scraps were used as blocks. They were better than those dinky squares the children had previously used for building.

Furniture for the housekeeping center had come from attics and basements all over the community. Doll bed, dresser, table, chairs, and an old cupboard were all painted blue. They really looked as though they were meant to be together. The dolls and doll clothes were cleaned and repaired. The new toys added to this center were some play and/or real tools in a small tool box and some durable, good-sized play dishes. Mrs. Furushima, who had set up this interest center, planned to add a child-sized broom and mop later.

Two new books, one about firefighters and one about babies, an airplane puzzle, and a duck puzzle had been laid on top of two crates that were nailed together to make a low, square table. This was placed near the rug. The crate-table was definitely makeshift until a bookrack and a puzzle rack could be completed. The rug was one of those limp kinds woven from reused wool, but it was large and warm and did not skid on the concrete floor.

For the creative art activity the teachers had felt that dough clay would be appealing on the first Sunday. It was Mr. Greene's responsibility to make it and to take charge of it on Sunday. The only table was a long, low, church dining table. The chairs were small, wooden ones (folding chairs can be dangerous with small children). They were not the best, but they had to do for a time. It was fortunate that

Photo by Rohn Engh

the room was large enough so that the table did not take up too much of the space.

The custodian had obligingly attached a board three feet off the floor along the wall of the hall outside the basement door. Coat hooks, twelve inches apart, were screwed into the board. There were just fourteen. "It certainly should be enough, but you never can tell."

Mrs. Kaufman's responsibility had been to set up the special table. Her husband had produced a low table by shortening the legs of an old stand. Covered with a white cloth it was passable, but it was on the list for the next round of painting. Mrs. Kaufman had placed her own Bible, the offering basket, and a white pitcher full of bright orange bittersweet on the table. She had put her "story chair" beside it.

Mrs. Kaufman had also made a picture stand. (See page 230 for directions.) She had mounted a picture of people going to church to put in the stand and had placed this on the table too.

The three teachers had called on the twelve children whom the church records showed were ready for the preschool class. Seven of the twelve had even visited the preschool room with a parent on Saturday morning and had chosen their coat hooks, had helped put up their name cards, and had played for a few minutes with the toys.

NOTES ON PREPARATION

Everything was ready—equipment, materials, records, registration forms, name tags, including a few extras for newcomers. The teachers were free to get acquainted with, listen to, and respond to children. This was a good first step in showing a child the teacher's (and God's) love is present within the church.

GREETING THE CHILDREN

All the teachers were on hand early to finish the last-minute preparations. The blocks and toy cars were in place on their new shelves. Mr. Greene was seated at the too-long table with a ball of yellow dough clay in front of him. Three other balls were in place before empty chairs. Mrs. Furushima was dressing a baby doll in the housekeeping center.

Putting name tags on the children was fun to do and provided a point of conversation right at the beginning. Ping didn't want his name on. That was all right—no one would forget who he was. Louis wanted to have his name on, but he wanted his big brother to pin it on, not the teacher. That was all right too. Shelley looked so distrustful and frightened as she and her mother entered the room that Mrs. Kaufman decided not to approach her at all at first. Instead she walked over and introduced herself to Shelley's mother.

"Good morning. I am one of the preschool teachers—Mrs. Kaufman."

"How do you do, Mrs. Kaufman. I'm Mrs. Ridge, and this is Shelley."

"Hello, Shelley," said Mrs. Kaufman.

Mrs. Ridge went on, "We're rather new here and this is our first Sunday. She won't want me to leave."

"We understand that. It takes time to become acquainted with a new place. Have a chair here at the edge of the room, Mrs. Ridge, and enjoy your visit. Before you leave, will you complete this registration card so we'll have Shelley on our roll?"

Then Mrs. Kaufman stooped to talk to Shelley, who peeked from behind her mother. "I'm glad you came to our church, Shelley. If you see something you would like very much to do this morning, just go and do it, won't you?"

Shelley said nothing. Mrs. Kaufman gave the mother an understanding nod and returned to the door. Mrs. Furushima was helping to greet and tag children now, since they were coming into the room two and three at a time.

Rhoda bounced in, a short, cheerful three-and-a-half year old. "Hello, Mrs. Kaufman. Here I am. I comed to school."

"Hello, Rhoda, I'm glad you came. We are all wearing our names today so that we shall know who one another is. Here's yours. It has a picture of a kitty pasted on it. See it? It has blue eyes. Please stand very still, and I'll pin it on you very carefully." With her name tag on, Rhoda headed for the blocks.

Then came another new one not on the list—a petite blonde girl dressed in pink with a matching pink purse. She looked like a pink cloud.

"Hello," said Mrs. Kaufman, and she introduced herself to the newcomers.

The pink cloud's mother responded as though she had been waiting too long.

"How do you do." (She didn't introduce herself.) "I want to leave Carolyn here in the preschool while I attend church. This *is* the preschool, isn't it?"

"Yes, this is the room for the preschool. How old is Carolyn?"

"She's two and a half, but she plays with older children all the time. I'm sure this would be just the right place for her."

"She may be happy here, but we feel that it is better for all children to participate with their own age group in the program especially designed for them. The two year olds meet in the next room, and Mrs. Cook is their teacher. She will be glad to have Carolyn in her group."

"Oh, all right."

The pink cloud and her irritated mother left.

Mrs. Kaufman had no time to reflect on this episode because here was Joy, looking like a sober brownie with her heavy, straight brown hair in a becoming bob with bangs. She recognized Mrs. Furushima, but she didn't know what to do. Mrs. Furushima and Joy went off together.

Behind Joy was Zachary with the laughing dark eyes, a book about Peter Rabbit in his hand. Shuntel was at the door holding a much-loved and well-worn doll with matted hair. Working together, Mrs. Kaufman and Mrs. Furushima greeted each child and her or his guardian, put on name tags, and completed the registration of the newcomers. (Joy was now happily playing in the housekeeping center.) Mrs. Kaufman was glad she had asked the adults to come early this first Sunday. Many of them had, making it possible to receive the children without hurry or pressure.

NOTES ON THE OPENING

Each child was personally received and the adults greeted—by name. (You need to know the families of your children and they you.)

The registrations were completed.

Each child began their relationship to the preschool in their own way. Some children walked right in and made themselves at home. Some were more careful about it. Still others needed a parent for moral support for a time. Some were not able to stay at all. The teachers offered understanding and acceptance to parent and child alike.

This is the nature of Christian living. Jesus accepted the rich young ruler, the poor, the sick, the despised Zacchaeus, the fearful Nicodemus, the woman caught in adultery. Jesus loved and helped men and women in whatever condition they came to him. He welcomed them all.

FREE PLAY TIME

At last there were no more children coming. It was 11:05. Mrs. Kaufman looked around the room. Mrs. Furushima was sitting on the rug near the block center, watching and listening. Rhoda was building a high tower with the odd-shaped blocks. Rafael and Naisha were building side by side and talking to each other. Zachery came up to Mrs. Furushima and asked her to read his book. Mrs. Furushima began reading, still watching the block play.

Mr. Greene was as busy as he could be with the modeling clay. Either three year olds have hot hands or the clay had absorbed moisture from the air overnight. Was it sticky! It strung out from the children's fingers in long yellow strands, and they loved it. Joy, Kathy, Shamik, Charles, and Marcia were pulling it, squeezing it, and laughing gaily about it.

"I've got long snakes," said Shamik, holding his hands high and letting the clay stretch down to the table. "Whoosh." He made a fast motion toward Marcia. "My snakes will bite you."

"No, they won't," said Marcia.

"Yes, they will," said Shamik.

Joy and Kathy were watching, much amused. Mr. Greene was watching too, glad that he had his pail of warm water and paper towels handy.

In other parts of the room each child was differently occupied. "No name" Ping was sitting with his hand on the large toy plane, looking around. He caught Mrs. Kaufman looking at him, and the plane took off at a terrifying speed. Louis was standing close to his mother's side holding the box of tools. Shuntel left the dolls for a moment to ask Louis for a hammer. He made no reply, turned his head, and hid the tools behind him. She shrugged her shoulders and returned to her doll babies.

Peter was sitting on the rug exactly where his mother had left him; a small wagon pull toy was beside him. From time to time he looked at Ping with the plane and at Naisha and Shuntel playing with the blocks and cars. Then he picked up the wagon, carefully examined each of the four wheels, put it down again, and resumed his watching.

Shelley and her mother changed their seats of observation from time to time to watch the activity better. Shelley was fascinated by the too-soft clay and really wanted to play too. Mr. Greene sensed this and placed an empty chair at the table right in front of where Shelley was standing. He placed a lovely smooth yellow ball at the empty place, but Shelley didn't feel certain enough to leave her mother and play with it.

Mrs. Kaufman spent her morning with many children in many activities. She helped Naisha and Zachary work out their problems about who should have the firefighter book. When Ping roared his plane past Kekoa with his wooden wagon, she engaged Kekoa in a conversation about planes. Luckily, planes seemed to be his favorite subject. Soon the wagon, the plane, Kekoa, and Ping had achieved a miraculous unity and found playing together fun.

Mrs. Kaufman invited Shelley to look closely at the bittersweet to find the seeds inside the orange shell. Exuberant Rhoda joined them and nearly, but not quite, frightened Shelley back to her mother. Then Mrs. Kaufman made a name tag for Shelley, who proudly took it to her mother to be pinned on.

Mrs. Kaufman showed Louis where the blocks were and a small wagon to load and unload. He happily left his tool box and loaded the blocks into the wagon and walked back to his mother to show it to her, only to discover that she had slipped out of the room. Mrs. Kaufman saw what had happened before Louis missed her. He was about to cry out "Mother" when Mrs. Kaufman said, "Louis, your mother went to the sanctuary where the other grown-ups are. She will be back quite soon, when worship is over. I shall be here with you while she is gone."

"But I want my own mother."

"I know you do, Louis." Mrs. Kaufman took him on her lap, and he responded by snuggling in. "Your mother is right here in this same building. She knows where you are, and she knows that I will take care of you. She will be back quite soon."

Mrs. Kaufman felt Louis' tense little body relax and then she felt herself relax. "A good beginning almost spoiled," she thought. "I must talk with Louis' mother." In another moment Louis was down from her lap pulling the wagon of blocks over to Rhoda.

NOTES ON THE FREE PLAY PERIOD

At the beginning of the free play period what each teacher said and did depended upon the feelings and concerns of the children. The children pointed the direction; the teachers read the cues. One child needed a suggestion about what to do; one needed to find a like-minded friend; another needed a boost to a faltering security. *Each one always needs to feel they belong, are loved, and will be cared for here.*

Listen to what you say and how you say it. Be aware of where you can be supportive rather than negative. I hasten to note that there may be a Louis who cannot be so easily reassured. You may have to send for this parent. *Do not keep a child in your group against his or her will.*

PICK-UP TIME

At 11:35 the teachers began helping the children to pick up the toys and put them away. Gradually most of the children came to the rug, where Mrs. Kaufman was passing graham crackers. Mr. Greene sat on the rug with the children, facing Mrs. Kaufman. Mrs. Furushima sat at the puzzle table, a little apart from the rug, so that she could be with the children who did not join the group, both to help them and to prevent undue noise and interruptions to the group. Mrs. Kaufman was speaking to the children as they were eating.

GROUP TIME

"Boys and girls, did you notice that everyone has on a name tag today? Shelley and Rhoda and Zachary and Marcia and who else? Kathy and Louis and. . . ." (She included every child.) "Oh, yes, Ping, you don't. Oh, you want your name now? OK. Mrs. Furushima will get it for you." (There were not "just like a child" attitudes here, no "looks" between teachers. There was sincere acceptance of a child who had changed his mind.)

"How many children are here today? Let's count and see. Mr. Greene will touch your heads as we count. Are you all ready? One, two . . . fourteen children! That's wonderful.

"We have three more names we didn't count. Does anyone know who they are? Yes, the teachers. I'll tell you our names so you'll know who we are too: Mr. Greene, who helped us with our clay this morning; Mrs. Furushima, who helped in the housekeeping center and with the blocks; and I am Mrs. Kaufman. If you forget our names you may call us Teacher. That's easy to remember, isn't it?

"Shamik, how old are you? Do you know? Three? That's right; I know you are three. And Rhoda . . ." She mentioned several others. The children all talked at once. Mrs. Kaufman tried to respond to each one and made some effort at order, but she did not belabor it.

"You know, *everyone* here is three or four years old. This is the room in our church for three- and four-year-old children."

She talked *with* the children about where the other children and the mothers or fathers go. "Everyone has a place in our church" was the recurring idea of this conversation.

"It's pretty special to be in the preschool. When you were a baby you were about this big. You couldn't walk or talk or sit up or look at books or play with toys or anything. About all you could do was drink milk and sleep and cry." There was lively talking, led by the children, about babies, mostly their babies at home, how they eat and sleep and cry. Mrs. Kaufman listened and responded and understood.

Twice Mrs. Kaufman interrupted this babble of "When I was . . ." and "At my house . . ." and "My baby . . ." in order to continue her plan leading to the story. But the children could not follow her. They had more to say about their own babies. Then she realized what was happening. "We are really getting acquainted," thought Mrs. Kaufman. "They want to tell me about themselves. If I cut them off, they'll feel I don't really care about them the way they thought I did. This talking together is far more valuable for the children today than the story I had planned. The story will wait."

So Mrs. Kaufman encouraged the talking. Louis reported that his baby cried all the time and he didn't like that. Marcia declared that she had never been a baby, she had always been a big girl. "What does this mean about the way she feels about herself?" flashed through Mrs. Kaufman's mind. Rhoda said their family had no babies and no big kids—just her. Raphael said their kitty had babies and two died. Patricia said her goldfish died too. Joy and Kathy said nothing.

Zachary looked at his book. Ping crawled under the dough table. Shamik and Naisha were in the block center. Mrs. Furushima was with them.

"No one here is a baby any more," Mrs. Kaufman told those who were left in the group. "You grew and grew just the way God planned for you to grow. Now you are big enough to come to the preschool room in our church. I know a little song and game about that. It goes like this.

"When I was one year old,
I was very, very small,
But now I'm three years old,
And I've grown up big and tall."

As she sang, Mrs. Kaufman showed the children how to stoop down close to the floor and stretch up high on "big and tall." (See page 96.)

"You can do it!" Mrs. Kaufman told the children. "Make yourselves as little as you can, as small as babies, and then slowly, slowly grow big and tall. Ready?" They sang it twice with the motions.

Then Mrs. Kaufman had them all sit down cross-legged in front of her again and she said, "Every morning when we come to the rug for our story and song and cracker we also say a prayer. When I say a prayer I bow my head and close my eyes.

"Dear God, we are glad we have grown big enough to come to church school. Amen."

Several children bowed their heads and closed their eyes during the prayer.

NOTES ON THE GROUP TIME

It is as important in story-conversation time to follow the lead of the children as it is in free play. Sometimes the group will follow the teacher. But often at the beginning of the year there is little group participation in the story, singing, or prayer. The ability to think and listen and talk together grows as the children grow. The teachers create the opportunity for this group activity, but they do not try to coerce it.

GOING HOME TIME

The children did not know quite what to do next. Mrs. Kaufman stayed at her chair on the rug and read *Now It's Fall* to Joy and Kathy and Zachary. Mr. Greene showed several children the large crayons and paper on which they could draw. Ping, Louis, and Rhoda crayoned. Mrs. Furushima helped Shamik and Naisha put away their blocks. Shuntel went to the housekeeping center, where she wrapped her doll to take home. Marcia stood and watched. The others wandered about, tired and ready to go home. Then the parents came.

AFTER THE SESSION

As the three teachers finished straightening up the room after the children left, they compared notes. All agreed that the morning had seemed to be a good one for most of the children. The teachers wanted to talk longer than they could at this point, so they decided to meet at Mrs. Kaufman's house on Monday evening to plan the next Sunday.

Your first session will very probably be similar to this one in many ways. You have the same job to do the first day that these teachers had: to get acquainted and to help the children feel secure. The children's responses will probably range from immediate acceptance of you and the preschool to a very tentative "stand by the door, watch and see" attitude.

And, like these three teachers, you will undoubtedly feel that you must talk things over and make some plans for the next session. You probably will want to discuss the ideas and goals you need to keep in mind as well as the type of questions and conversation that may help the children grow in their awareness of God's love for them. Here are the notes from their teachers' meeting.

A LIST OF PLANS FOR NEXT TIME

1. Visit the three new children. Each teacher will visit one child.
2. Suggest to Louis' mother that she tell him when she is leaving. (Mrs. Kaufman)
3. Telephone Scott's mother to see if he is sick. He is the only one on the roll who did not come. (Mrs. Furushima)
4. Put the clay in an accessible area for the children. (Mr. Greene)
5. Make new name tags to replace those the children wore home. (Mr. Greene)
6. General program same as last week. Try a story. (Mrs. Kaufman)
7. Make a birthday schedule so that no child will miss getting a birthday card. (Mrs. Furushima)
8. Questions: Why did Ping crawl under the table? Is Louis having problems with "his" baby? Has petite Marcia "always been a big girl?" What does that mean? Listen to, observe, think about these children particularly, but pay attention to all. Quiet Joy and gentle Raphael need our individual attention too. All of us agree that we must continue to observe and think.

Photo from Sunrise/Trinity Photos

Letter 7 The Second Sunday

The second Sunday was more relaxed than the first one. The children felt more at ease and so did the teachers. Everyone was a little more certain of where they were, who the other persons were, and how the morning would go. All the children, including Ping, wanted their names on, "the same name as before." Mrs. Kaufman had to explain over and over that the name was the same but the picture was different. The children were not quite satisfied. Some of them took the name tags off.

Scott, who had not come the first Sunday, arrived crying. He did not want to come, and Mrs. Kaufman suggested that he not be expected to come. His stepfather was willing to wait a few months.

It was interesting to watch the children as they arrived. Some remembered their coat hooks and went to find them, although they had nothing to hang on them.

"Why, these children are already feeling that they belong here and are happy about it—in one short Sunday!" Mrs. Kaufman felt that all the hours of extra work had been rewarded.

Other children, who did not remember or care about the coat hooks, did remember what they had done the previous week. Mr. Greene had the same children at the dough clay table that he had had the first Sunday—Joy, Charles, and Kathy. Marcia and Shamik were absent. The children did not seem to remember one another particularly; they remembered the clay and Mr. Greene. When Shuntel arrived with an old pink bunny, she told Mrs. Kaufman all about the bunny and two other bunnies she had at home. Shuntel also said that her clothes were new and asked if the clay would get on them. Mrs. Kaufman assured her the clay would brush off if a bit did get on her clothes, so Shuntel joined the "clay people." Mrs. Kaufman made a mental note to get aprons or old shirt cover-ups for the children.

Shelley arrived, looking happy enough about being there, but sticking close to her mother. Her mother sat in a chair at the edge of the room; Shelley stood beside her, watching. Mrs. Furushima approached to greet them.

"Good morning, Shelley. Do you have a new purse today?"

Shelley nodded affirmatively, a slow, definite up-and-down yes.

"It's very pretty. Do you have something in it?"

Another slow, definite, up-and-down yes, as she fumbled with the catch on the purse to open it. Inside were a mirror, a comb, and a dime.

"Shelley, is your money for the church?"

Another wordless affirmative.

"Right here on this special table is the basket for your money. It will be here every Sunday, so you can put your money in the basket the first thing you do. Then it won't be lost." Shelley was listening carefully, and understanding too, Mrs. Furushima thought. She was almost tempted by such rapt attention to say something about the whys of the money but then decided that Shelley probably was not curious about that at this point. She needed, and wanted, to become part of the room. Mrs. Furushima looked around and caught Mr. Greene's wordless communication through a nod of his head. There on the table before an empty chair lay a smooth ball of yellow clay.

"Shelley, Mr. Greene has clay ready for you to play with if you would like to. Here's your place right beside Joy and Kathy. I'll help you get seated."

Shelley wanted to play, but she hesitated and looked at her mother. Mrs. Ridge nodded encouragingly. "I'll stay here, Shelley. Go ahead and play."

Shelley did. This time three teachers were glad about the work and the planning they had done together that made it possible for them to think and feel together about Shelley without saying a word to one another.

Louis came in holding tightly to his mother. Mrs. Kaufman felt as she greeted him that he was no longer uncertain about the preschool; he was now uncertain about his mother.

"Do you need your mother to stay today, Louis?"

"Yes," he said, barely audibly.

"All right, that will be fine. Mrs. Martin, you can sit over here while Louis plays." Mrs. Kaufman was glad that she had been able to talk with Mrs. Martin during the week and that they had an understanding which they need not work out now.

FREE PLAY TIME

Mrs. Martin sat down. Louis went to the cupboard of the housekeeping center. Ping was there, cooking. Louis took a cup out of the cupboard and pretended to fill it with milk. He turned to Ping, who was now putting a doll to bed.

"Here's some milk for your baby."

Ping said nothing. Louis put the cup down and examined the stove. He felt the top burners, turned the switches (some ingenious parent had put knobs on the front that would turn forever), opened the oven, and took out the small frying pan. He put that on the table, picked up some more cups, including the one he had given Ping, and crossed the room. He set them in the small wooden wagon in the block center. David joined him and tried to take the cups. Louis objected. Mrs. Kaufman knew now why her teacher's guide had suggested *two* of many items. She suggested that Louis show David where the other dishes were. Louis did, and the two of them played together with great good humor and wit.

"Now is the time," thought Mrs. Kaufman. She approached Louis. "Louis, it's time now for your mother to go to church. Will you go tell her she can go now, so she won't be late? Then you can come back to your work."

Louis didn't budge, and Mrs. Kaufman thought she had timed her help wrong. But not so. Instead he spoke across the room to his mother. "You can go now, Mommy. I'll be right here." Then he returned to the housekeeping center.

Louis and Shelley both had a happy, comfortable morning. Shelley's mother stayed the whole morning. Shelley returned to her side several times during the morning, stood there a few moments as though she were receiving a new charge for her batteries, and then ventured forth again.

The morning was under way. Zachary was poring over the firefighter book. Later he joined the clay table. Again, this time Rhoda was bent on building a high, high tower with uneven, different-sized blocks. She showed considerable skill in balancing them. Naisha, who was last Sunday's engineer, found the wooden engine again and loaded beads in the tender. Mike was working on a block road.

Suddenly and with no apparent reason Raphael kicked the road apart. Then he knocked over Rhoda's tower and stood there kicking the blocks with his feet.

Mr. Greene offered him some clay, in the hope that some of the bad feelings could be pounded out into the clay. He didn't use it that way. Instead he sat there and slowly picked the big ball into little crumbly bits; then he scattered them with his hand and left the table.

Raphael was uneasy the whole morning, apparently under strain. From time to time he let out loud yells as though they were not his doing and he could not help himself. Each teacher in turn tried to be of some help, and each teacher failed. It was a strange kind of disquiet. He did not attack any other person, but he raised havoc with the peace and order. What was the trouble, and what would help?

GROUP TIME

Mrs. Kaufman began the group time with the finger play "Here's the Church" (page 91). Then they all sang and acted "This is the way we wash our face . . . So early Sunday morning" to the tune of "Here We Go Round the Mulberry Bush" (page 95). They repeated last week's "Growing Song."

During this time Ping remained in the doll center, where he had been all morning. He watched and listened from there but did not join the group.

Shamik looked up from his blocks occasionally but went on playing. Zachary read his own book. Shuntel worked a puzzle.

Raphael made noise, lots of it. Mrs. Furushima got his attention and asked him if he would like to take a walk. He would, and they left. Mrs. Kaufman held up a five-inch boy paper doll that she had made by cutting the figure from a mail-order catalog and mounting it on heavy cardboard. She had intended to use it last Sunday.

"I will tell you a story about this boy. If everyone will sit flat on the floor, cross your legs in front of you, you will all be able to see." Mr. Greene helped the children to get settled.

"This is Ronnie. He is three years old, just like you. Something very pleasant happened to him today, and I want to tell you about it." (She told the story of "Ronnie and the Pancakes," page 81.)

Mrs. Kaufman then held up the picture of people going to church. "Our picture today shows how Ronnie and his friends might be going to church." She and the children talked a little about the picture.

"Why do you like Sunday, Joy?"

" 'Cause I can come to church like Ronnie," Joy replied simply.

Shuntel looked up from her puzzle and announced that she liked wearing her best shoes because they were so slippery. Zachary liked making popcorn with his daddy. Naisha was going to see her gran'ma in the afternoon; she had a big black dog named Rex. Kekoa found a black bug in his sandbox.

"Let's put these ideas about Sunday into our prayer to God this morning," Mrs. Kaufman suggested. "Do you remember how I pray? I fold my hands, close my eyes, and bow my head like this.

"Dear God, we are glad when it is Sunday and we can all come to church and do other things that are fun with one another and people at home. Amen.

"I said our prayer this morning. On other mornings you may say it, for it is your prayer to God as well as mine."

Mr. Greene passed the crackers. He and Mrs. Kaufman talked with the children in small groups as they were eating. Raphael and Mrs. Furushima returned. Raphael ate four crackers! Then the adults came and everyone went home.

Photo © Kathryn Abbe

Letter 8 Love and Understanding

Have you ever had a preschool room full of fifteen children, an assortment of mothers, fathers, and grandmothers, and three teachers and wondered how to get them all in their right places so that you could start? Most of the assorted adults usually stay just long enough to see that their children are settled; then they go to church. But there are others who stay session after session. They become bored with just sitting. They would rather be in church or class with the other adults, and they are beginning to wonder what is the matter with their children when all the others are happy in the room without their parents. They start urging the children to go do something. The more they urge, the less they succeed. They look to you to help them out. You feel that you should be able to help children stay without their parent, but you don't quite know how to do it.

The separation of young children from their mother or father, or whoever represents a secure relationship, is an experience so common, so much misunderstood, and so fraught with distressing emotions on the part of adult and child alike that it must be considered one of the major areas of the course of study of this year.

Seems funny, I know. We are not used to thinking of such things as gaining independence as proper subject matter for a church school curriculum. After all, it is something each child does or does not do, and what can the church school do about it? In fact, is it the church school's business even to be concerned?

Yes, it is, for this reason: The children's first feeling toward the church will depend on how they feel about the preschool—the other children and the teacher—in connection with their parents' leaving them. Subsequent experiences in the church school will be interpreted, at least in part, in terms of this first experience and their feeling about it. In fact, there are many people who believe that unhappy and meaningless experiences in the early church school years are a major reason for adolescents leaving the church.

FROM A CHILD'S POINT OF VIEW

Let's think of how the experience of coming to the church preschool feels to Zachary. Think of the location of your room and the approach to it. Does Zachary have to walk down a dimly lit flight of stairs, turn a corner, open or walk through a narrow door, cross the basement hall, where the church suppers are held, and end up in the kitchen? Or must he toil up a flight of stairs and walk the length of a long hall, busy with people going in each direction who often do not see him and whom he cannot see through or around or over, before he gets to his room? Once he is there, what then? Lots more legs of grownups standing around in the hall, in the doorway, in the room, so he can't tell who belongs where? He begins to feel that certainly *he* does not belong here.

Apart from the possible perils of the route from the church door to the preschool, Zachary will have some expectations and some anxieties about the preschool class long before he gets there. He may have been wanting to go for months with his older brothers and sisters. Now that he is old enough he can scarcely wait for everyone to get ready. Or he may feel that his mother or father want him to go to the preschool for reasons he cannot appreciate; he is a little anxious that others may be trying to get rid of him.

Zachary may be a child whose mother has told him about the preschool—who is there, what is there, and what he will do there—but he may come with no definite feeling either of wanting to be there or of not wanting to stay. He is interested and curious. Or he may be a child who has had almost no preparation for the experience other than getting dressed to go to church with the neighbors one bright sunny morning.

KENDRA'S FEELINGS

All children who approach the preschool door during these first sessions bring their own particular set of feelings. Kendra has feelings about herself: what she likes to do, what she can do, whether she likes other people, whether other people like her. She has feelings about her parents: whether they want her to come because the preschool class may prove to be a worthwhile experience for her, or because they want to be free of her for an hour, or because they want her to be as grown-up as the child next door, who goes every Sunday. She also has all kinds of feelings about strange places and strangers, adults and children. Sometimes adult strangers say, "I'd like to hug you. Would you be my little girl"? Sometimes they stick you with needles and put sticks down your throat. Sometimes they give you candy or cookies. Sometimes other children push you off your tricycle. Sometimes strange children become new friends. Strange places are unpredictable; some are okay, some are scary.

NO CHILD COMES TO YOU EMPTY, EVER

In fact, just the opposite of that is true. Their interior world, which is made up of all their experiences, their feelings about those experiences, and their understanding of the meaning of the experiences, is complete. There is no vacuum, no pie-shaped wedge anyplace labeled "church experiences" waiting to be filled in as the child has experiences with the church. Each comes to the preschool class on that first day with some quite clear attitudes and feelings toward it *without having had one single bit of firsthand evidence to work on* beyond the walk from the church door to the preschool room. The child is not just being childish. We all do the same thing.

How each of us behaves in a new situation depends in great part on how we understand what happened to us in previous similar situations and how we feel about what happened. If the first boss you had was a democratic, understanding, fair person, you greatly hope and to some degree expect that your second boss will be the same kind of person. If that boss is, and you work with that boss long, you come to have quite a clear picture of the kind of person a boss should be and the kind of behavior on your part that is acceptable and necessary. If the first strange grown-up children deal with asks them for their big brown eyes, and the second one wonders if the cat has got their tongue, and a third gives them a shot that hurts, you can guess that the child might be a little wary of you, a teacher. The child has no way of knowing what teachers do and say to children and may not take any chances until finding out.

If the suggestions you made in the last committee or planning group you worked with were misunderstood or ignored, you will be less likely to make contributions in the new committee you are on, even if the people are different and the task is different. If a child has had a bewildering, hectic, perhaps even unhappy time with a group of children under the care of sitters while a parent attended a church meeting, the child may not be happy about coming to the church preschool even if the people are different, the purpose is different, and the place is different.

This is behavior characteristic of intelligent human beings. We approach all new situations with the understandings and the feelings and the expectations left over from previous similar situations. The understandings may be completely incorrect, the feelings wholly unjustified, and the expectations inappropriate, but telling us so will not change them one iota. Only a new and different experience will change our feelings and actions.

Helping children feel comfortable and secure in the preschool is not just a matter of showing them the interesting things to play with and assuring them that you will take care of them while a parent is gone. It may be that Cineca is not a bit concerned about the things to play with or about who will take care of her, but rather whether the children will push her down. Masaki may be afraid that his mother will not come for him on time, like last week, when he stayed all morning at Jacque's house and even had to eat lunch there. Becky may not want to stay because her mother is just home from the hospital with a new baby brother, and Becky wants to be home with her. Jad, with no siblings at home and no close neighbors to play with, may be entranced and at the same time a little anxious about the bustle of activity and the "lots" of children in the room. Lorita, her eye on the doll buggy, doesn't hear or need your reassuring invitation. She has already sized up the situation and taken hold of it.

A GIANT STEP

For a preschooler to feel adequate to handle the world—even a world of other young children and fascinating playthings—alone, without a parent, is a tremendous step in growth. It is so great a step that kind, reassuring words by an adult will often not be of sufficient help to enable a child to take it. Some children are able to take this step in three short years. Some children will accomplish the task during their first weeks of the first grade of school. There is no "right" or normal age, up to six or seven years, at which a child's separation from home "ought" to take place. Many factors—home life, good or poor health, happy or unhappy experiences—enter into the child's ability to function happily, confidently, without his or her parent.

It is often an error in judgment and a grave mistake in action to try to separate or wean a child from the parent. All children wean themselves, given the opportunity, when they are able, when they find the situation trustworthy—just as they walk when they are physically able, when their leg muscles and sense of balance are trustworthy. You cannot teach the child to walk before the time has come. You can provide furniture for the child to walk around and offer an outstretched hand to hold, but each person will finally walk when the time is right. No one knows when that is.

A child's separation from a parent is something like walking. When the child is ready and secure enough, he or she will be happy to come to the preschool. Your job is to provide a book to look at or a jeep to run. Should a child need it, you have an outstretched hand for holding or a lap for sitting in. Although unfortunately, you *can* forcibly produce a separation and wait out the tears, such a method is almost always a mistake.

GOALS FOR THE PRESCHOOL

One of our goals for the preschool is to *help children become competent, happy, creative persons.* Another is to *help them discover that the church is a place where they are loved, understood, and helped.* Keeping children in the church school who, for any reason, are not ready to stay alone, teaches them the very opposite of what we intend.

Think of the two goals mentioned above. They will help you know what is the good thing for you to do or say to each child who comes to the preschool room. Think of the many kinds of experiences the child might have had. Then you may begin to understand the meaning behind what each child says or does. Let us look at these children and think about their needs.

Ruby comes into the preschool room clinging to her mother's hand, walking close by her side. After three sessions with her mother sitting quietly, apparently relaxed, in a corner of the room, Ruby still spends the whole morning watching, not moving more than six inches away from her mother.

Luke comes in each session carefully, uncertainly, not clinging to an older sister but looking tense and fearful. She stays a few minutes, says good-bye. He responds quietly, picks up a small object in each hand—a car, a figure, a small bell, whatever is right at hand—and stations himself in some inconspicuous place apart from the activity of the room. He does essentially the same thing the first three times he is in the group.

Gretchen comes the first session looking pleased with her grown-up state. She says "Bye" cheerfully to her grandmother and spends two-and-one-half sessions apparently enjoying the whole adventure. Suddenly she begins to cry for no reason anyone can see. A lap is little comfort. Feeding the goldfish is no distraction. She wants her grandmother.

What will you say to each of these children? What will you do for them or with them? For each one it will be quite different, depending on how you understand what each one is feeling. In whatever you say or do, however, you must try to make sure that the child's sense of adequacy and "all rightness" will be increased; that you as teacher will be seen as one who understands feelings and is ready to help when needed; and that the church preschool will be experienced as a place that cares deeply for each child. It is a safe place to be.

If after some time (from four to six consecutive sessions) the child does not want to stay without mother or father, it may be better for the child to stop coming to church school for three or four months rather than to make the parent discouraged about the child's behavior and to make the child uncertain about being left alone. Most parents will welcome an opportunity to talk with you about their child. They may be relieved to discover that you do not think their child babyish, spoiled, or slow. You can visit the child at home from time to time. Take books and talk and play if you can take the time. Become a friend, but *do not put pressure on the child to return.*

Some months later you could invite the child to come to visit the preschool, but never give cause to feel any disappointment on your part. Believe yourself that the child will attend when ready and able, at the appropriate time. Children want to play with other children. They are eager for new experiences; they long to try out their wings, to assert increasing independence, and to discover new strengths and skills. They are made that way. All they need is time to grow and some patient understanding.

Why is this long discussion a proper concern for the preschool teacher of the church school? Because a child's religious growth cannot be separated from all other aspects of growth.

Nor can a child's religious growth adequately be measured in terms of the prayers, the Bible stories, the verses, and the songs that are learned. Religious growth is bigger than that, more basic than that, more important than that. Religious growth can really be measured only in terms of one's ability to give and receive love, to extend trust, to accept oneself and other people, to forgive and to be forgiven. These are experiences characteristic of Christian people as they relate to each other and as they relate to God. A person's religion is the base of operations for their *whole* life. How one *lives* reflects one's religion much more than what is known or recited, whether adult or child.

Even though we often fail, we Christians try to love others, are concerned for others, give of ourselves in the service of others. We believe that in loving and serving other persons we are loving and serving God. This is the kind of life Jesus lived and taught. How can one grow toward being this kind of person? By experiencing the love and concern of adults when life is young and the world is new. "We love, because God first loved us." Therefore, the basic curriculum of the preschool in the church is to provide each child with repeated experiences of being loved, understood, accepted; of finding people trustworthy and dependable; of discovering the church to be a place that knows each child personally and cares for each child deeply.

Any curriculum used in the preschool that ignores or denies these basic experiences actually teaches the opposite, gives the lie to the gospel, and provides the beginning of hypocrisy. Why? Because you are talking about, but not practicing, the love of God.

Letter 9 Teachers Are Dependable: All Children Have Rights

I saw Wendy's mother showing Wendy's grandmother around the church last Sunday. As they paused at the preschool door Wendy's mother said, "This is the preschool room. Wendy loves to come here."

The grandmother replied, "Is it any wonder? It is certainly an attractive room. They don't do anything with the little kiddies but let them play the whole hour, do they? They don't teach them anything, I mean."

Have parents said much the same thing to you? Or perhaps at this point you are asking the question yourself. Why, when we have the children only such a short time each week, do we schedule most of the time as free play? How can children learn anything about the Christian faith if they spend all their time playing?

Let us look at some anecdotal records of children "just playing" in a church preschool class and try to understand what they may have been learning through this method.

9:35 The hour has just begun when Ms. Colson sees Juan try to take the large van truck away from Jimmy. Jimmy holds on, objecting. Ms. Colson says, "Juan, Jimmy is using the truck right now. Jimmy, will you give Juan the truck when you have finished?" Jimmy nods assent.

Juan seems to accept that arrangement and walks over to the shelf of blocks and cars. Ms. Colson turns to the table where some children are pasting, only to hear Letticia yelling, "No." She looks up to see Juan trying to take a dump truck away from Letticia.

Ms. Colson goes to Juan again. She takes him by the hand and says, "I know you want a turn, Juan. All the trucks are being used right now, but pretty soon someone will be finished. For now, if you'll sit down, I'll tie your shoe, and then we'll find a puzzle, shall we?"

Juan willingly sits down, and Ms. Colson talks with him about shoes and his toes inside. He smiles, and together they walk to the table where Ms. Kay is giving Wendy and Jennifer some puzzles.

"We want a puzzle, Ms. Kay," says Ms. Colson. Still holding Juan's hand, she walks with him a few steps to the rug, where they sit down together. Juan begins to work the puzzle. Ms. Colson helps him when he needs help by suggesting, "Turn it a little until it fits" or "Try this piece there."

9:40 Both Juan and Ms. Colson look up when they hear Ms. Kay say firmly, "Wendy, if you throw one more piece of that puzzle, I shall take it away from you." Wendy throws one more. Ms. Kay removes the puzzle. Wendy does not object, but immediately begins to suck her thumb.

Ms. Colson leaves Juan working at the puzzle. He finishes it. Then he goes back to Letticia and this

Photo © Kathryn Abbe

time succeeds in taking the dump truck. Letticia protests angrily, and Ms. Colson helps Juan return the truck, saying, "We don't take toys from other children, Juan. We take turns. Letticia, will you be finished in a few minutes so Juan can have a turn?"

Letticia says, "Yes."

"Here is the rocking boat, Juan," says Ms. Colson. Juan climbs in and rocks vigorously for several minutes. Then he sees that the large wooden tractor is not being used, so he hurries to it and begins to ride. Ms. Colson sees, too, and gives a nod of approval. She seems to be saying, "I see you got a turn. I'm glad."

9:45 Letticia pushes her dump truck full speed ahead into Juan's tractor. Now Juan objects. After a few more assaults, Letticia leaves. Then Jimmy comes and stands on the tractor, and Juan cannot dislodge him, nor can he ride the tractor away with Jimmy on it. Juan is becoming more and more angry, and Jimmy seems to have no notion of leaving. Ms. Colson helps, this time by directing Jimmy to the pounding board.

9:50 A few minutes later the picture has changed again. Juan is on the floor assembling the cars of a large wooden train. Jimmy is vigorously bouncing on the horse. Wendy is playing alone with the trucks. Then Juan sees Jimmy on the horse, leaves his train, and tries to pull Jimmy off. Jimmy holds his own but calls for the teacher to help.

"After a while you may have a turn, Juan," she says in the same even, sincere way. He turns from her and Jimmy, walks straight toward Wendy, who is playing with a pushcart, and takes it right out of her hands. She yells and quite naturally protests.

Ms. Colson takes Juan by the hand and says, "Let's go over here and sit down a little while and talk, Juan." He goes with her without objection. She shows him a new book, and they talk for a few minutes. Then Juan, looking quite at ease with everything and everyone, returns to his wooden train and settles down to loading the beads in the freight car. Seung comes by driving the tractor. He stops to watch Juan. Juan takes a wooden figure of a man from his train, places it on the tractor, and knocks it halfway across the room with a wild swing of his right arm. Seung says nothing and rides away. Juan goes back to loading his train. He is now almost alone in the block and truck center.

9:55 Wendy and Jennifer, who have been loading blocks into the pushcart and transporting them across the room, tire of that and enter the rocking boat. Soon Jennifer leaves the boat and returns to the puzzles. Wendy follows Karen into the bathroom. Eight minutes later Wendy emerges drenched in front. Ms. Colson changes her into the spare clothes and puts Wendy's wet clothes near the heating unit to dry. They talk about what happened. Wendy says it was an accident, and she doesn't like the wet feel on her tummy.

"I bet you don't, Wendy. If you need help the next time in the bathroom, ask me, won't you?" Wendy nods yes and skips off to the housekeeping center, where she makes a number of "important" phone calls.

Juan has momentarily left his train and is getting out all the large, hollow pasteboard blocks. Three girls approach Juan and ask him if they can use some of the blocks. He gives willing assent. At the moment he seems more interested in getting the blocks all out than in going to work with them; the blocks out, he returns to the train. Jeanie joins him and they begin to play together.

The girls are building a church. Juan joins them, works hard at the stairway, which he reiterates is "not for people." (He may mean that no one should walk on it lest it fall down.) The girls soon leave, but Juan stays with the church construction until he notices the fun they are having in the rocking boat. He joins them once again, and helps them rock the boat faster. Then he leaves, comes back to his church, and knocks the whole thing down.

Ms. Kay admonishes, "We don't knock down blocks, Juan. We only build them up."

He makes no response to Ms. Kay but goes to work picking up and restacking in its original place along the wall every one of the knocked-down blocks. He works hard, steadily, apparently very interested in what he is doing. It is as though this is exactly what he had planned to do, whether Ms. Kay had said anything or not.

10:05 Jimmy is now in the housekeeping center, where he is intent on cooking. He adds one thing after another from empty food cans and boxes to a pot. He stirs it carefully. From time to time he tastes the mixture, then bends his head down and carefully "adjusts the flame." Finally, he loads the empty cans and boxes into the small shopping cart and starts off across the room with it.

Juan is alone in the corner with the blocks and trucks. He is having his turn with everything. There is no competition. He plays happily and busily, going from one thing to another, paying no attention to any other part of the room.

10:15 Ms. Neal is helping Jimmy dress his baby, and they are talking together, nodding and smiling. Wendy approaches Ms. Neal with a large crayon picture that she has just completed and painstakingly and crookedly folded. "It's for you," she says.

"Oh, how nice!" Ms. Neal carefully unfolds it and looks at if thoughtfully. She puts her arm around Wendy and says with genuine appreciation, "I like it very much, Wendy. It was thoughtful of you to make me a picture." Wendy beams happily and walks over by the window, where she checks her wet clothes and then stands looking out, or lost in thought, for long minutes.

Ms. Colson sits in a little chair at the edge of the rug doing finger plays with a few children while Ms. Kay and Ms. Neal are working with the others, picking up and putting away the toys. The group on the rug have snacks, count noses, name one another's names. "We have thirteen noses today. That's very good. I'm glad you are all here. We need you here so that we'll have fun in our preschool room."

Ms. Colson reads a story. Juan, appearing to be quite tired, approaches Ms. Neal. She offers her lap. He accepts and sits looking as though he might fall asleep. Wendy sits very close by her side. Jimmy sits almost off the rug, banging his feet on the floor. Yuriko walks over to the basket of beads and empties them with a clatter in order to string them. Ms. Kay helps her do it quietly.

The adults come from church and the children leave.

JUAN'S MORNING

It may seem apparent to you reading this record, as it did to me as I was making it, that something was bothering Juan this morning. It seemed to me that he was mad at the world; that he was feeling badly about something—what, I could not say. Perhaps something had gone wrong before he came and he had to express his feelings. Whatever child was around became the target.

It is a temptation to try to figure out what was taking place inside Juan: Why didn't he express anger when the teachers continually directed him? What did he mean by saying the stairway was "not for people"? Why did he knock the church down with so much feeling and knock the wooden man halfway across the room? Why did he want whatever some other child had? Without a great deal of experience and know-how, we would only be second-guessing the situation—reading our own feelings into Juan's actions. The best we could do would be to become sensitive to Juan as a person and attempt to recognize his feelings.

Ms. Colson became aware of Juan's feelings. She recognized that he was mad at the world. She did not condemn him for this, scold him, or tell him the other children didn't like the way he was treating them. If she had, she would have been dealing negatively with Juan. Negative responses offer little help, for they do not provide possible and acceptable ways of expressing the energy that strong feelings engender. Negative responses such as these are really just one response: *"Don't!"*

Some of the intensity of Juan's feelings and some of the anxiety he felt because of his behavior and his uncertainty about how the teacher would respond were relieved when Ms. Colson changed the focus. She tied his shoe, and they laughed over a joke about his toes. She took him lightly by the hand and said, "*We* want a puzzle." She sat down with him and they put the puzzle together. Her suggestions for turning the puzzle pieces, her attitude, and her sensitivity helped Juan have his first successful experience of the morning.

No one thing Ms. Colson said or did that morning turned the trick to change Juan into a happy, free, creative child. Moods and strong feelings are not flippant, lighthearted, or whimsical. They usually cannot be dissipated easily or quickly; they have to be lived through. This, Ms. Colson helped Juan do. The puzzle, the rocking boat, and the train all to himself helped. The courteousness of the three girls who did not trespass on his right to all the blocks helped. Fifteen uninterrupted noncompetitive minutes with all the trucks and blocks helped. Finally, a lap to sit in for story time and a warm person-to-person good-bye ("I'll be looking for you next time, Juan") sent Juan home a much more relaxed and reassured little boy than when he came.

Ms. Colson accepted Juan and his feelings, but not his aggressive, bullying behavior. She reminded him of the limits but was not irritated when he persisted in breaking them. She helped him engage his energies creatively, then vigorously, in something else until his turn came. She tried not to let his attacks on other children go so far that they would reject him. He already was feeling out of kinship with people, and she took care that he did not alienate himself further.

So Juan worked out some of his feelings without damaging his relationship with people. Perhaps he gained a new sense of self worth through Ms. Colson's and Ms. Neal's warm acceptance of him and through his one successful play experience with the three girls. He repeatedly experienced love and understanding and was offered help at every point where he needed it, without his being made to feel inadequate or unwanted.

WENDY'S MORNING

Now let us see what happened to Wendy on this particular morning. I cannot say anything about her as she arrived, for I did not notice her. It seemed to me that when she threw the first puzzle piece it was out of exasperation that she could not get it to fit. Ms. Kay did not understand and dared her to throw another. Wendy did. Looking hurt and bewildered as Ms. Kay took her puzzle away, Wendy began to suck her thumb vigorously.

Several minutes later she left the puzzle table and began playing with the pushcart that Juan tried unsuccessfully to take away from her. Jennifer joined her in play, but only for a few minutes. Alone again, she wandered into the bathroom. She must have had a wonderful time squirting water, for she emerged looking much happier, although very wet. Here again, as with Juan, Ms. Colson did not judge the behavior solely on the basis of what it *appeared* to be. She tried to get a glimpse of the *meaning behind the behavior* and to help the child discover a more satisfying and acceptable way to accomplish what she wanted or needed to do.

All children—in fact, all persons, you and I, too—constantly seek acceptance and assurance of worth and adequacy. Once is not enough. Wendy discovered that Ms. Colson did not treat her as a naughty girl when she got her clothes wet. She felt assured of her worth when Ms. Neal accepted her crayon pictures and hugged her. Ms. Kay's rejection and lack of understanding were, for the moment, forgotten. Wendy likes church school. Is it any wonder?

I discovered later that Ms. Kay was a new teacher. Her intention was not to dare Wendy to throw another puzzle piece, but to give her another chance. With helpful guidance from her coteachers and her own eagerness to learn, Ms. Kay can become, I feel, an effective teacher. In time she will realize that the child experiences a feeling of accomplishment in completing a puzzle, in building blocks up *and* in knocking them down. she may also learn (I hope) that doing things quietly is not *the* criterion for *all* behavior in the preschool.

STANDARDS AND UNDERSTANDING BEHAVIOR

"Aren't there *any* standards of behavior or performance in the preschool?" I can almost hear you asking. "Will Ms. Colson accept *anything*? Some behavior is right and good, isn't it? And other behavior if not wrong and bad, is surely, at least, less right and less good?"

Certainly, but which is which? Beyond the basic limitations that we must adhere to in the interest of the health and safety of the children, we must be flexible. What might appear to be the same kind of behavior on the part of two different children very likely would have two vastly different meanings. For instance: a child returns from the bathroom soaked to the skin, and the bathroom looks as though a hippopotamus had been bathing there. If the child had been Wendy, the water play would have been therapy for her. It washed away her aloneness and restored her sense of "all rightness." I don't know how soapy water does this, but it does. Incidentally, her clothes got wet. That fact is truly incidental to the value of the experience.

But if the child had been Carl, whom I knew well a few years ago, the water play would have had a very different meaning for him. With a mother too busy with a large family and new twin babies to give him the attention he wanted, he could always count on water play to bring her around. True, she scolded and was angry, and he often was deprived of something, but all of that was preferable to being ignored. When Carl's mother set aside a special time each day for some personal attention to him alone, the bathroom drenching stopped.

What would you do to become a helpful effective *teacher*—rather than a kindly, authoritarian keeper of order and respectability—for Wendy and Carl? You might give Wendy a large pan of soapy water, roll up her sleeves, protect her clothes with a plastic apron, put papers on the floor, and let her play. You might hold Carl on your lap and read a book to him, sing to him, or spend a few special minutes talking just with him. There are other things you could do too.

Your purpose with both children would be the same: to help them discover that they are all right, acceptable as they are, and that they belong to the preschool class and are worthwhile, desirable people. As children have these experiences, they may continue to build trustful relationships with their teachers and to feel that they are a part of the Christian fellowship.

All behavior is caused—yours and mine too! To label behavior—or a child—as good or bad, happy or hostile, mischievous or destructive is often more misleading than helpful. The reason for this is that the label indicates the meaning the behavior has for you, from your point of view. What we need to know in order to do our best for the child is *what the behavior means to the child.* To proceed in our relationship with a child on the basis of a label which we have affixed to behavior is to focus on symptoms without being aware of or concerned about the causes. This is not good pedagogy. It is possible to alleviate or eradicate the symptoms without remedying the problem which is at their source. For instance, eliminating splashing water all over the room without dealing with the feelings that make water play such a needful and satisfying experience is like giving aspirin for a fever without dealing with the source of the infection. In fact, you may complicate the underlying problem.

JIMMY'S MORNING

Now let us look at Jimmy's morning. The significant part of his morning was spent in playing in the housekeeping center, cooking, shopping, and caring for the baby. Perhaps we can understand as much about Jimmy's own life as he perceives it by observing what he did *not* do as by noting what he did. He did not spank, threaten, scold, or misuse the baby doll. Nor did he play the part of a baby himself. He worked cheerfully and happily at the business of keeping house, with no fretting or complaining about all the work. It is probably a pretty accurate guess to say that Jimmy has a strong sense of identification with his parents, that they include him in the constant business of taking care of a house and a new baby, and that he feels pretty sure of his worth and his place in the family. Ms. Neal did not intrude on his play with any such remark as, "Isn't it fun to help your parents?" or "Aren't we glad that God has a plan for families to have babies?" Sometimes it's fun, and we are glad; and sometimes it isn't, and we are not. By showing her hand, disclosing her own attitudes, the teacher says quite clearly, "These are the attitudes about families and babies that are acceptable to me." If the child has strong feelings otherwise, such comments are not likely to change the feelings. In fact, they may prevent the teacher's ever discovering the real truth. The only one fooled by this kind of talk is the teacher.

THE VALUE OF PLAY

There will be sessions when some of the resources which you had planned do not get used. You will be so busy with the children's living and learning at play that the time runs out. There will be other days when the story, the song, and the prayer will be the joyous expression of the living and loving and learning that has been part of a happy session. Both are valuable to the child.

Play is the business of the young child. If we cannot understand its importance or its meaning, it does not mean the play has none. My son once said to me, "All you do is work, work, work." He could not understand the meaning behind my activity and so it seemed senseless. We often make the same mistake about children's play. We do not understand it, so we think of it as unimportant, insignificant, interruptible. That is not so. Children's play is laden with meanings, subtle, infinite, profound. To be aware of this fact is to begin to be a teacher.

Photo © Kathryn Abbe

Letter 10 A Change of Session Plans

It is always a happy experience to observe a preschool class where the teachers are alert to the experiences and interests of the children. Sometimes this means that the teachers have to make a quick shift in their plans as my friend Mrs. Badami did one Sunday. Let me tell you about it.

TO UNDERSTAND AND EXPERIENCE RAIN

Sunday dawned gray. Soon it began to rain, a hard steady rain. Mrs. Badami set out a pail to catch rain water for the preschool.

She loaded her large dishpan with some quickly improvised aprons cut from discarded plastic curtains, several sponge and small pie-dish "boats," some clothes, a box of detergent, and a spoon.

Every child, upon arriving, talked about the rain. Juanita brought her red umbrella with an "elfin" (elephant) on it. Ellen had on her brother's raincoat, which on her nearly touched the ground. Yuki wore a rain hat designed like a firefighter's hat. Alan said that his daddy's "windshields" wouldn't work and his daddy couldn't see very well. Mario arrived with one foot wet from investigating a puddle too enthusiastically.

The present vivid experience of the children coming to church in the rain became the background for the entire morning's plan. Think how much less interesting this session about rain would be on a sunny Sunday even if it had poured down the day before.

Mrs. Badami asked Susan if she knew the song "Rain, Rain, Go Away." Susan did, and she sang it. Several children listened. Mrs. Badami and Susan sang it together a second time, and two children joined the singing. Other children joined the group. "I know another rain song we can sing," Mrs. Badami told them. "It goes like this:

It's raining, it's raining
It's raining all around
It's splashing in puddles
With circles going round."

(This is the second verse of the song "It's Snowing," page 163.)

The children enjoyed this. They stood up and "made it rain" with their arms and fingers.

Mrs. Badami had her dishpan full of equipment at her side and her pail of water in front of her. "Do you know where I got this water?" she asked.

"It's got dirt in it," said Billy.

"Out of the faucet," said Russ.

"At your house," said Becky Sue.

"Yes, at my house, but not out of the faucet. It does have a twig and some leaves in it, Billy, and they wouldn't come out of the faucet, would they?"

"No."

No one suggested that the water was rain water. Mrs. Badami told them how she had caught it.

"Why does it rain?" she asked.

"To give flowers a drink," said Juanita.

"It rains on umbrellas too," said Alan.

"My daddy's got a boat and it got full of water last night," said Yuki. "He forgot to cover it."

Mrs. Badami said, "That's right," to Alan, and "Oh, did he?" to Yuki. Each child nodded his head, and she went on.

"Where does rain come from?"

"From heaven," said Juanita.

"Where's heaven, Juanita?" asked Mrs. Badami.

"You know . . . where God and Jesus is. When it rains, Jesus comes out with his big hose."

Mrs. Badami could barely restrain her amusement.

UNDERSTANDING "FACTS"

This comment of Juanita's seems ridiculous to adults and perfectly logical to Juanita. It is very likely that no one had told her about the hose. She had been told, apparently, that heaven is in the sky and that God and Jesus live there. She knew that when her father or mother watered the lawn and flowers, they got out the big hose. Jesus must surely have one too.

The points to note here are how an easy conversational manner of questions back and forth provides both a clue to the facts or concepts children have and an opportunity to straighten out some of the facts. This is teaching children effectively.

When you have led a child to answer your questions, it is important not to ridicule or reject the answer. Most children respond in good faith with good intentions. They believe that you really wanted to know what they think. Let them know that you respect them while you correct the facts.

Sometimes you cannot correct all the facts at once. Mrs. Badami could not. Her answer to Juanita was not scientifically correct, but it did help the children to begin to associate clouds with rain:

"I don't think Jesus has a hose, Juanita. Rain falls when two clouds full of drops of water bump into each other. Bang! The water spills out, and we say it's raining. But you are right about why it rains. God planned for the rain so that all the flowers and trees and the grass could have a drink. The rain is good for other things too. Can you think of any?" The children talked about this, but they made no connection between the rain that falls and the water that comes through their faucets.

"When the rain falls, it falls in lakes and reservoirs, which then give us water to wash our dishes and our clothes." Mrs. Badami held up some clothes, and the children began talking again about dishes and clothes and water and baths. "It fills the lakes and the rivers so that boats can sail, like Yuki's daddy's boat. Today we will try out a little rain water. Would you like to do that? Some children may sail these little boats, some may wash doll clothes, one can water our plants."

WATER ACTIVITIES

For the first day that year Mrs. Badami really appreciated her kitchen preschool room. She put two children, wearing aprons, on high stools to sail boats in the rain water she had poured into the sink. Others, also in aprons, washed doll clothes in more of the rain water in the big dishpan set on a low table. They hung the clothes to dry on the clothesline stretched between two drawer pulls at the far end of the kitchen. Newspapers underneath caught the drips. Ellen had a watering can full of rain water to water the plants.

Everyone wanted to get into the water, so Mrs. Badami beat up a big bowl of soapsuds finger paint with a little water—of course—and soap. (See page 222 for recipe.) The children took turns playing with the egg beater, and each one took several large spoonfuls of thick suds. Six children, up to their elbows in white, billowy, beautiful soapsuds, stood around a long low table.

Ken and Louise washed their hands in it.

Patrick carefully picked up gobs of it and placed them in a considered arrangement before him.

Takeenya moved her hands and arms in rhythm, singing "It's Raining."

Raul named his artistic efforts—after he had completed them, of course. First he was a ballet dancer. Then he was a figure skater on ice. His hands and feet and body and voice were all part of this activity.

Then Takeenya suggested they all go walking around the table one after the other. They kept one or both hands on the table as they walked. This became a kind of dance and the children enjoyed it thoroughly. Around and around they went, making wide swaths through the suds.

Carrying on this variety of activity requires good alert teachers. Children need help with aprons and occasionally with mopping up in water play. This morning's program required three active teachers. No one could stop to count the offering, take attendance, or stand and talk to a visiting adult.

GROUP TIME

About 11:40 the teachers began helping children clean up these activities. There were many opportunities to talk about rain with the children during this hour of free play.

The children who came to the rug heard the story "The Storm" (page 153). At its conclusion each child had a paper cup full of cool fresh water to drink and a graham cracker to eat.

Juanita said the prayer. "Thank you, God, for all this water. Amen."

Some heard the story "Four Looking Walks" (page 150) read by one teacher. Others tried to do some finger plays and talked about the mounted pictures with a second teacher. A few children played with the puzzles and the dolls.

Church was over then and everyone went home again—in the sun!

I hope that you and your children will have equally rich, spontaneous learning experiences. To take advantage of these opportunities you must know your children, know your resources, and use your imagination!

An Extra Letter

How to Use the Resource Sections

The three resource sections of this book contain stories, poems, songs, games, finger plays, and activities for you to use as you plan your sessions. I have tried to arrange these materials in an order that will be helpful to you.

SEASONS

The resources are in a seasonal sequence:

Section I, Fall and Early Winter (September through December)
Section II, Late Winter and Early Spring (January through April)
Section III, Late Spring and Summer (May through August)

Suggestions for alternate use of these resources in other times of the year are given under "Teaching Plans" in each resource section.

EXPERIENCES

The arrangement is also based on experiences common to children. I have tried, therefore, to imagine what the thoughts, feelings, and curiosities of preschool children might be at any given time and have tried to develop the teaching materials accordingly.

For example, when preschoolers first come to church an entirely new experience is ahead of them. They know almost nothing about what happens in the preschool or what is expected of them. To help them understand and digest this new experience there are stories, conversations, and activities about the church and the church preschool. You may not want to use all of these resources, but they will help you begin.

Summer activities are in Resource Section III, beginning on page 208. Groups beginning their year in July or August will want to use some of these activities as well as those suggested for the introduction to the church preschool in Resource Section I.

SPECIAL DAYS

Thanksgiving and Christmas resources are included in Resource Section I for use in November and December.

Materials to help you plan your sessions from January through April are in Resource Section II. Easter resources are included here.

Church School Day or Children's Day is sometimes also celebrated as promotion Sunday. Suggestions for this day will be found on page 198.

APPENDIX

The Appendix contains recipes and instruction for art activities, plans for building equipment, room arrangements, the bibliography, and addresses of sources.

BASIC THEMES

Three themes run throughout this material. These are the three questions that most preschoolers are asking: "Who am I? Who are you? What is the world like?" (Be sure to read the three letters I wrote to you about these questions. The letters begin on page 107.) These questions are the unfinished business of preschoolers. They, you, and I will spend our lives defining and redefining the answers. It is the purpose of the preschool program during the entire session—not just the story time—to help the children find good, satisfying, Christian answers at their own level.

We cannot separate the questions and deal with them one at a time. All these questions may be felt by the child at the same time. Different children may be concerned with different aspects of them. An answer to one question also gives partial answers to the other two. Examine each story or activity carefully and you will see that it provides some answers to all these questions.

USING THE RESOURCES

Let us look for a minute at how the stories and other resources may be used. The stories about families and going to church, for instance, are not intended primarily to teach the child a specific interpretation or behavior, or to entertain them, although these things may happen. Rather, they are intended to help children understand what church is like and how they are a part of it.

The interest centers, finger plays, songs, prayers, and special activities used should also help the children to learn about the church and themselves in relation to it. The pictures around the room and the books in the book center are important resources for helping the child develop answers to the questions: "Who am I?" (Am I a person of worth in this church?) "Who are you?" (What kind of persons are these children and teachers?) "What is the world like?" (What is this world called "the church"? Does it have a place for me? Is it a place where I want to be?)

It is logical that the children will be interested in the stories and conversations about the church when they first enter the preschool, but it is not inevitable. Circumstances may make a story, song, conversation, or activity about pets or friends or a new baby much more valuable and appropriate. As soon as you can, become acquainted with the resources from all three sections. Then you will be able to change your plans to fit the interests and experiences of a particular session.

TO PLAN A SESSION

First choose a story, a book, an activity, or a conversation idea as the "kernel" of the session. Then select songs, pictures, activities, or stories that relate to the kernel and that will stimulate the children's interest and response.

Additional resources you will need are library books, pictures, and special supplies for the interest centers and activities. Suggestions for these are found under "Teaching Plans" in the resource sections and in the letters "Company's Coming!" (page 7) and "Lynn's Father Asks: Is This *Christian* Education?" (page 171).

Before you make plans for your first session, *read all of this book*. In the letters in the other two sections I have written about the use of the Bible and prayer, about the big (theological) questions children ask in their own way, more about ways of working with preschoolers and their parents, and many other things to help you in your task as a preschool teacher. Become familiar with the resources in all three sections so that you can turn quickly to the song, story, or activity needed by one child or the whole group at a particular moment.

As I have said many times before, use the materials to suit *your* situation. Build the program to fit *your* children; deal with *their* questions. Do not stick to one part of this book just because it happens to come next. It may not suit you at this point at all. What happens to be last in this book may come first in the lives of your children. Turn the resources around, adapt them, change them, or use them as idea starters and create your own materials. Remember to be flexible even after careful preparation for a session, for an opportunity for learning may necessitate a quick change of plans.

SUGGESTED SESSION SCHEDULES

Sessions for the preschool group must be, above everything, flexible. Teachers should be alert to the interests and needs of the children, to signs of fatigue or overstimulation, and be ready to vary the program accordingly. However, here are some basic schedules to guide you in your plans. If there is an extended session, perhaps a system of teacher rotation will provide the needed constancy of teaching staff while allowing for participation in the Christian community at worship.

A ONE-HOUR SESSION

If your session is 9:30 to 10:30	If your session is 11:00 to 12:00	
9:00	10:30	Teachers arrive and make last-minute preparations
9:15–10:00	10:45–11:30	Greet children, free play time
10:00–10:20	11:30–11:50	Group time
10:20–10:35	11:50–12:05	Free play, going home time, pick up, put on coats, say good-bye
10:35–10:50	12:05–12:20	Teachers finish picking up, cleaning up, putting away; begin evaluation and plans for next session

A TWO-AND-ONE-HALF-HOUR SESSION

(9:30–10:30, regular church school; 11:00–12:00, extended session during worship or a weekday "Children's Morning Out" session)

9:00	Teachers arrive and make last-minute preparations
9:15–10:00	Greet children, free play time
10:00–10:10	Restroom time
10:10–10:30	Group time: story, music, finger plays, cookies (If some children may go home during this time, one teacher should be available to these children.)
10:45–11:05	Quiet activities—looking at books and pictures, playing with puzzles, and similar quiet activities—some children may even need to lie down and listen to quiet music.)
11:05–11:40	Special activities, such as walks, planting, having a visitor, "show and tell" time, or outdoor play in good weather (You might serve a second snack at the end of this period if the children seem tired.)
11:40–11:55	Group time: music, songs, finger plays, stories
11:55–12:05	Free play, going home time, pick up, put on coats, say good-bye
12:05–12:20	Teachers pick up, clean up; begin to evaluate and plan next session

Photo from Sunrise/Trinity Photos, © Shirley Haley

Resource Section I Contents

TEACHING PLANS 56
Theme: The Child Goes to Church 57
A Sample Teaching Plan for *The Child Goes to Church* 58
Theme: The Child in the Family 60
A Sample Teaching Plan for *The Child in the Family* 62
Theme: Falltime and Thanksgiving 64
A Sample Teaching Plan for *Falltime and Thanksgiving* 67
Theme: Christmas 69
A Sample Teaching Plan for *Christmas* 72

BOOKS 74

PICTURES 74

ACTIVITIES 75
Getting-Acquainted Activities 75
- Ball Rolling 75
- Count Noses, Name Names 75
- Taking Turns 75

General Activities 75
- See How I Am Growing 75
- Take a Walk 75
- Snapshots 76
- Visiting the Church Sanctuary 76

Falltime Activities 76
- Making Fall Leaves 76
- Playing Squirrel 76
- A Scuffing Walk 76
- Planting Bulbs 77
- Apple Seeds 77
- Making a Halloween Pumpkin 77
- A Turkey Visit 77
- Thanksgiving Place Mats 78

Christmas Activities 78
- Playing Christmas 78
- The Friendly Beasts 78
- Jingle Bells 78
- Decorating Paper Christmas Trees 78
- Making Christmas Tree Ornaments 78
- A Birds' Christmas Tree 79
- Making Christmas Presents 79

STORIES 79
- *Karen Goes to Preschool* 80
- *Ronnie and the Pancakes* 81
- *Why I Like Sunday* 82
- *Jenny Lee* 83
- *Marc's Sunflowers* 85
- *Fun for Joey* 86
- *What Do You Think of That?* 87
- *The First Christmas* 88
- *Jesus* 89

FINGER PLAYS 90
- *Bedtime Story* 90
- *Here's the Church* 91
- *The Fine Family* 91
- *The Apple Tree* 91
- *The Turkey* 91

POEMS 91
- *Baby Seeds* 92
- *Whisky Frisky* 92

PRAYERS 92

SONGS 92
- *God, We Thank You* 94
- *This Is the Way* 95
- *Growing Up* 96
- *Open, Shut Them* 96
- *Today Is Sunday* 97
- *This Is the Fall-time* 98
- *Away in a Manger* 99
- *Bye-low, My Baby* 100

TEACHING PLANS

The following plans suggest enough materials for several sessions on each theme. Do not try to use all the resources suggested for the theme on any one day. Choose what seems good and possible for you and your children. Most of the material can be—indeed, should be—used many times. A story is no more worn out by one reading or telling than a song or finger play is. In fact, just the opposite is true. Children's appreciation and enjoyment grow as they become familiar with the story or song.

SUGGESTED THEMES

Suggested themes in this resource section are:

> The Child Goes to Church ("Karen Goes to the Preschool," page 80)
> The Child in the Family ("What Do You Think of That?" page 87)
> Falltime and Thanksgiving
> Christmas ("The First Christmas," page 88, and "Jesus," page 89)

These are suggested for major use from July through December or September through December, depending upon the date and the beginning of your church school year.

THE FIRST SESSIONS

What happens to the children the first session or two is most important. This is when children will decide that they want to come to church school or that it is a place to be feared and disliked. You will need to have read all of the letters before you teach this first session, but reread "The First Sunday" (page 23) and "The Second Sunday" (page 31) for specific help in planning your first sessions.

NEW SUMMER GROUPS

Churches that begin the preschool year in July will want to spend a number of sessions during July and August on the theme "The Child Goes to Church." Admission on the basis of school dates may bring some children not much more than two-and-a-half years of age into the new group. Certainly you will have very young threes. This means spending a much longer time helping children adjust to you, the room, the equipment, and the other children. It may be four or five sessions before you can even begin to have a group time involving more than three or four children. To further complicate matters, summertime brings visiting cousins to the preschool and may take children out for a vacation just as they are beginning to feel at home. It is important to establish simple routines to give these young children a sense of security. Special activities should not be planned until children feel at home in the preschool.

Take advantage of outdoor play during the summer months. Observe one caution, however: Be sure the children feel at home with you, the room, and the other children before you introduce them to another new experience such as going outdoors or to a nearby park. You will want to check the activities suggested in Resource Section III as well as those in this section in planning your summer sessions. Also reread the letter "Summertime" (page 191) before you begin to make your plans.

The organization of the resource materials and teaching plans are only suggestions. Materials related to the children's experiences in the church are given first, but the resources related to "The Child in the Family" might just as well be your first unit. Stories or activities about family life may give the children a feeling of security during their first days in the church preschool. Or, you may use resources from both themes in one session, such as a getting-acquainted activity suggested in the teaching plans for "The Child Goes to Church" along with a secure-feeling family story.

Again, the number of sessions in which you use a particular group of materials depends upon the experiences the children are having. You need to learn to be aware of what is a new experience for each child, when it is new, how long it is new, and plan your sessions accordingly. The child's experience of feeling wanted and at home in the preschool has no end, even after six or eight weeks. In every session the child must experience it anew in the living together that goes on in the preschool.

Theme:
The Child Goes to Church

Going to the church preschool may be one of the first experience of being on their own for some young children. Here the child is separated from home and family and becomes part of a group of children the same age in a place called the "church." How they are going to feel about the church in the years to come and whether or not they will commit themselves to God through Jesus Christ when they are young persons or adults depends to a large extent on the experiences they have in the preschool group. How do you think Shelley and Louis ("The First Sunday," page 23) will feel about the church? Or perhaps you will have a Juan ("Teachers Are Dependable: All Children Have Rights," page 39) in the very first session. Will his experience in your class help him to feel good about himself and the church? If it does, he probably will want to keep coming to this place called the church where he may sense that friendly and loving people care about him.

PURPOSE

You will be especially concerned these first sessions in the preschool class *to help the children feel loved, wanted, and secure in this new "world."* This is a big order. You will not accomplish it in four to six sessions; you will work at these purposes throughout the year. But, during these first few weeks, the way you approach and respond to each child, the stories you tell, the activities you plan, and the routines you develop will all be geared to help each child have a happy first experience in church.

THE ROOM

Before you begin to prepare your room or space, you will want to reread the letters about room arrangement ("Company's Coming!" page 7, and "Doing Big Things in Little Space," page 11). See Appendix (pages 233–34) for illustrations of room arrangements. The setup of the room or space in which your group meets is very important. It tells children at a glance whether there is a place for them in their church. Children learn by doing, as do people of all ages. The equipment and materials for the free play period are important for learning about themselves, others, and the world in which they live.

Does your housekeeping center say, "Come, cook breakfast" or, "This doll needs to be cuddled and fed"? A pan of soapy water (protect the floor with papers, and protect shirts and dresses with plastic aprons) for washing dishes or doll clothes will help children feel relaxed and at home in the preschool.

If you have room for a block center, are the trucks, tractors, and interestingly shaped blocks placed to engage children in constructive play?

Are there tables, chairs, and materials that invite children to quiet play—working with clay, pasting, putting puzzles together, "reading" books?

These and other books from your basic library (see Appendix, page 235) might be placed in the book center for the sessions on the theme "The Child Goes to Church":

Big Red Barn
Home for a Bunny
The Runaway Bunny
Baby Animals
Most Ministers Wear Sneakers

A Bible, an offering basket (if you have one), flowers or something lovely to look at, or a teaching picture may be put on the special table placed near the rug or wherever you plan to gather the children together for group time. (See "Company's Coming!" page 7.)

Place around the room—at the child's eye level—seasonal pictures, an enlarged photo of your church, and possibly an enlarged snapshot of your minister shaking hands with a child at the door of the church. Cut from magazines and mount pictures of children playing together, taking turns; children or families in church or walking or riding to church; families doing things together that your children might do with their families. These pictures may be put up in the interest centers or on a picture board or rail. You could ask parents to send photographs from their home, and these could be shared and displayed.

ACTIVITIES

You will probably use very few organized activities early in the church school year. The following activities are suggested to help the children feel at home in the church school and with one another.

Use name tags. (See "Company's Coming!" page 7, and "The First Sunday," page 23.)
Choose individual pictures for the coat hooks. (See above letters.)
Play getting-acquainted games (page 75).
Ball Rolling
Count Noses, Name Names
Taking Turns

Use art activities.
Dough Clay, page 223
Pasting, page 224

The child's enjoyment of working with clay or pasting increases with continued use. These activities may also relieve tensions children develop as they adjust to the new environment of the preschool room or space.

GROUP TIME

This will be only a few minutes for the first few sessions. Later, children may enjoy a ten-to-fifteen-minute group time for story, conversation, songs, prayer, finger plays, or games. Some children will not be ready to join the group. Do not force them. One teacher should be free to work with the children who do not join the group.

The resources listed below are to be used for several sessions. Prepare your group time plans for each session using several of these resources, but do not try to use all the songs or finger plays on any one day. Plan according to the needs of your children.

Finger plays
Here's the Church, page 91
A Bedtime Story, page 90

Stories
Karen Goes to the Preschool, page 80
Ronnie and the Pancakes, page 81
Why I Like Sunday, page 82

Songs
This Is the Way, page 95
Open, Shut Them, page 96
Today Is Sunday, page 97

Prayers
See page 92 for sample prayers.
Your prayers should grow out of the children's experiences during the morning. When a morning has been a happy time for the children, talk about "the happy times we had this morning" in your prayer. Read again "What Kind of Prayer for Preschoolers?" (page 179). Be prepared to offer prayer whenever and however it will be meaningful for a child, the group, and yourself.

A Sample Teaching Plan for *The Child Goes to Church*

To develop a plan for any session, your first consideration is the children you teach. What experiences did they have the last time? Was Max still unwilling to leave his mother's side? Did Aruba find washing dishes in the housekeeping center so satisfying that she spoke to you for the first time since entering church school? What will help both Max and Aruba to feel wanted and at home?

By the third or fourth session most of the children may feel sufficiently at home in the preschool so that you can plan ways of *emphasizing the joy and anticipation of coming to church school.* Events that seem commonplace to us as adults are often exciting and important to preschoolers. These include riding or walking to church with mother or father, going to their own room, and playing with other children. Some may have a special breakfast, as in the story "Ronnie and the Pancakes."

Special preparation for sessions emphasizing the joy and anticipation of coming to church school includes obtaining activity materials, pictures, and books and selecting a story, games, finger plays, songs, prayers—whatever you need—for the group time.

The following sample teaching plan suggests a way you might develop your own teaching notebook as well as an outline of a session schedule and a group of resources which you might use for one session early in the church school year. I have written the plan for my own group, including reminders to myself about setting up the room, special needs of some children, approximate time schedule I plan to follow, and page references of resources I may use so that I can turn to them quickly. You may add notes in brackets of additional things you might do or materials you may want to review before making your own plan.

PREPARATION

The Room

- Set up interest centers so that they say, "Come in. There are lots of interesting things to do here for children just your size."
- Bring flowers, a Bible, and a picture of the church to put on the special table. (See "The Use of the Bible with Preschool Children," page 175.)
- Select two or three books about church and human or animal families for the book center.
- Put the church puzzle and two or three others on the small table.
- Cut out paper shapes for pasting.
- Make green, yellow, or pink dough clay for the art activity table.
- Have crayons and paper handy on the shelf or in supply cupboard.
- Find pictures of families going to church, driving or walking together, or of children playing together to place in the interest centers and on the picture board. Be sure some pictures represent single parent families and that racial and ethnic diversity is evident in the pictures as a whole.

Special Equipment

Bring a large ball for rolling.

SESSION TIME

Greet Children and Parents

You may still need to use name tags unless your group is small. Be sure each teacher also wears a name tag. Sit on a low chair or bend down to the child's level when you say, "Good morning." Greet the parents also, but keep your conversation brief. Your first concern is the children.

Free Play (about 30 to 35 minutes)

[Reread "Company's Coming!" page 7, and "How to Teach When You're Not Talking—and When You Are," page 103].

Observe what is happening and make appropriate suggestions. See that Tom has a turn at the dishpan again if he wants one.

Sharon seems interested in the blocks. She might begin to play if her mother sat near the block center.

Group Time (about 10 to 15 minutes)

(When children are new to one another and their teachers, the group time will be very brief. During the first session or two you may not even tell a story. Use a finger play to gain the children's attention and then talk about their activities during the free play period.

If the group seems ready, you might sing a song or say a brief prayer. For other sessions you might tell a story, look at pictures, or sing an action song during group time, as in the following outline. Not all children will be ready to join in the group time. One teacher needs to be free to work quietly with the children who do not join the group.)

Finger Play: "Here's the Church" (page 91) or "A Bedtime Story" (page 90)

Game: "Count Noses, Name Names" (page 75)

Story: "Ronnie and the Pancakes" (page 81)

Conversation: Let the children tell about getting ready for church school. They may want to tell how many pancakes they can eat!

Do they ever sing a little song while they are getting dressed? Perhaps they will talk about being big enough to come to church school.

Prayer: "Dear God, we are glad we can come to church with our friends and families. Amen."

The prayer should grow out of the conversation or activities of the morning. See "What Kind of Prayer for Preschoolers," page 179.

Songs: "This Is the Way" (page 95)
Use actions about getting ready for church.

"Today Is Sunday" (page 97)
Use with story.

Going Home Time, Cleanup, Pick up, Saying Good-bye (about 10 minutes)
Make picking up an enjoyable part of the morning.

Suggest that some of the children try counting while they put the blocks on the shelf. Others might arrange the cars in "garages." Say good-bye to the children individually. Tell each one that you are glad he or she is a part of our preschool group and that we are looking forward to seeing each child again next time.

AFTER THE SESSION

The children will not have put away all the toys. Finish this job and discuss the events of the morning as an evaluation of this morning's session and as a beginning of planning for the next session. Schedule a meeting time and place for your teaching team.

Remember, what you plan may not be used at all! See "A Change of Session Plans" (page 47). This tells how a teacher made a sudden change of plans because of rain. Be ready to adapt or abandon your plans to meet the needs and interests of the children in your group.

Theme: The Child in the Family

All young children live in a family. But these families vary greatly: families consisting of father, mother, and possibly brothers and sisters; one-parent families; divorced families with joint or shared custody; three-or four-generation families; biracial or bicultural families; familes of wealth and families with few material things.

Experiences in family living will be different for each child, but they provide some common ground for stories, finger plays, and other activities in the church school. It is most important for you to know the kind of homes from which your children come as background for the sessions in this unit. Reread the letters "Meeting Charles" (page 3) and "Love and Understanding" (page 35).

PURPOSE

Your special concern for the sessions planned around the theme "The Child in the Family" is *to help children discover further answers to their basic questions as they think about their relationships with other members of their families.* To find answers to "Who am I?" preschoolers need to know that they are significant persons who live and learn and grow in families. To begin to answer, "Who are you?" children need to discover their special place in their homes, the special things that families do together, and how the members of families may help each other. To help children discover Christian answers to these questions you need to know each child and the family personally, provide interest centers to stimulate dramatic play, and tell stories and talk together about living in families. Most of all you need to listen and be sensitive to the particular circumstances of each child's family situation and the concerns and needs—whatever these may be—of each individual child.

ALTERNATIVE SUGGESTIONS

If your preschool class began its year in September, you may want to combine some resources related to suggested materials for this theme with "Falltime and Thanksgiving" to take advantage of any seasonal changes in your part of the country. Later in the church school year you may plan other sessions on the theme of "The Child in the Family."

THE ROOM

By now you and your children have "lived" in your room or space for several weeks. You may have discovered that your equipment needs to be rearranged to provide better light for art activities and more space for the block builders. Or perhaps you have too many chairs and tables and not enough space for interest centers. Find a place to store the excess furniture. If you need an easel or other equipment, work with your children's parents and/or the Christian education committee to make or obtain the items you need.

Check your equipment and supplies and change your interest centers to provide opportunities for experiences related to the new theme. If you are using the theme of "The Child in the Family" early in the year, do not make radical changes. This would confuse the children. But change pictures, puzzles, books; and add items related to the theme to the interest centers.

Provide a box of dress-up clothes for the housekeeping center: hats, purses, gloves, blouses, shirts, vests, overalls, jeans, shoes, wallets, ties, scarves, and sashes. Add small suitcases or briefcases for "traveling," a lunch box for "packing lunch," or a basket for "picnics."

If you have not had wooden or plastic figures of a family in your block center, add these figures for this theme. Usable figures may be made by pasting catalog cutouts on oblong blocks. Be certain the figures are racially and ethnically diverse.

Put away one or two of the puzzles the children have been using and bring out a new one, perhaps one of a family or a house.

In the book center you might put out:

Make Way for Ducklings
Goodnight Moon
See How You Grow
How You Were Born
The New Baby at Your Home

See the list of basic books on page 235 for other suggestions. Do not crowd your book table. Remove the books used in the last unit except for one or two favorites.

Provide equipment and materials for easel painting or finger painting as a change from pasting and dough clay. (See pages 221–22.)

Flowers might be put on the special table, in the housekeeping center, or wherever your room needs a bright touch.

Seasonal pictures and pictures related to family life which you have gathered from magazines and other sources will be useful.

ACTIVITIES

Choose from these activities the ones that seem most appropriate to the needs of your children. If you are using this particular theme when fall is at its height in your part of the country and you have access to the outdoors, you will surely want to take a scuffing leaf walk and plant bulbs, if this is at all possible. Continue getting-acquainted activities:

Ball Rolling, page 75
Count Noses, Name Names, page 75
Taking Turns, page 75

New activities

See How I Am Growing, page 75
Snapshots, page 76
A Scuffing Walk, page 76
Planting Bulbs, page 77

Art activities

Continue dough clay and pasting.
Easel Painting, page 222
Finger Painting, page 221

Easel and finger painting are good activities for preschoolers because these activities utilize large muscles and provide release for expression of feelings or tensions. Protect the floor with newspapers or drop cloths. Protect clothes with coverall aprons made from old shirts or plastic. See page 221 for instructions for easel and finger painting. Do not do both activities in one session unless you have lots of space and extra teachers to supervise each activity.

GROUP TIME

More children may be coming to the group time now than at the beginning of the year. Others are staying for a longer time. Do not rush your children into joining in group time if they are not ready for it. Be sure that there is always a teacher free to work with the children in the interest centers. On the other hand, be alert to the children's needs. They may not want to join the group because they are particularly busy in an interest center at the moment; they are not aware that they are getting tired and need the relaxation of sitting on the rug, having a snack, and listening to a story. Assure these children that they may go back to their play, if they want to, after they have come to the rug and have had their snacks.

Select from the following list, or from any of the other resources in this book, the materials you plan to use for each session. Your knowledge of your children and their interests should be your guide.

Finger plays

The Fine Family, page 91
A Bedtime Story, page 91

Stories

What Do You Think of That? page 87
Jenny Lee, page 83
Ronnie and the Pancakes, page 81
Why I Like Sunday, page 82

Poem

Baby Seeds, page 92

Songs

Growing Up, page 96
Repeat the ones you have already used.

Prayers

If you have been talking about baby brothers or sisters, you might say a thank-you prayer for babies. If the conversation has been about helping in the family, mention in the prayer some of the things children do to help. See page 92 for sample prayers.

CHECK UP ON YOURSELF

Do you know by name and sight every child who has been in your group three or more times? Do you know about the child's family? Does the child have brothers and sisters? Is it a one-parent home? Does the child have playmates the same age in the neighborhood? Are there any families which need special help that the church can give to them? If you know these things, you may be more aware of opportunities to be a channel of God's love to these children and their families.

A Sample Teaching Plan for *The Child in the Family*

As you begin your planning for a session, remember what happened the last time. Did you have to comfort any children by holding them on your lap? The kinds of experiences that a child has in the family are reflected in behavior. One may have felt left out of the family circle because of a new baby. Perhaps another kept asking when mother was coming back because her mother had been at the hospital most of the week before with a sister who was having surgery. Both children may need a little extra attention in church school for a few sessions while their parents are busy with others.

As you think about your individual children and prepare your session plan, you may want to devote one or more sessions to *helping the children discover that all of them are important to their families.* The core for this sample teaching plan is the group conversation. The story and other resources are chosen to stimulate this conversation. You may want to adapt this sample teaching plan to fit your own group and situation.

PREPARATION

The Room

- An attractive room encourages participation. Your room teaches!
- Repair or wash dress-up clothes as needed.
- Place a family of wooden figures or stand-up paper dolls on the special table. The children may talk about the doll family or their own families as they put their offerings in the basket.
- Select at least one book about a new baby for your book table.
- Find several pictures of families doing things together, of children doing grown-up things, of families with grandparents. Place these around the room where they will be at the eye level of the children. Be certain the figures, dolls, and pictures represent different kinds of families and racial and ethnic groups.

Special Equipment

- Cut several large sheets of heavy wrapping paper or other strong paper, such as the kind used to cover church dining tables, for the activity "See How I Am Growing" (page 75).
- Easel and materials for painting
- Glazed paper and finger paints
- Newspapers and aprons
- Prepare paper dolls or mounted individual pictures of family members for use with the "Jenny Lee" stories. You may want to paste a copy of each story on the back of the appropriate picture so that you can read the story easily while holding the picture for the children to see.

SESSION TIME

Greet Children

Greet the children individually. If parents want to talk to you, suggest a time when you might call or visit them at home. The greeting period is important. Do not use it to catch up on the latest news with your coteachers or the parents who are your special friends, or for last-minute preparations such as mixing paint.

Free Play (about 30 to 35 minutes)
The activity "See How I Am Growing" may continue for several weeks unless your group is very small. Some children will not want to be a part of this activity during this session. Next week these same children may remind you that it is their turn to have their pictures drawn. At least one teacher should be free from this activity to work with children in the interest centers.

Group Time (about 10 to 15 minutes)
Group time is significant for the children who share in it. The teacher should not do all the talking. As you move from finger plays to songs to story, visit with the children and accept their contributions to the conversation. You may find on occasion that children will respond to your conversation with "stories" of their own. Wonderful! Save your story or other plans for the next session.

Finger Play: "The Fine Family" (page 91)

Story: "Jenny Lee" (page 83)
There are five separate "Jenny Lee" stories in this resource section. Any of them would be suitable for this session. You will probably want to begin with "What Jenny Lee Can Do." "Jenny Lee and Josie" and "Jenny Lee and Jim" might also be used today.

If your children are more interested in talking about their mothers and fathers, you will want to use "Jenny Lee and her Parents."

Conversation
Encourage the children to talk by using the questions in the story "Jenny Lee." Help them to think about what each member of the family does. Let them tell you about their families.

Prayer
Perhaps you could use one or two of the ideas about family relationships suggested by the children in your prayer.

Song: "Growing Up" (page 96)
You may not have time for a song if the children are responsive in the conversation period.

Free Play, Pick-up Time, Saying Good-bye (about 10 minutes)
As you help children put on their coats, you may talk personally about their own families. Let the children know you are glad they are in your group and that you want them to come again for the next session.

AFTER THE SESSION

If you cannot leave the outlines of the children on the wall during the week, pack them away carefully. You will want to put them up again next week and draw outlines of the other children who did not take a part in this activity today. Keep all of the outlines until spring, when you can look at them with the children again to see how much each child has grown.

As you are doing your final cleanup, talk over the session. Think about special things that happened to the children during the morning, and begin to plan ways of working with the children next week.

On-the-spot evaluations are very helpful, but they do not take the place of thoughtful, during-the-week evaluation and planning.

Theme: Falltime and Thanksgiving

SOME THOUGHTS ON THANKSGIVING

Some of the child's good experiences with friends and family and falltime can be thought of as preparation for Thanksgiving. The experiences of falltime will vary in different parts of the country. In some places the coming of the fall rains that make the brown earth green again is the most important seasonal change. In some of the southern areas there may be no really noticeable changes in nature which say, "Now it is fall." But to preschoolers all the world is very new; and you have the privilege of seeing it afresh through their eyes as you help them to see all around them. Most of the stories and activities suggested in this unit can be adapted for use wherever you live.

Teachers in areas where fall brings definite seasonal changes must pick and choose among the suggested activities so that the children will have time to live with each experience.

A scuffing walk through leaves; gathering nuts, acorns, or pine cones; helping to make a jack-o'-lantern; helping put the garden to bed; watching the birds flying in flocks and the squirrels burying their nuts; finding colorful leaves; blowing the seeds of dried milkweed pods—all of these (and you'll think of more) can be rich falltime experiences for those living in suburban or rural areas. Such falltime experiences can enrich the meaning of Thanksgiving for preschoolers.

By experience I mean more than just pointing out things such as falling leaves and telling a story about them. Plan for the children to hear or feel, see or touch or smell the new event. Knowing it is new to them, you should try to imagine how it must feel to them. Enjoy it with them, feel it with them, talk about it with them, listen carefully to their comments and questions, then share your understanding and appreciation of the event with them.

I have some question about how thankful and grateful children can really feel. But I have no doubt that they take great pleasure in some things and do feel glad about them. Their pleasure is, in the main, physical enjoyment—hearing the rustle of the leaves as they scuff through them; feeling, taking apart, or amassing a bagful of acorns. "What makes the leaves turn lovely colors?" is not typically a three-year-old question. But the fact that they are not curious about the *why* of the colors does not make the experience any less important or meaningful to them. You already know about walking through piles of brittle, rustling leaves, but they don't. Their response to having fun with delight may be as close to worship for them as your response to feeling wonder with appreciation is for you. Children also experience awe and wonder at times, and this feeling is akin to worship. But these moments are not nearly so frequent as the happy, pleasurable ones.

SHARING PROJECTS

Bringing canned goods to be delivered to food pantries is of questionable value as an experience of sharing for the preschoolers. In the first place, the canned goods are not theirs to share; they are their parent's, and hence cannot be an expression of the child's gratitude for abundance. In the second place, children may not understand all the reason for bringing them. They are here-and-now children. They understand—sometimes—sharing a big lot of clay with a child who has too little. Yet they have not lived long enough to be able to give themselves with feeling and concern to people whom they do not know. However, homelessness and hunger are problems in many communities, and young children may be aware of needs. Giving some of a favorite, nonperishable food such as peanut butter or jelly might be most appropriate. Use your judgment on this. If the whole church is joining in such efforts, this can be one way of helping children know that they are a real part of the church community.

THANKSGIVING SERVICES

A word about family services in church at Thanksgiving, or any time, for that matter. I have seen excellent ones with preschoolers in attendance. They have been services of prayer and praise, not formal or stilted, and only about twenty minutes long.

It is very desirable for preschool children to have the opportunity to visit the church sanctuary with their families. It is good for them to hear the organ; see the pulpit, communion table, and flowers; hear and see all the people worshiping under the leadership of church members, the minister, and the choir. (In some churches the children may be in the sanctuary briefly on some Sundays. In some small church buildings, class may be held in the sanctuary. They need to experience church worship as well as their own activities in their special area.)

If the Thanksgiving service is not too long for the children, by all means plan for them to attend with their parents or with you. But if the service is longer than half an hour, it would be better for the preschoolers to visit the opening ten or fifteen minutes of the service and spend the rest of the time together with their teachers in the preschool room.

PURPOSES

Your purposes for these four to eight sessions are *to enjoy the wonder of falltime and to help children relate this joy and wonder to their question "What is the world like?"* (Read "And 'What Is the World Like?' " page 117, to understand the importance of this question for preschool children.) The children will begin to find answers to this question as they experience pleasure and joy with the world about them, as they respond to the world with gladness and delight.

THE ROOM

Surround the group with signs of fall. If possible, take the children outdoors to enjoy the falltime world. In any case, bring the fall (or other wonders of nature) inside.

Set up a new interest center, a "wonder table." This will be in addition to the table that contains the Bible, offering basket, and teaching pictures. Your wonder center may be a table, a window sill, a large flat box on a pew, a fruit crate, an old bookcase, whatever is available. On it (or in it) put the leaves, pine cones, gourds, cattails, cocoons, colored corn, milkweed pods, and other nature objects that you and the children bring.

Have vases for leaves and flowers and bowls for nuts and seeds available for decorating the housekeeping center. You might add a few empty food containers and special dishes for "cooking Thanksgiving dinner."

Choose some appropriate books for the book center from your basic library (see Bibliography, page 235) such as:

When Autumn Comes
The Very Hungry Caterpillar
The Thanksgiving Story

Borrow from your church school or public library two or three autumn books. Children can learn many things from the pictures in such books.

Use seasonal pictures cut from magazines or old calendars. Place these at the children's eye level. Remember, children "see" with their fingers as well as with their eyes, so protect permanent pictures with plastic or place behind glass.

ACTIVITIES

Select four or five of the following activities on the basis of the interests of your group and the part of the country in which you live.

Making Fall Leaves, page 76
Playing Squirrel, page 76
Planting Bulbs, page 77
Apple Seeds, page 77
Making a Halloween Pumpkin, page 77
Visiting the Church Sanctuary, page 76
A Turkey Visit, page 77
Thanksgiving Place Mats, page 78

Some mornings you may use an activity instead of a story. Another time an activity may take most of the morning. Never use an activity for the sake of the activity. Keep in mind the needs of the children—what activities will help them find answers for their question "What is the world like?" Allow plenty of time for each activity: time for children to get ready to participate, to carry through the activity with a sense of satisfaction, and to talk about it afterward if they wish.

The last three activities listed above may be used a session or two before Thanksgiving. Otherwise these sessions will be similar to other days in the preschool. Read the "Fun for Joey" stories and the accompanying suggestions for conversations about being glad or thankful.

Art activities

Red, yellow, brown, or green paints will be good choices for easel painting. (Use one color to an easel.) Unless children wish to take their pictures home, put them up around the room for all to enjoy. Have materials for the activity "Making Fall Leaves" (page 76). Omit clay for a few sessions.

GROUP TIME

Are your children beginning to follow the routine of the morning more easily? Do the children put away their toys after free play time and settle down on the rug to talk, listen to a story, and eat their cookies? By November most of the children should be taking part in the group time. A few children may still need to play quietly in the centers rather than join the group. Use the finger plays, songs, and stories the children have enjoyed previously, as well as the following:

Finger plays

The Apple Tree, page 91
The Turkey, page 91

Stories

Marc's Sunflowers, page 85
Fun for Joey, page 86
Jenny Lee and Nighttime, page 84

Songs

This Is the Way, page 95
This Is the Fall-time, page 98
God, We Thank You, page 94

Poems

Baby Seeds, page 92
Whisky Frisky, page 92

Prayers

Let your brief prayers with the children express your and the group's real feelings of thanks or feeling glad about events of the morning. "It is good to feel the wind" or "It is fun to kick leaves" may be included in a prayer after you have taken a scuffing walk.

These resources will help you plan for your sessions during the fall and Thanksgiving time. There are many more resources than you can possibly use in four to eight sessions. Do not try to do too much. Enjoy the falltime with your children and discover some adult answers to the three big questions too!

A Sample Teaching Plan for *Falltime and Thanksgiving*

HOW TO BEGIN A UNIT

Note: An inner-city, urban church may not be able to use this session as there may be few signs of falltime visible outside.

To the children in your group, one session is much like every other session. The simple routines, the familiar interest centers, the pleasant story time and conversation have helped the children develop a sense of trust, a feeling of being liked and wanted in their church. The children are unaware of themes or units. These are devices to help you plan activities and use materials that will enrich the children's experience.

Moving into a new theme does not break into the continuity of the children's experiences. However, they will appreciate a certain amount of change in the room and in the activities. For the next several weeks you will want to provide opportunities for the children to become vividly aware of falltime in God's world and to begin to express their delight, wonder, and awe. You, their teacher, will want to use the words "Thank you, God" or "God planned for juicy red apples to grow from little brown seeds." The children may repeat some of these words; but they will have little meaning except as smelling, touching, and tasting that move them to be glad, to be a little awed by the wonder and mystery of the world.

This sample teaching plan suggests one way to introduce the theme of falltime and Thanksgiving. "A Scuffing Walk" is the kernel for this session.

PREPARATION

The Room

- Remove pictures and books related to the previous unit.
- If you have children's paintings or drawings or the growth charts on the wall, take these down also.
- Check equipment. Good housekeeping is a must.
- Put away dress-up clothes for a few weeks. Put leaves or fall flowers in the housekeeping center.
- Have extra vases for bouquets the children may bring.
- If you live in a farming community, you may want to supply toy farm equipment in the block corner for the "busy farmers" in your group to work at the fall chores. (Always provide durable, well-constructed toys. Avoid small, breakable toys, toys that have sharp edges, or that are painted with toxic paint.)
- Provide a table or a special place for a wonder center.
- Bring two or three interesting signs of fall for this center.
- Bring new things each session rather than too many at one time. The children might bring some items to put in the wonder center. A magnifying glass will make the wonder objects even more wonderful.
- Prepare materials for easel painting and making fall leaves.
- Put some of the falltime books suggested on page 66 in the book corner. A story about all four seasons is *Big Tree* in Resource Section III, page 214.
- Place in the interest centers and about the room seasonal pictures, pictures of people working at fall tasks, pictures of farmers gathering fall crops, and pictures of children having fun in leaves.

Special Activity

Before the day of your session check the best places for taking a scuffing walk or a looking walk. Reread the suggestions for different kinds of walks on pages 76 and 148.

SESSION TIME

Greet Children
If fall has really come to your part of the country, children may tell you about the flock of geese they saw flying overhead. Another may arrive loaded down with purple asters or yellow chrysanthemums from a garden and will need help putting them in a vase for the housekeeping center or the wonder center. Be as appreciative of the single yellow leaf someone silently hands you as you were of the flowers. Take the child by the hand and go to place the treasure in the wonder center.

Free Play (about 20 or 25 minutes today)
Let the children work with the equipment according to their interests. If some are wandering aimlessly from center to center you might suggest that they paint at the easel or color fall leaves (see "Making Fall Leaves," page 76, for instructions about this activity.) One teacher should be near the wonder table to talk with the children as they examine the various objects. After about 20 minutes move from child to child and tell each that it is time to finish their play, put things away, then come to the rug for group time. You might tell the children that you have a special surprise for them.

Group Time (about 10 minutes this morning)
Group time should be short today to allow a good twenty minutes for the scuffing walk and to still get back to the room before parents come.

Conversation
Look at the objects on the wonder table and talk about them.
Feel their fuzziness, smoothness, or prickles.
Let the children who brought signs of fall tell about them if they wish.

Song
"This Is the Fall-time" (page 98) or "God, We Thank You" (page 94). If you sing "God, We Thank You," insert appropriate words for lines two, three, and four. If you have been looking at seed pods, you might sing, to the tune of "Are You Sleeping?":

God, we thank you; God, we thank you
For the pods hiding seeds,
Brown and fuzzy seed pods,
Brown and fuzzy seed pods,
Thank you, God; thank you, God.

Scuffing Walk
This is the special surprise you promised. Talk about the things you will do or may see when you get outside. Make this conversation brief. The real value of this walk is to let the children experience the sound and feel and color of the leaves, to enjoy the crisp fall air, the warm sunshine. (Note: If you are taking the children off of church property, get written consent from a guardian first.)

Include in your conversation "good rules to remember when we take a walk" (page 75). If this is the first walk the group has taken, be sure the children understand the rules so that the walk will be enjoyed by everyone.

Put on coats (if necessary), and gather at the door. Have at least one adult for every four children. If you have to cross a busy street or highway, you will need even more adults. Enjoy scuffing (or looking) with the children.

Prayer
When you return from the scuffing walk (or while you are outdoors), if the children seem ready for it, say a brief prayer of gladness for crisp, crunchy leaves. You might sing "God, We Thank You" as a prayer song rather than saying a prayer.

Free Play, Going Home Time, Cleanup, Pick up, Saying Good-bye (about 10 minutes)
Place on the wonder table any signs of fall the children brought back from the scuffing walk. If there is time, children may help pick up and put away the rest of the toys. Ask the children who brought objects for the wonder table if they would like to take them home. Some items might be left for a week or two. Let each child know that you have enjoyed having them in the group today. Suggest that perhaps they will find something this week to bring next time for the wonder table.

AFTER THE SESSION

If some children made especially interesting paintings during free play time, you might plan to put them away to use as Christmas presents (see page 79). As you and the other teachers do the final pick up and cleanup, talk about the children and their responses.

Did the children find some answers to "What is the world like?" on the walk? Were there any special problems? Do you need to make a call to someone's home? What objects in the wonder center were most interesting to the children today? Does this suggest something you might bring for the next session?

Theme: Christmas

SOME THOUGHTS ON CHRISTMAS

The Sunday after Thanksgiving is the first Sunday in Advent, the season of preparation for "the coming." Time was when we would not have thought of planning for Christmas with preschoolers four weeks ahead of time. But I think that time is past.

In some towns the merchants announce Santa's arrival by helicopter or rocket ship the first or second weekend in November. Christmas parades are televised all over the country as part of the networks' special program for Thanksgiving Day.

By Advent most of our children will have been seeing, hearing, and talking Christmas for weeks. You may decry all this ballyhoo—as I do—but we will do well to recognize the situation for what it is.

THE REAL MEANING OF CHRISTMAS

How shall we observe Christmas in the preschool? First, by living the meaning of Christmas. I know we do this all the time—or we try to. But there is something different at Christmas. It seems to me that people are more generous, more tolerant, more sensitive, and forgiving in their relationships to other people at Christmas than at any other time of the year. If that is not true, it ought to be. At Christmas, God, who is Love, became incarnate in Jesus of Nazareth. Jesus lived a life of love with such persistence and conviction that he changed the world for all who live after him. He told us that there are two great commandments: to love God and to love one's neighbors. In fact, we show our love for God through our love for others. Peace and joy, two of the traditional words of our Christmas greetings, are real and constant evidences of this life of love.

This is not the meaning of Christmas which the hundreds of bewhiskered Santas and the Thanksgiving Day paraders proclaim. Unfortunately, it is also true that this meaning of Christmas may not be a part of the child's experience in the home. Attention is focused on getting and giving for Christmas and on the busy preparations and events preceding Christmas.

CHRISTMAS IN THE PRESCHOOL

If the preschool is a place of love and peace and joy with no rush, no tension, no hurry, no pressure, the meaning of Christmas may be felt there. For this to happen, you must be relaxed yourself. If you make plans for too many special activities or too many changes in the usual routine, you will feel harassed. I do not mean that you should do nothing special for Christmas; I mean that whatever you do should be relaxed and easy and fun.

Be particularly aware, as Christmas approaches, of the children who may be worried, unhappy, or tense and keyed up. If you are not trying to do too many extra or different things in the preschool, you will have a chance to give special attention to anyone who may need it. This may be just holding a child in your lap for a little while, engaging in understanding talk with another, or reading a favorite book to a third.

A second way you will observe Christmas in the preschool is by talking about it, of course, and by doing a few special things. Christmas is Jesus' birthday. The Christmas story of the birth of the baby will be the center of most of the conversation. You can use it several times in different ways.

SANTA CLAUS

I do not mention Santa Claus in the preschool. Santa Claus is not the reason for Christmas. Also, you do not know what the children think about Santa. There may be some preschoolers who scarcely know the name or recognize his picture. Children with different nationality backgrounds may think of Santa Claus in a somewhat different way. It would also be well if the church preschool could provide another understanding of Christmas that will eventually take Santa's place in the child's thinking.

On the other hand, do not try to disclose Santa Claus as a hoax or in any way do away with him. To do that might be most unsettling to a young child. Just try to avoid Santa—that's all.

CHRISTMAS PAGEANTS

It is a rare church pageant in which preschoolers can participate or can watch with meaning. It is a good experience for them to play the Christmas story in their room. They can take turns playing or watching or listening. What each child does will have meaning for that child, and that is what we are after.

CHRISTMAS GIFTS

Teachers often want to give Christmas presents to the children in their group. Sometimes this is a good experience and sometimes it is not. It depends on the children, the teacher, and the gift. Many of the children in our country have too many things, and teachers can hardly afford to compete. But even if you can, don't. Our gift to our children is our love. No one can offer anything of greater worth. A Christmas card from the teacher with a drawing or painting of Mary, Joseph, and the baby Jesus given by you to the child would be appropriate and meaningful.

May you and your children have a joyous and blessed Christmas.

PURPOSE

Beginning the session after Thanksgiving and continuing for one or two sessions after Christmas, you will want to center your sessions on *living the meaning of Christmas*. The Christmas story will be your basic resource. Preschool children who have experienced their parents' love will have an understanding of the love and joy expressed in the biblical story of Jesus's birth. Celebrating Christmas through loving and sharing will help children live the meaning of Christmas.

THE ROOM

How can you begin to surround your group with peace and joy through the arrangement of the room? You will need to consider the activities you plan to use, the children's need for familiar objects in familiar places, the kinds of decorations that will be joyous but not overwhelming.

Put a box of scarves and sashes for dressing up in the housekeeping center.

If you need extra space for special activities such as finger painting, you many want to put away the large hollow blocks. Keep the smaller ones for building roads, garages, or airports. Grandparents may be coming by car, train, or plane to spend Christmas; and eager grandchildren may anticipate the event in their play. Supply wooden or plastic animals and figures of Mary, Joseph, and the baby Jesus. Some children might want to build a block barn as they play with the crèche figures.

Have copies of Christmas books, such as *Christmas in the Barn* in the book center or on the table with the Bible and offering basket. A record or tape player in either of these places could provide quiet listening to the lovely music of Christmas.

Plan to use art activities that will provide an outlet for excitement and tensions. Clay, painting, finger painting, and easel painting are the best. Allow plenty of space and materials for each activity. See "Making Christmas Presents" (page 79) for ways of using these art activities to make gifts.

Put a picture of the nativity on the special table or in one of the interest centers, wherever children will be able to see it best. If you have a picture of Jesus and children of several cultures, place this near the nativity picture. This will give you an opportunity to remind children that the baby Jesus grew up to be a kind, loving adult who cared for children.

Even at the preschool level it is wise to comment that "this is the way the person who made the picture thinks the baby Jesus and his mother and father must have looked. See how happy they are!" This is a first small step in helping children understand that we have no photographs of Jesus, that the pictures of Jesus we have in our homes and churches are the artists' attempts to show the kindness, the courage, the love, and the strength of Jesus.

Pictures of babies and their parents, pictures of people going to church at Christmas time, or families setting up crèches will add emphasis to the real meaning of Christmas. Use pictures sparingly if you plan to have special Christmas decorations.

A small tree that the children can decorate themselves is more useful than a large tree elaborately decorated by grown-ups. See page 78 for suggestions of tree decorations children may make.

Observe fire laws regarding the use of greens in public buildings. *Never* use lighted candles in the preschool. Colorful cutouts will add to the festive appearance of your room. Add one or two new decorations each session. Children's own creations will be as pleasing to them as adult-made decorations.

ACTIVITIES

Making Christmas presents to take home may be a major activity for the first few weeks of this unit. Several of the gifts suggested for children to make (see "Making Christmas Presents," page 79) may be part of your regular art activities:

A Painting
Candle Holders
Making Christmas Tree Ornaments
Decorating Paper Christmas Trees
Table Decorations
Christmas Cards

Other activities you may want to do are explained under "Christmas Activities" on pages 78–79.

GROUP TIME

A quiet time to sit down, listen to a story or a record, and eat a cracker. Do not crowd your morning full of activities, songs, or finger plays. Use your resources as you think they will fit the needs of the children.

Finger plays
Use familiar ones the children have enjoyed in previous units.

Stories
The First Christmas, page 88
Jesus, page 89

Songs
Bye-low, My Baby, page 100
Away in a Manger, page 99

Prayers
If the children have been talking about their friends or love or sharing at Christmas, mention these in your prayers. See page 92 for sample prayers.

Use the story of Jesus' birth and the story of Jesus, the friend of children, in Resource Section I over and over again. Sing the Christmas story, using the lovely carols and lullabies. Let the children play the story. Celebrate Jesus' birthday with peace and joy in the preschool group.

A Sample Teaching Plan for *Christmas*

What was the atmosphere of the preschool last session? Did you have to drop your session plans because one child began to cry and another was on a destructive rampage, upsetting an activity here, kicking a carefully constructed block garage there, snatching a piece of a puzzle, leaving a string of unhappy children behind? Perhaps as you talked with the children you discovered that many of them had already been to see Santa Claus or were allowed to stay up a little later than usual to see a special television show. Tiredness and excitement show up in the children's behavior, sometimes as withdrawal, sometimes as aggressiveness.

The experiences of the past session (whether they were similar to the ones just described or quite different) offer you clues for planning.

The overall purpose for sessions on the Christmas theme is "living the meaning of Christmas." For several sessions you may wish to emphasize *loving and sharing.* You will want to use the Christmas story to help children understand better what we mean by loving. Making Christmas presents will be one part of learning about giving as an expression of love. Experiences of working and playing together and of sharing equipment and materials will be others.

PREPARATION

The Room

- Dolls, scarves, and sashes in the housekeeping center may suggest playing the Christmas story or singing a lullaby to baby as Joseph and Mary might have sung to the baby Jesus.
- Crèche figures (preferably, sturdy ones) may be used in the block center during free play period and brought to the special table for group time.
- Puzzles may be kept on the shelf but should be where a child can get one if wanted. If you have colored beads to string, children will enjoy this activity.
- Have a Bible, a nativity picture or crèche figures, and perhaps a few greens or pine cones on the special table. If your group meets in a corner of the sanctuary, cover part of a pew with an attractive cloth and place these items on it.
- A picture of Jesus and some children or a picture of a family putting up a crèche and pictures of babies with their happy parents may be placed in the interest centers or on the picture board or rail. (Use easily removable tape to attach pictures to pews or walls if you meet in the sanctuary.)

Special Equipment

- Scarves and sashes for "Playing Christmas" (page 78)
- Glazed paper, such as shelf paper, finger paints, and aprons (See Appendix, page 221, for recipe for finger paint.)
- Red or green candles and clay for candle holders, white paste and cut-up paper for snowflakes.

SESSION TIME

Greet Children

Enjoy the children's tales of getting ready for Christmas—or whatever item of interest they want to talk about—as you help them out of coats, snow pants, and boots. Tell them you have some special paints, if they would like to paint a picture to give someone for Christmas; or candles, if they would rather make candle holders out of the dough clay to give as their special surprise.

Free Play

Help an overtired child rock a baby to sleep as you sing a lullaby. Put the overexcited child to work with clay or finger paint. It may calm your nerves to read again about the struggles Juan had one Sunday and how Ms. Colson helped him work out his problems while protecting the rights of the other children in the group ("Teachers Are Dependable: All Children Have Rights," page 39).

Give some extra attention to the child who is feeling lonely because both parents are especially busy during the Christmas rush or because his or her parents do not live together.

One teacher should work with the children who are making Christmas gifts. Check the instructions for the activities "A Painting" and "Candle Holders" (page 79). Let all the children know that they may make presents. No one has to make one. If you have made Christmas cards of snapshots of the group as suggested on page 79, every child will have at least one gift to take home a session or two before Christmas. It is a good idea, however, to offer these same activities for making gifts again the following session. What does not appeal one day may do so the next time.

Allow plenty of time for cleanup at the end of the free play period.

Group Time

As the children gather, one teacher may give each child a snack. Another teacher (sitting facing the group) may be rocking a doll and singing "Bye-low, My Baby" (page 100).

Conversation

Talk about babies and how parents love their children. "Does your parent sing a lullaby when he or she put the baby to sleep?" "Did they sing to you when you were a baby?" (They will not remember, but most parents will have told them about the time when they were babies.) "Do they still sing to you sometimes when you go to bed?" Let the children tell about their experiences.

"Mothers and fathers are happy when their babies are born and when their babies grow to be big boys and girls. They show their love and happiness in many ways." Talk about some of these ways. The children may suggest some too.

Story

The First Christmas, page 88

Introduce the story from the preceding conversation: "The story tells about how happy Mary and Joseph were when their baby, Jesus, was born." Show some pictures or use the crèche figures as you read the story. After the story, pick up the Bible and open it to Luke 2. Show the children where the story of Jesus' birth is told in the Bible.

Prayer

Your prayer might express the children's gladness that mothers and fathers love them and show their love in many ways.

Be specific. Mention one or two of the ways that were talked about during the conversation period.

Song

Play Jingle Bells (page 78)

This will give the children a chance to stretch their muscles and relax.

Free Play, Going Home Time, Cleanup, Pick up, Saying Good-bye

The finger paintings and candle holders will not be dry enough for the children to take home today. Tell the children who made gifts that they will be ready for them to wrap and take home the next time they come to church school. Keep this part of the morning as relaxed and happy as the other portions. The children will look forward to coming back again.

AFTER THE SESSION

Finish picking up and putting away. Be sure children's names are on the gifts. If it is necessary to remove the finger paintings from the rack or floor or wherever you have spread them to dry, stack them loosely with a clean piece of paper between each painting. Pack the candle holders carefully in a box. They should be put near a radiator or into a warm oven for a couple of hours to dry.

Talk over the morning as you pick up. Make plans for the next session. You may want to follow exactly the same plan, except to center the conversation period on sharing as a way of showing love. Your prayer could mention one or two instances of sharing you observed during the free play period.

BOOKS

BASIC LIBRARY

Books are valuable resources. If your church or church school does not have a library containing reading and picture books for preschoolers, borrow books from your public library or bookmobile. A list of excellent books for a basic library is included in the Bibliography (page 235). Under "Teaching Plans," books related to the theme are suggested as resources. Another excellent source of thematic songs, poems, and stories is the monthly magazine *Ladybug*, which is for children ages 2 to 7. (For the address see the Bibliography.)

PICTURES

PICTURE FILE

Pictures on the following themes would be especially useful with the stories and activities suggested for use in the fall and early winter:

A family or children eating
People playing games
Fall pictures
Squirrels
Simple nativity pictures

HOW TO USE

A picture helps children focus their attention and visualize a story. If a picture illustrates a story, hold the picture where all can see it while you tell the story. Children "see" with their fingers as well as with their eyes, so let them touch the picture. Later they may tell *you* a story as they point out the different parts of the picture.

When you are through talking about the picture, place it where the children can see and touch it as they go about their other activities. It may be put on a picture board or rail at the child's eye level or placed on an easel on the special table.

Seasonal pictures and other appropriate pictures cut from magazines may be placed on the special table, in the book center, on a dividing screen, or wherever children may look at, touch, and talk about them. Maybe there's a person in your congregation who can draw pictures to accompany some of the stories and conversations.

ADDITIONAL USES

One of your best resources for pictures to use with preschoolers is a do-it-yourself project. Pictures cut from magazines, calendars, and advertisements, mounted on colored construction paper, can be used in housekeeping, block, and book centers. Indeed, they can be used everywhere in the room to stimulate conversation and play, illustrate stories, or satisfy children's needs and interests.

Select pictures that show people doing interesting things: a family having a picnic, a child helping a parent at a workbench or painting; farmers, road builders, firefighters, and others at work; parents taking care of children. Try to select pictures that are in keeping with the main theme of your sessions, and keep in mind the purpose you hope the picture will serve. A black-and-white picture which shows real expression on the people's faces is more interesting to a three year old than a brightly colored picture that is cluttered or is poor art. Mount the pictures for convenient handling and storage.

You will be able to make better use of pictures if you have them sorted by subject matter and stored where you can get them easily. A deep box or cardboard carton makes an excellent picture file. Make a folder for each subject by taping together two pieces of cardboard. These folders should be large enough to protect the edges of your largest picture. The back of the folder should be about an inch higher than the front cardboard so that you can label the folder for easy reference.

PICTURES TO LIVE WITH

Children need to live with one or two good pictures for several months at a time. These picture should be framed, covered with glass or plastic (for "looking" with fingers), and hung at the child's eye level.

ACTIVITIES

Getting-Acquainted Activities

This first group of activities will help the children learn to know you and the other children. Getting acquainted will help the children feel at home in the church, to become a part of the fellowship.

BALL ROLLING

The teacher organizes this activity. Seat two children about six feet apart on the floor. Have them spread their legs and roll a large ball back and forth to each other. Each calls the other's name as he rolls the ball "Cineca" . . . "Carlos" . . . "Cineca" . . . "Carlos." Sometimes you may join in the ball rolling with one or two children.

COUNT NOSES, NAME NAMES

When the children gather for group time, count noses or heads or whatever else you think of. Use the names of the children as you do it. After some weeks the children will begin to call out one another's names.

TAKING TURNS

As children are helped to form a line for "taking turns," use these words so that children will learn what this expression means. When they line up to take turns at a slide, a rocking boat, or a block walk of large blocks placed in a line, call the children by name as they play. For example, you may say, "There goes Jill down the slide . . . and Juan's turn is next. David and Kim are rocking the boat. Wait a minute, David, until Juan gets back on. He lost his balance and stepped off. Okay. Now it's your turn to start. Fine!"

General Activities

SEE HOW I AM GROWING

Make records of each child's height in the fall and again in the spring. Place a large sheet of sturdy paper (wrapping paper or the like) on the floor or tape it to the wall. Place each child against the paper and draw his or her outline with a colored crayon or a big marker. Put the chid's name on the paper. The child might paste a picture on the paper to help identify the outline.

Keep the papers in a safe place until late in the spring. Then repeat the activity. Use a different color for the second outline so that the growth is easily seen. Let each child have the paper to take home.

You do not need to draw all the children at one session, use several sessions at the beginning of the year and again in the spring.

TAKE A WALK

Certain precautions are necessary to make this a safe activity for preschoolers:

1. Have one adult for every four children, but never fewer than two adults.
2. Decide which children need special watching.
3. Assemble the children in a group and work out rules for a safe walk. They may suggest some.
4. Do not make too many rules.
5. Be sure the children understand the rules. This is important, for they must learn safety. I have used these rules.
   Stay with the teachers.
   Stay on the sidewalks (or paths).
   Wait at the corners (or to cross the street).
6. Some teachers like to have a rope or piece of clothesline long enough for each child to hold on to.

See "A Scuffing Walk" (page 76) and "Looking Walks" (page 147) for suggestions about taking walks. The children and you might gather some pretty leaves, small stones, or grasses to take back to the preschool or to take home. If your group cannot go outdoors, you can lead them in a "pretend" walk, describe things to them, and try to have them imagine seeing different things.

SNAPSHOTS

Have a parent or chuch member take a picture of your church and a picture of the preschool group (teachers and children together). An enlarged print of the church would be a valuable picture for you to have in your file. Small prints of the church picture might be treasured by the children. Put prints in envelopes for the children to take home. You may write a note to send home with each child's picture. The note might read:

> We have been hearing stories, talking, singing, and praying about our church. This snapshot, which Mr./ Ms. [name] took for us, will help your child remember friends at church and will help us all remember that *we* are the church, together.

You might add an invitation to visit the preschool. Ask people to please phone before they come so that there will not be too many visitors at one time. Or you might ask them to help with such activities as planting bulbs or cutting Halloween pumpkins. Or you might include a brief explanation of your fall season activities.

Keep the group pictures for making Christmas cards (page 79).

VISITING THE CHURCH SANCTUARY

The preschool children should visit the church sanctuary several times during the year if they meet in another room. If your church has a balcony, a teacher and five or six children may sit there a few minutes before church begins and during the first few minutes of the service. Or you might arrange to have the children sit in a front row pew for a few minutes at the beginning of the service. Plan with your minister about the best time to leave without disrupting the service.

Unless you have a small group and know that you will not have any visitors or late arrivals, plan for a few children and one or two teachers to go one Sunday and the others on following Sundays. Always leave someone in charge of the group.

Falltime Activities

MAKING FALL LEAVES

Cut out large leaf shapes from paper. (Use twelve-by-eighteen-inch paper if possible; cut one leaf from each sheet.) The children will enjoy crayoning these shapes to resemble fall leaves. (In some areas this will mean fresh green leaves. In other areas, where seasonal changes are less noticeable, there may be leaves of unusual shape or color that you can use as your sample.) Children may take the leaves home or may want to use them in the preschool during the fall to remind them of the outdoor colors.

PLAYING SQUIRREL

Give each child a nut of some kind. Tell the children to pretend they are squirrels and hide their nuts around the room. When the children have hidden the nuts, call them back to the rug and have them pretend to go to sleep. After a few moments tell them it is time for the "squirrels" to wake up and go find their nuts. You might use "Playing Squirrel" after telling the story "Marc's Sunflowers" (page 85).

A SCUFFING WALK

Take a scuffing walk through the leaves if the leaves are crisp and not dirty or far away. Enjoy the sight, the sound, the feel, and the smell of the leaves. You might sing the song "This Is the Fall-time" (page 98) or make up words to "God, We Thank You" (page 94) to sing when you rest. If you cannot go out, take a "pretend" walk. Scuff through crunched-up newspapers. Jump over a pretend stream or puddle. Look for "birds" in "trees." See how many things the children can imagine discovering.

PLANTING BULBS

Where possible, plant fall bulbs in the churchyard. Be sure to get permission from the proper board or committee. If you need it, get some advice about the kind of bulbs to plant and where to purchase them. Plan well and prepare the children before you begin so that they will know what they are doing and why. If possible, have a picture taken of the children planting the bulbs. Have pictures of the flowers that the bulbs will produce. This experience can be fun and educational. When the bulbs bloom, if the congregation has been informed of the preschool activities, some will remember the children planted them. Have another picture taken with the children and the flowering plants together.

APPLE SEEDS

During group time cut shiny apples (washed, of course) into sections. Help the children find the smooth, brown seeds inside. They may have the seeds to take home or you may collect them in a small jar and save them to use on a bird feeder (see page 149 for having a bird-feeding station). Cut one apple crosswise so that the children can see the star design of the core with the little pockets containing the seeds. Eat the apples, and enjoy!

MAKING A HALLOWEEN PUMPKIN

The session before Halloween you and the children might carve a face on a pumpkin together. Let the children decide whether to make round eyes, square noses, sad or smiling mouths. The teacher does the cutting, of course. This activity is not to celebrate Halloween, but is another opportunity for the children to experience firsthand the world about them. They can take turns reaching into the pumpkin and pulling out the seed membranes with their hands or with a large spoon. They can separate the seeds and put them in a pan.

The seeds can be given to the birds, or you can toast them during the week for the children to eat the following session.

With the children, enjoy the pumpkin's color, its smoothness, its special odor, the fun it provides. Much learning can take place with this activity.

Some children are afraid of carved faces on pumpkins. They might overcome this fear after talking together about the *funny* face you are making on the pumpkin. "The face may look fierce, but it isn't real; it's just a funny orange pumpkin."

Some children do not like the feel of the wet, stringy membranes. Others are afraid that their hands will get dirty. Respect these points of view. But you and the children who have no such inhibitions can demonstrate that the slippery feeling inside is very different from the hard, smooth outside and that the stringiness can be washed away.

One teacher should not have more than four to six children when cutting a pumpkin. Perhaps for this session you can recruit some other helpers. Instruct them about the how and why of this activity—how to include the children and how much time it may take.

A TURKEY VISIT

If the children in your group have not seen live turkeys, a visit to a turkey farm would be ideal, although very unlikely. If such a trip is possible, secure written permission from all the parents. Ask several parents to accompany the group so that you have one adult for every two or three children. Make arrangements with the farmer ahead of time about what the children may see and do.

Or you might have a turkey or a chicken in a crate brought to visit your group one session. One teacher I knew managed this in a suburban community with such success that the children talked about it from time to time all year. Let the children feed the turkey or chicken if possible.

THANKSGIVING PLACE MATS

In preparation for the session before Thanksgiving, cut the corners off sheets of colored construction paper to make "place mats." The children can decorate them with crayons and take them home to use for their Thanksgiving dinner. Let the children make as many as they want. Some may wish to make a mat for each family member; others will make just one; some may not be interested at all.

Prepare more materials than you think you will need for this activity (as you should do for all activities with preschoolers). Putting clear contact paper around the construction paper (front and back) makes the placemats wipeable.

Christmas Activities

PLAYING CHRISTMAS

Provide a few head scarves, a box with straw for a manger, a big doll, and a walking stick for the children to use to play the Christmas story. The children may all want to play the story at the same time. That's fine. They are not staging a play; they are trying to understand an experience. The children may need help in getting dressed up, but do not tell them what to do or say. You may find the children "playing Christmas" (with only a doll) months after the actual day if this has been an enjoyable, meaningful activity for them.

THE FRIENDLY BEASTS

Learn the carol "Jesus Our Brother, Strong and Good," also known as "The Friendly Beasts" (*Sing to God*, United Church Press). Do not expect the children to sing the carol. Their school-age brothers and sisters may be just learning it. Make or buy some animal figures for the children to place in the crèche as they listen to this version of the nativity story.

JINGLE BELLS

Small metal bells are usually available near Christmastime. One teacher provided each child with a small bell, a heavy ribbon with a jingle bell, or a wrist bracelet with small bells. The children shook the bells to the music of the song "Jingle Bells." The teacher sang it, and they sang along.

DECORATING PAPER CHRISTMAS TREES

Cut Christmas tree shapes from large (12 x 18 inch) sheets of green construction paper. Provide glue sticks and interesting shapes of foil and colored papers to be pasted on the trees for decorations. Some children can paste on bits of cloth or bright ribbon or cotton; others cannot. Do not provide materials the children cannot handle easily.

Another way to decorate the Christmas tree shapes is to cover the cutouts with paste and have the children sprinkle them with hard colored candies used for cake and cookie decorations.

Punch a hole in top of each tree, strengthen the hole with notebook paper reinforcers, and loop a piece of yarn through the hole. Let the children take their "Christmas trees" home. A few trees may be used in the preschool as room decorations.

MAKING CHRISTMAS TREE ORNAMENTS

Paper balls and chains are ornaments for a Christmas tree which young children can help make.

You might plan to trim a tree in the preschool several sessions before Christmas. At the close of the session right before Christmas, each child could take home an ornament for their own tree at home.

Balls

They can make simple Christmas tree balls by decorating four-inch circles that you have cut from construction paper or poster board. The decorating may be done with crayons or by pasting brightly colored paper shapes on the balls. String a loop of yarn through the ball for hanging it on the tree.

Chains
Some children can make paper chains; others cannot. You will need to cut the strips ahead of time. Strips should be at least an inch wide and nine or ten inches long.

A BIRDS' CHRISTMAS TREE

For the session after Christmas it is fun to trim the preschool Christmas tree with food for birds and to take the tree outdoors. Before the session, the teachers string the dry bread, suet, sunflower seeds, or whatever you use, on heavy thread. The children can hang the food on the tree.

Plan this activity for the first part of the session. The children could leave their coats on while they hang the food on the tree and be ready to go outdoors with you while you put it in place.

MAKING CHRISTMAS PRESENTS

All these ideas for gifts will require your help and some supervision, but the making of the gifts should be the children's work. Resist the temptation to make the crooked straight and the bumpy smooth.

Handprints
Parents treasure these gifts from their preschoolers.

Use any soft—but not sticky—dough clay (except the salt-cornstarch recipe) or plaster of Paris. The clay may be tinted a pastel color by using food coloring. Put the clay in greased paper plates. The plates should be about six inches across. Show the children how to make a handprint by making one of your own hand. (You will need a larger plate to make your own.) Help each child to place a hand on the clay in the plate. Press the hand and each of the fingers gently and help lift the hand out of the clay. Write the child's name on the plate.

Allow two weeks for the mold to dry. Various kinds of attachments for hanging the mold are available at hardware and discount stores. Hangers may be inserted in the wet clay or attached to the backs of the finished molds. Or punch a hole through the wet clay with a straw, then hang with a ribbon or yarn after the clay dries.

Table decorations
Children can make a table decoration by placing a small evergreen branch or a large pine cone upright in the center of a mound of soft clay or dough clay. Allow a week or two for the clay to harden.

Candle Holders
Children can fashion simple candle holders out of balls of dough clay by boring the stub end of a candle into the clay to make a hole. Add red or green vegetable coloring when you make the dough clay to give the holders a festive touch. When dry (allow a week or two), the children can smear the candle holders with paste and sprinkle glitter on them. Let them dry again before sending them home.

A Painting
During the fall keep any easel or finger paintings the children do not take home. Press the backs of the finger paintings with a moderate iron to make them lie flat.

Cut out the most interesting sections of the painting and help the children mount them on suitable pieces of construction paper. Punch two holes at the center top and loop a ribbon through them.

Christmas Cards
If you had snapshots taken of the preschool group earlier in the fall, these may be mounted on attractive paper to make Christmas cards for the children to give to their parents. Place the cards in envelopes for protection. The children can help "wrap" these cards as gifts by pasting Christmas stickers on each envelope.

STORIES

Stories used with preschoolers help the children find satisfactory interpretations of many of their experiences. The stories are not intended to teach children specific facts or to change their behavior or to entertain them, although any of these may happen.

Through feeling the same way as the main character of the story does, a child may discover a new significance (see "Jenny Lee"), a new sense of belonging (see "Karen Goes to the Preschool" or "What Do You Think of That?"), or a new appreciation of being part of the family (see "Ronnie and the Pancakes" or "Why I Like Sunday").

The stories dealing with the seasons, Thanksgiving, Christmas, and families interpret the world of people and their relationships as well as the world of nature and its importance to the preschool child.

The authentic story of Christmas should be the main content of the Advent season. There are many other whimsical, delightful stories about little angels, the smallest fir tree, and the "engine that could," but we would do well in the church preschool to neglect these in favor of the story of Jesus' birth. Read the story "The First Christmas" to your group. Tell the story once or twice with crèche figures. (Small figures of Mary, Joseph, Jesus in the manger, and the animals may be made by mounting pictures on heavy cardboard; or you can purchase inexpensive plastic figures at most variety stores. Do not have shepherds, Magi, or camels.) Perhaps the children will tell *you* the story one session!

Use the story of "Jesus" (page 89) during the Christmas season also to help the children associate the baby Jesus with the man Jesus. You will probably want to read "The First Christmas" early in Advent.

See "The Use of the Bible with Preschool Children" (page 175) for a discussion of the place of Bible stories in the preschool.

Karen Goes to Preschool

Many preschoolers are emotionally ready to be separated from their parents and play in a group of children their own age, but the experience may be a new one for them if they have not been in day-care. Not all children will have visited in the preschool before their first session or will know any of the other children. The only person the child might know is the teacher who called in the child's home. Thus, the first session may be filled with questions and fears for the child. The brief recital of events in this story should help the child face and overcome these fears. It should help the child feel at home in the room and relaxed with the other children and the teachers.

Fit the story to your own situation. You may use either the suggested details or mention the toys and objects in your own room so that your children may identify with the experience of this story.

Children enjoy a story that is illustrated. Try drawing a series of stick figures or simple line drawings to illustrate the high points of this story. You don't have to be an artist!

Karen was three years old. She was going to the preschool room at church for the *first time.*

Karen wondered what the preschool would be like. Would it be like her room at home, where she had her dolls and her blocks? Would it be like the doctor's office or clinic, where there were goldfish in a bowl? Karen didn't know. Karen wondered about the children who would be there. Would they be big or little? Would they be happy children or crying children? Would she find a friend to play house? Karen didn't know.

Karen wondered about the teachers. Would the teachers be smiling grown-ups or grouchy grown-ups? Karen didn't know.

Karen wasn't sure she wanted to go to the preschool. She held tightly to her mother's hand as they went into the church and through the door to the preschool.

My, it was a big room!

Karen looked and looked. She saw a shelf full of blocks and a table with dishes. There was a dump truck, a firefighter's hat, and some books to look at. There were goldfish, too, just like her doctor had. But there were more fish, and this was a *much* bigger bowl.

There were oh, so many children in the preschool. Some were pasting colored papers. Some were building with blocks. Some were playing with the dolls, and others were playing with the dishes. They were all happy, not crying. And they were *all just her size.*

A smiling lady said, "Good morning, Karen. I'm Ms. Fay, your teacher. We are glad you are old enough to come to our preschool."

Karen watched and watched. She saw Ms. Fay help Sally put pajamas on the doll. She saw Akio riding the dump truck. She saw Wanda and Lee working puzzles. She saw Neva painting a big green picture with a big, big brush. Neva had an apron on. Karen loved to paint.

Ms. Fay said, "Karen, would you like to paint? We have more paint and another apron and brush."

Karen painted a beautiful red picture. She covered the whole paper. She showed it to her mother. "I'm going to play with the dishes," said Karen to her mother.

"I'll go to church while you do," said her mother. "I'll come back for you when church is over."

"All right," Karen said.

Karen's mother went to church. Karen played with the dishes. So did Skippy. Karen poured some pretend tea. So did Skippy. Karen fed the doll some breakfast. Skippy fried some fish. They had fun.

Ms. Fay told a story. Ms. Fay and the children talked. Ms. Fay said a prayer. Then it was time to go home.

Now Karen knew about the preschool. Karen knew what the preschool room was like. She knew about the teachers who help children have a good time. She knew about the happy children just her size. Karen had found a new friend, Skippy.

Karen liked the preschool. She could hardly wait to go back again.

Ronnie and the Pancakes

"Ronnie and the Pancakes" helps preschool children think about the fun of getting ready to go to church school. Others in the family look forward to Sunday as a special day. Ronnie shares fully in the preparations and in the joyous anticipation of going to church.

The children will enjoy the story more if you actually sing the song "Today Is Sunday" when you come to it. The tune is found on page 97. As you repeat the story again and again, the children will begin to join you in singing the song.

Something smelled good. Ronnie smelled it the minute he woke up. What could it be? Sniff, sniff. Now Ronnie knew! Bacon!

"Oh, boy-oh, boy-oh, boy-oh, boy!" said Ronnie. "If that is bacon, *maybe* we are going to have pancakes." Ronnie did love pancakes. Why, he could eat sixteen or maybe thirty-four at one time! This morning he felt specially hungry.

Ronnie put on his red slippers and his striped bathrobe. Paddity-pat, paddity-pat, paddity-pat *[pat your knees like footsteps]*. "Pancakes!"

Ronnie ran into the kitchen. "Hi, Mommy," he said. "Are we having pancakes for breakfast?"

"Yes, we are," his mother told him. "How did you guess?"

"Because I smelled the bacon," Ronnie said.

"How many do you want this morning?" Mother asked.

"Oh, about fifty-two," said Ronnie.

Mother laughed. "Fifty-two is a good many pancakes. You must be very hungry today! That's good. When you are hungry and eat a lot, that means you are growing strong and tall." Then she asked, "Do you know what day this is, Ronnie?"

Ronnie thought and thought and thought. "A working day?" he asked.

"No."

"Saturday?"

"No, not Saturday."

Just then Daddy came into the kitchen. He had that good smell that meant he had just finished shaving. He had on *his* striped bathrobe and *his* red slippers too. He was not in a hurry to go to work. Then Ronnie knew what day it was.

"I know," he said. "It's Sunday 'cause Daddy and you don't have to go to work today and you have time to fix pancakes for breakfast."

Ronnie was right. It was Sunday. Today he could go to church preschool. Ronnie was so excited, he could hardly eat his pancakes quickly enough.

After breakfast, Daddy helped Ronnie put on his pink shirt and his pants. Then Daddy went to get dressed.

Ronnie put on his brand-new striped socks. He put them on all by himself. First he pulled off the label that was stuck to the socks to hold them together. He licked the label and stuck it on his toy shelf. (Yes, he did. That's exactly what he did.) Then Ronnie carefully pulled on each sock so that the heel would be right where it should be. Last of all he put on his shoes.

Then he heard Daddy singing a song:
Today is Sunday, today is Sunday,
Sunday, ch---urch;
Everybody ready?
Off to church we'll go.

Mother sang it too:
Today is Sunday, today is Sunday,
Sunday, ch---urch;
Ronnie, if you're ready,
Off to church we'll go.

Ronnie answered:
Today is Sunday, today is Sunday,
Sunday, ch---urch;
If you'll tie my sho-o-o-es,
Off to church we'll go.

Daddy and Mother and Ronnie all laughed at the good song they had made up. Mother tied Ronnie's shoes and off to church they went.

Ronnie liked Sundays. He liked to have pancakes for breakfast. He liked to have Daddy and Mommy at home. He liked to go to church.

Why I Like Sunday

The purpose of this story is to rejoice with the children in the special activities of Sunday. Family customs that make Sunday different vary widely. Adapt this story, therefore, to fit the homes of the children in your group. This story does not aim to set standards for how Sunday should *be observed or how people should behave. It is pure celebration of what* is.

At the close of this story conversation, include the children's ideas in a prayer. The children may suggest the ideas and create the prayer with you.

Use paper dolls made from a catalog or pattern-book pictures to represent the characters of this story. Or you may use boy and girl hand puppets with changes of collars, hats, or ties to represent the different children. Adapt the descriptions of Mary Lou's clothes, Tommy's breakfast, and the rest to fit your dolls and your local situation.

You may wish to use just one or two of these story conversations at a time. If the children do not join readily in the conversations, you could use more of the stories to encourage the children to talk about their own experiences.

This little girl is Mary Lou.

> Fiddledeedum, fiddledeedee,
> Hi-de-ho, and all the rest;
> Of all the days that are in the week
> Sunday's the one that I like best.
> Do you know why?

"Because I can put on all my dress-up clothes and go to church school. I put on my shiny black shoes. I wear the dress Grandma made for me. I take my red purse with a handkerchief and my money, and off I go."

Do you know anyone who has some special Sunday clothes like Mary Lou's? (At this point, talk with the children about their Sunday clothes, how they get ready for church. Make the questions you ask fit the children in your group.)

This is Mark.

> Fiddledeedum, fiddledeedee,
> Hi-de-ho, and all the rest;
> Of all the days that are in the week
> Sunday's the one that I like best.
> Do you know why?

"Because on Sunday we have the best breakfast. We have scrambled eggs and coffee cake. I eat a whole big piece of coffee cake all by myself. Sometimes I cut it with my knife. Sometimes I butter it. I like butter."

Do you have a special breakfast on Sunday or a special dinner or supper? Who do you know who eats by the television or by the fireplace? Do you pop corn or make cookies with someone? (Most families have some different eating habits on Sunday. Make up your questions. These are suggestions only.)

This is Lia.

> Fiddledeedum, fiddledeedee,
> Hi-de-ho, and all the rest;
> Of all the days that are in the week
> Sunday's the one that I like best.
> Do you know why?

"Because that's the day I go to school—church school, I mean. Other days I can't go to school. My brother Bruce and my big sister Leslie go to school. My daddy and mommy go to work. I stay home with Grandma. I am not big enough to go to school every day. But I can go to church school on Sunday. Everybody in our family goes to church. Nobody stays home, only our house. It is all alone by itself and I am here!"

When is your house at home all alone too? Do you know where the adults are in the church? Do you know where the big children have their classes? What special things do you do on Sundays besides go to church? Do you ever go anywhere or visit anyone? (Questions such as these may help in your conversation.)

This is Danny.

> "Fiddledeedum, fiddledeedee,
> Hi-de-ho, and all the rest;
> Of all the days that are in the week
> Sunday's the one that I like best.
> Do you know why?

"Because I can be with my daddy. We have the most fun on Sundays. Sometimes he helps me saw and hammer. Last Sunday I made this airplane. [If you use this sentence, have two pieces of wood nailed together as a body and wings of an airplane. Show this as you tell the story.] Sometimes we take a long walk or go to the park. Sometimes we play ball. Once in a while we wrestle and roughhouse on the floor. I like it best."

Do you know anyone who does things like that with his or her daddy?

Jenny Lee

Preschool children need to acquire a sense of importance in the family circle. The story of Jenny Lee may help children recall the ordinary occasions in their own home situation when they have contributed to the family life. The growing awareness of enjoyable give-and-take relationships in the family may help the preschoolers answer the questions "Who am I?" and "Who are you?"

These stories can be told with paper dolls or with pictures cut from magazines and mounted individually on construction paper or cardboard or pasted to narrow wooden blocks. A copy of the story can be pasted on the back of the pictures for easy reading, or the story could be memorized and practiced, since the rhythm is an important part of the story.

You may use these stories for a period of several sessions. The first time you might tell "What Jenny Lee Can Do." The next session, tell this story again and introduce the next story "Jenny Lee and Her Parents." On the following days, you can introduce the other members of the family and tell the nighttime story. Plan a conversation time with each story. Use the suggested questions.

Sometimes you may wish to tell all the stories without interruption for conversation. When you do this, use an introduction with the first story and omit the questions until the end.

WHAT JENNY LEE CAN DO

I'm Jenny Lee Brown.
I'm a big girl, you see.
Do you know the reason?
I'm already *three.*

(Are you three too?)

I can do lots of things.
I help make my bed.
I go shopping with Mother.
To buy milk and bread.
I can put on my shirts Even over my head!
I can wash my own hands
And brush my own hair;
Help Mother make cookies,
And run up the stairs
For her slippers sometimes.
I get my own too,
And then we sit down
And have "eats," just we two.

(What things can you do?)

JENNY LEE AND HER PARENTS

I'm Jenny Lee Brown.
I'm a big girl, you see.
Do you know the reason?
I'm already *three.*

(Are you three too?)

Here are my folks.
They work all day long.
They go on the bus,
Take their lunch boxes along.

(How do your folks go to work?)

At night when they're home,
They play with me.
I climb on Daddy's back
And he tickles my knee.
Then Mom stands me up straight
'Gainst the wall, and she marks
With a pencil. "My goodness!" says she,
"How tall you are growing, my dear Jenny Lee!"

(What games do you play with your folks?)

JENNY LEE AND JOSIE

I'm Jenny Lee Brown.
I'm a big girl, you see.
Do you know the reason?
I'm already *three.*

(Are you three too?)

My big sister is Josie.
There's a big bus that
Takes her to school.
She is learning to read
And can write her own name.
When she comes home
We play a good game.
Hide-'n-seek is the game I like best.
Do you know where I hide?
There's a good place inside
The closet, behind a blue suit.
Josie can't find me, unless I call "Toot!"
Then she opens the door,
"One, two, three for Jenny Lee!"
And we laughed so hard! You should see.

(What games would you play with
a big sister or brother?)

JENNY LEE AND JIM

I'm Jenny Lee Brown.
I'm a big girl, you see.
Do you know the reason?
I'm already *three.*

(Are you three too?)

I have a brother;
He's not very big.
Jim is his name.
He can't dig in the sand,
Or look at a book, Or swing on the swing,
Or help someone cook, Or play games with me.
He's much too little.
But he rattles his rattles
And sits in his chair
And bounces a little.
If I am there, he laughs and he gurgles
To see me do tricks.
If I have a sucker, I give him some licks.
Mom says she's glad for a big girl like me
To help her with him.
He likes me too;
And I like him.

(Do you know anyone with a baby?
How would you help?)

JENNY LEE AND NIGHTTIME

I'm Jenny Lee Brown.
I'm a big girl, you see.
Do you know the reason?
I'm already *three.*

(Are you three too?)

Evening's the time I like specially.
Everyone's home—Mother, Daddy, and me,
Josie, and Jim—our whole family.
We sit down for dinner, each in their place.
We hold hands round the table
And all say our grace:
  God is great, God is good,
  And we thank God for this food.

Everyone join, all except Jim.
He can't talk; and our food
Is too chewy for him.
(Do you know the grace Jenny Lee knows?)
Then Jim goes to bed.
I take a bath and one little swim.
I put on my blue nightie and run very fast
Into my room to see if it's dark yet,
To look for the moon, and find my soft blanket.
Daddy is there. He reads to me.
Then Daddy, Mommy, and I say prayers:
Dear God, I'm glad as I can be
For my Josie who plays with me.
I'm glad for my Daddy who reads me my book,
For Mommy who lets me help cook.
I'm glad for Jim, who is not very tall;
For me, who has the most fun of all. Amen.
I give Mommy and Daddy a kiss and I say,
"I love you. Good night."
"We love you, too, Jenny Lee," say they.
Then they give me a kiss and
Tuck me in tight.

Marc's Sunflowers

Whether or not fall brings a major change in your area, your preschool children may be eager to learn about the relationship between plant and animal life. In years to come the children may begin to think of the intricate relationships in nature as a part of God's creative activity. For now it is enough that they hear stories about and begin to observe the wonders all around them.

You may want to use this story even though you do not have sunflowers or squirrels in your part of the country. Or you may want to use the idea of the interrelation of plant and animal life and make up a story more closely related to the experiences of your children.

If you live in an area where sunflowers grow, bring one or two sunflower heads to show the children when you tell this story. The children can shell the seeds, put some aside for planting, and save the rest to feed the birds. Save the planting seeds until spring; then let the children have them to plant if they have their own gardens.

Marc liked to play in his backyard. He liked to play near the big, big tree that grew there. Two gray squirrels, Curly Tail and Squirrel Boy, liked the big tree too. Every day they chased each other up and down the tree. They ran along the fence and across the yard. Then they ran back up the tree and disappeared into a big hole.

Marc liked the garden in his backyard too. It was his flower garden. He had planted the flowers all by himself—well, almost. His daddy helped him a little, but it was Marc's garden.

Marc watered the garden. He pulled the weeds. He watched the flowers grow. There were daisies, marigolds, and tall, tall sunflowers. Marc had to look up high to see them. The sunflowers became so heavy they began to bend over.

One day when Marc went out to play, two big sunflowers were lying on the walk. Their seeds were scattered everywhere. Many seeds were gone.

"Mother," called Marc, "look at my sunflowers! Someone knocked them down."

"Who could it be?" said Mother. "They are so tall. Who could reach them?"

Marc didn't know.

Marc's mother didn't know.

Marc picked up the rest of the seeds. He put them into a paper sack to save them until wintertime. Mother marked the sack with a crayon *For Our Birds*.

The next day when Marc went out to play, two more big sunflowers were lying on the walk. Seeds were scattered everywhere. Many were gone.

"Mother," called Marc, "two more sunflowers are broken off. Who did it?"

Marc's mother didn't know.

Marc did not know. He saved the seeds for the birds.

The next day, two more sunflowers were broken down. Only two sunflowers were left standing. Marc wondered and wondered. Who was breaking off his sunflowers? Marc's mother wondered too. They were so tall. Who could reach them?

Marc's mother had a plan. "Marc," she said, "sit here by the window and watch for a while. Be very quiet. You may see who is knocking down the sunflowers."

Marc did that. He sat very quietly. He saw birds sitting on the branches of the big tree. He saw three big fat pigeons walking up the garage roof. He saw a little black kitten walk softly across the grass. He saw Curly Tail and Squirrel Boy chase each other down the tree and across the yard. They ran along the top of the fence and jumped right onto his sunflowers! Each squirrel clung tightly to a sunflower's thick stalk while it swayed back and forth. Then it broke. When it broke, it fell to the ground. The squirrels scampered down and picked out the sunflower seeds with their little front paws. They ate some of them. They carried some of the seeds up the tree and into their hole.

"Mother!" called Marc. "It's the gray squirrels who are breaking the sunflowers. Look how hungry they are!"

When Curly Tail and Squirrel Boy dashed back up the tree, Marc carefully picked up the rest of the seeds and put them into a sack that his mother had marked *For Our Garden*.

"Sunflowers are such fun," said Marc. "Next year I'll plant plenty for our birds, and for Curly Tail and Squirrel Boy too."

Fun for Joey

This is not a typical story of thanksgiving for the harvest or for the abundance of God's goodness to us. In our country most preschoolers do not generally feel thankful for food. Food is taken for granted. But little children can recall feelings of gladness in certain other experiences. This story is about these other experiences.

Thanksgiving is a response of gratitude to God. Preschoolers may occasionally have such feelings of gratitude. They may not express these feelings or say thank you to God in words, but the feelings are real and important. They may be the beginnings of a response of gratitude which marks the mature Christian person.

Use a paper doll or puppet to represent Joey as you tell these stories.

JOEY'S HAIRCUT

This is Joey. He likes to have fun. Do you? One day Joey's brown hair kept falling in his eyes.

"Time for a haircut," Uncle Joseph said.

Joey liked to have his hair cut. He got out the newspapers and the box to put on the kitchen table. He had to sit way up high so his uncle could cut his hair. Joey wore a big apron to keep his clothes clean. When Uncle Joseph finished, he brushed Joey's face and neck with a soft, tickly brush. It tickled so much Joey laughed and laughed. Haircuts can be fun.

JOEY'S SWIM IN THE TUB

Playing cowboy is fun. Joey raced around the backyard and crawled under bushes. He was hot and dirty when he got through playing.

"Come take a swim in the tub," Uncle Joseph called.

Joey liked to take a bath. In the tub he played with his sponge duck and his rubber boats. He washed his feet and his hands, his tummy and his neck with slithery soap. Joey liked the way the water felt when he poured it down his back. He liked to swim among the bubbles. Baths can be fun.

JOEY'S PET KITTEN

Do you have a pet? Joey has a little black kitten with a white face. He calls her Kitty. Joey likes to feed Kitty warm milk. He puts Kitty on his lap and pats her until she falls asleep. Kitty feels soft and warm. She makes a quiet, bumpy purr in her throat when she is going to sleep. Kittens can be fun.

JOEY PLAYS OUTDOORS

Joey ran out the back door. Joey liked to play outside. He especially liked warm days when he didn't have to wear boots or leggings or mittens or a heavy jacket.

Joey decided to dig a hole. What would he find? He found some brown, wriggly worms. He found a long, tough root that was hard to get out.

Then he chased a butterfly.

He stopped to smell pretty flowers.

He ran as fast as he could run. The cool wind blowing in his face felt good. Then he sat down to cool off and look around. "What fun the world can be," Joey said right out loud. No one answered. I guess no one heard.

GROUP CONVERSATION

These stories are suggestions for conversation that will give each child a chance to talk and be heard by the other children. Use the episodes of your story as reminders: haircuts, baths, games with sisters or brothers or friends, pets, music or books, playing outside. Of course you will not use all these suggestions in one session, and you will adapt these episodes and suggestions.

"Do you know how it happens that there is such a wonderful world or that there are so many things that are fun?

"God planned it to be this way.

"God planned the rain so that we could have water for our baths,

and water for good cold drinks,
and water . . . for what else?"

"Why do families have mothers in them? What does your mother or daddy or sister or brother or baby do in your family?

"God planned for families so that children would have

someone to sing to them,
someone to cut their hair,
maybe big sisters and brothers to play with,
or baby sisters and brothers to help care for."

"Do you have a pet?

God planned for animals—

pets like Joey's kitten,
brown, wriggly worms in the garden,
pretty butterflies."

(The children will all want to tell about pets, and in some detail.)

"Have you ever held a worm? Have you chased a butterfly?"

(These questions may or may not draw much response from the children.)

"God planned the whole, wonderful world we live in. I know a poem about that.

The world is so full of a number of things,
I'm sure we should all be so happy we sing.
Our friends and our families, our pets and our play,
The rain and the sunshine, God planned it that way.
We thank you, dear God, for all these good things;
We love you, we thank you. We're happy.

Perhaps you can put some of the children's conversation into the poem.

While you say the last two lines, you might fold your hands in an attitude of prayer. When you have finished, tell the children that part of the poem was a prayer. Perhaps they will want you to say it again or to repeat it after you.

What Do You Think of That?

All preschoolers—in fact, all human beings—need to know that they are worthwhile, valuable, acceptable just as they are. They need to be wanted and to be loved for no other reason than that they are themselves. That's what this story is all about.

On a big farm not far from here lives a mother sheep. She has two baby sheep, called lambs.

One lamb bleats and frisks and jumps around in the meadow from sunup until sundown. He is full of pep.

The other lamb plays all day long with grasshoppers and daisies. He is a quiet lamb. The mother sheep has two different lambs. She loves both lambs very much.

What do you think of that?

In the barn loft in the hay is a daddy cat with two little kittens. One is all black with blue eyes.

It is a teeny-tiny kitten. One is all white with green eyes. It is a roly-poly kitten. The daddy cat has two different kittens. He loves both kittens very much.

What do you think of that?

Over by the doghouse are a mommy and a daddy dog with two little puppies. One puppy has curly hair, long and red. The other puppy has straight hair, short and brown. The mommy and the daddy dog have two different puppies. They love both puppies very much.

What do you think of that?

In the white house on the farm live a mother and a father. They have two children. One has blue eyes and straight hair. One is small. One is tall. One plays noisy games. One plays quiet games. The two children are different. But they are also alike. Both of them cry sometimes and are happy most times. Both of them get dirty when they play and get clean when they take baths. Both of them can dress themselves, except for the hard buttons, and can feed themselves, except for cutting their meat.

Both of them love their mother and father. And their mother and father love both of them very much.

What do you think of that?

In the preschool of the church down the road from the farm, there are many preschool children. They are all different. Some are boys, some are girls. Some are tall, some are short. Some have light skins, some have dark skins. Some are lively and noisy, some are poky and quiet. One has curly hair. One wears glasses. One is hopping. One is singing. There are all kinds of children, and God loves them all very much.

What do you think of that?

The First Christmas

The real gifts of Christmas are peace, joy, and love. Intangible things, aren't they? Because they cannot be held or looked at, tried on or played with, they may not appear on your list of gifts. But love is real, as you well know, and life is lonely and barren without it. Where there is no love, there is no joy and there is no peace.

No gift is of greater worth to any child than the love of parents and family. The scarcity or abundance of presents under the tree is no measure of love and will not take its place.

If all of us, parents and teachers, try harder than ever to make love and joy and peace part of our everyday *living together, the real gifts of Christmas will pervade church and home as surely as the fragrance of the pine. Then, in actual practice, we shall be experiencing the realities of Christmas about which we sing: "Love came down at Christmas" with "tidings of comfort and joy."*

This simple Christmas story was written to help your children feel Christmas. They, who so recently were babes in arms, rejoice in the love that they know when hearing and seeing and feeling the love of other parents for another baby. No matter that it happened long ago; it happened yesterday, and it will happen again tomorrow.

Do you know how it looks on a clear cool night
When the sky is deep blue
And the stars are all bright?
You feel so small
And the sky is so tall
It stretches and stretches way out of sight . . .
There's a nearby star that seems specially bright.
  That's how it was the first Christmas.
Have you smelled the good smell
Of a barn filled with hay?
It smells fresh and sweet.
It feels warm and deep.
Hay makes a fine bed
For a cow, or a sheep,
Or a donkey gray,
Or even a child with no place to stay.
  That's how it was the first Christmas.
Have you ever heard animals sleeping at night?
Listen, sh-h-h . . .
There is hardly a sound . . .
Just heavy breathing, whispery, slow, Then the cooing of doves.
They seem to know of the coming of day.
A lamb starts to bleat,
The cow munches hay,
The horse stomps his feet.
In his stall

Gray donkey watches them all.
  That's how it was the first Christmas.
Do you know how it feels
To be held warm and tight
In somebody's arms
As you say good night?
It feels loving and happy; everything's right.
  That's how it was the first Christmas.

  Here's how it was the first Christmas.
On a bright clear night
In a barn sweet with hay
A dear little babe
In his mother's arms lay.
He was *born* in the barn
Near the cows and the sheep.
His crib was a bed in the hay
Warm and sweet.
Mary, his mother, sang him to sleep.
Then, bowing their heads, Joseph and Mary
Together thanked God
For Jesus, their baby.
  That's how it was the first Christmas.

Jesus

Do your children have a grown-up friend who talks with them, reads to them, or tells them stories? The children in your preschool do. Most children enjoy having such a friend.

It would seem from the very short account which is in the Bible that Jesus was such a friend to children. Preschoolers can imagine a grown-up like Jesus. They know what fun it is to make plans to do special things with adults. They have had some experience with disappointment when plans did not work out. For these reasons this story has been chosen. It is real, and it is filled with understanding for young children.

There is another reason why this Bible story has been chosen. The meaning that the child gets from this story is not different from the meaning that the original author intended and the meaning that the story has for adults. It may be less complete, but its meaning is not different. Children are *a bother, sometimes, but they are also of great worth. Jesus honored them and loved them and told them God loves all persons—little and big, children and grown-ups, all the time. It is a cause for rejoicing, isn't it?*

After telling the children the story, show them where it is found in the Bible (Matt. 19:13–15).

The baby Jesus who was born at Christmas grew tall and strong until he was a grown-up man. Jesus knew about many things. He knew about making things of wood. He knew about catching fish with nets. He knew about helping people who were sick or sad. He had many friends.

Jesus was a teacher. He taught grown-up people, mothers and father, grandmothers and grandfathers. Jesus loved the people whom he taught. One day the mothers and fathers had an idea. They made a big plan. They planned to take their children to see Jesus.

So the mothers and fathers, the grandmothers and the grandfathers, and all the children—big sisters and little sisters, big brothers and little brothers, and even the babies—went to see Jesus.

They walked. They skipped. They ran ahead. They were having fun. Then—something happened. Jesus' helpers saw them coming.

"Oh no. Here come those children," they said. They sounded angry.

"You must not bring the children here. They will bother Jesus and everyone else."

The mothers and fathers felt bad. The children felt bad. Slowly they turned to leave. No one was laughing. No one was skipping. No one wanted to go away.

Then they heard Jesus say, "Don't send the children away. Let them come to me. I want to see them and talk with them. I love children, all children."

The children heard. The mothers and fathers heard.

"Oh good! Let's go!" the children cried.

"What good news! We can stay!" the mothers and fathers said.

Everyone was happy again. The children ran up to Jesus. Some sat on his lap. Some stood at his side. Some sat on the ground in front of him. Jesus told stories to the children. He told stories to the grown-ups.

Jesus said, "God loves us. God loves you, and God loves me. God loves everybody."

The children were happy. They had found a new friend, a grown-up friend—Jesus.

FINGER PLAYS

Finger plays are primarily a tool for the teacher. Every session needs some active time, some quiet time; some time for children to do their own playing and experimenting; some time to enjoy having the teacher take over.

Finger plays are basically a device to help children relax, sit down, and enjoy some little "plays" with you. Begin a finger play as soon as a few children gather on the rug. Others will join the group as they see the first children enjoying the activity.

Make no effort to have the children do the finger plays properly with the right fingers in the right order. That spoils the fun for everyone. Some will imitate you; others will watch with pleasure. After a time they will know some of the finger plays.

Using finger plays, reading or telling a story, passing and enjoying crackers, and counting noses are various ways to arrange for a brief rest when the children are tired. This time comes naturally toward the end of your program.

The Eentsy, Weentsy Spider: Fingerplays and Action Rhymes, by Joanna Cole and Stephanie Calmenson (New York: Morrow Junior Books, 1991), is an excellent, paperbound collection, including some musical arrangements.

Bedtime Story

(Note: "Girl" can be substituted for "boy" for a second verse.)

This little boy is going to bed; *(First finger of right hand in palm of left)*

Down on the pillow he lays his head; *(Thumb of left hand is pillow)*

Wraps himself in his covers tight—*(Fingers of left hand closed)* This is the way he sleeps all night.

Morning comes, he opens his eyes; *(Blink open your eyes)*

Back with a toss the cover flies. *(Fingers of left hand open)*

Up he jumps, is dressed and away, *(Right index finger jumping up and down)*

Off to church on a bright Sunday.

—*Author Unknown*

Here's the Church

Here's the church, *(Face palms, interlace fingers)*
And here's the steeple, *(Index fingers raised and touching)*
Open the door, *(Thumbs together are door)*
Where are the people? *(Hands open wide, fingers at back)*

Here's the church, *(Place hands back to back, interlace fingers, turn hands over)*
And here's the steeple, *(Same steeple)*
Open the door, *(Same door)*
And see all the people. *(Open hands and show fingers)*

—*Traditional*

The Fine Family

(Note: Create other verses using aunt, uncle, and grandparent for variety.)

This is the mother *(Raise index finger)*
So fine and good.

This is the father *(Raise middle finger)*
Who buys our food.

This is the brother *(Raise ring finger)*
So big and tall.

This is the sister *(Raise little finger)*
Who loves her doll.

This is the baby, *(Raise thumb)*
So little, you see,
Short and tall is this family.

—*Traditional*

The Apple Tree

'Way up in the apple tree, *(Point up)*
Two little apples smiled at me. *(Make circles with thumb and forefinger of each hand)*
I shook that tree as hard as I could, *(Grab imaginary tree and shake it)*
Down fell the apples—
(Raise hands and arms high, then let fall)
M-m-m were they good! *(Rub tummy, satisfied smile on face)*

—*Author Unknown*

The Turkey

"Gobble, gobble," says the turkey.
(Fist of left hand, thumb out to make turkey's head, against palm of outstretched right hand, making turkey's tail fan)
"Soon 'twill be Thanksgiving Day—
How will you treat me?
Will you eat me?
I will run away." *(Right hand chases left hand behind back)*

—*Author Unknown*

POEMS

I have used the following poems by pasting them to the backs of pictures I have found. That way I could read the poem as we talked about the picture.

Children love to look at pictures. There are many good pictures in magazines that can be cut out and mounted to use with poems.

You might use "Whisky Frisky" with the children during a story conversation on animals. Attach a copy of the poem to an appropriate picture and place it on the wall at a level children can see and teachers can read.

BABY SEEDS

In a milkweed cradle,
  Snug and warm,
Baby seeds are hiding.
  Safe from harm.
Open wide the cradle,
  Hold it high!
Come, Mr. Wind,
  Help them to fly.
—Author Unknown

WHISKY FRISKY

Whisky Frisky,
Hippity hop, Up he goes
To the tree top!
Whirly, twirly,
Round and round,
Down he scampers
To the ground.
Furly, curly,
What a tail!
Tall as a feather
Broad as a sail!
Where's his supper?
In the shell.
Snappy, cracky,
Out it fell.
—Author Unknown

PRAYERS

Do not feel bound by these sample prayers. You may never be able to use any of these suggestions because they may not fit any of your situations. Keep your prayers short and simple and relate them to the experiences of your children.

Dear God, we are glad to have a place at church with our mommies and daddies. Amen.

Dear God, it is fun to have good friends. Thank you for our friends. Amen.

Dear God, we are glad for our parents and others who take care of us. Amen.

Thank you, God, for our warm clothes. Amen.

Dear God, we are glad when it is Sunday. We like to come to church and do other things that are fun with our families. Amen.

SONGS

Music can be a most enjoyable part of children's preschool experiences. Sounds and rhythms are a part of their world. Children sing and hum tunes of their own creation as they go about their work and play. This natural response of children gives us the clue for the use of music with them.

Music may be used any time during the session. A child putting a doll to bed may croon a little made-up lullaby or be delighted to have a teacher who is standing nearby sing or hum a lullaby. Children in a rocking boat may join the teacher singing in rhythm with their rocking:

This is the way we rock our boat,
Rock our boat, rock our boat,
This is the way we rock our boat,
So early in the morning.
  (Tune: Mulberry Bush)

Sometimes a song can point up a high moment of achievement or wonder. This may be an impromptu chant or a song such as "God, We Thank You" (page 94).

During the group time, music is used for relaxation, for developing group feeling, or to accentuate a high moment.

HOW TO TEACH SONGS

You need not be a skilled musician to use music with children. Just follow a few simple rules:

1. Sing pleasingly, accurately, and unselfconsciously. Have a good repertoire of songs so that you can use whatever is appropriate.
2. Keep the atmosphere informal. Encourage children to sing but do not coerce them.
3. Sing the whole song through. The children will learn it by listening and will sing it along with you as soon as they are ready. Early in the year you may want to start with a song the children know, such as "Jingle Bells," before singing a new song. Do not use accompaniment at first, and only the melody when accompaniment is used.

4. Repeat the songs frequently. Work for accuracy and sweetness of tone, not loudness.

HOW TO CHOOSE SONGS

Many songs that children have enjoyed are included in these resource sections. They all have words within the children's vocabularies and ideas within their experiences. Avoid using songs that contain symbolism. A candle is a candle to a preschooler, not a symbol of the light of the world. Repetition of words and phrases in a song makes it easier to learn. Vivid, dramatic songs have the most appeal to preschool children.

The music also should be simple and alive. The best range for young voices is within the staff. Avoid songs that use half tones, slurs, or tricky rhythms. A fairly rapid tempo and simple 3/4 or 4/4 rhythm is best.

See *Sing to God: Songs and Hymns for Christian Education* (New York: United Church Press, 1984), especially numbers 5, 22, 24, 25, 28, 42, 50, 55, 65, 74, 77, 78, 120, and 125 for use with preschoolers.

MUSICAL GAMES AND RHYTHMS

Some of the songs included in the resource sections, such as "High Stepping Horses" (page 164) are for rhythm activities. The teacher does the singing of these musical game songs. The children are too busy doing the activities to sing. (See pages 218–220 for musical games.) Some songs may be used as finger plays rather than as rhythms.

A piano, guitar, keyboard, omnichord or Autoharp is helpful for rhythm activities. Rhythm records or tapes are also available. Write to one of the companies listed on page 239 for a catalogue and information.

Rhythms should be simple, obvious, and well defined. They should be interesting, joyous, relaxing, and expressive of mood. We do not tell preschoolers what to do to any music. Let them listen, then respond as they will—walking, running, hopping, bending and stretching, swinging and swaying, turning and twisting.

Sometimes you may wish to use rhythm instruments. Directions for making instruments are found on page 228. Show the children how to use the instruments and let them experiment freely. Then play the music and help them feel the rhythm before joining in. Rhythm instruments will be more interesting to children toward the end of the year because their use is a group activity.

Listening to music on a record or tape player is also a very pleasant activity. Choose good music and good words to fit the mood and experiences of the children.

From *Summer with Nursery Children*, by Florence Schulz (Boston: Pilgrim Press, 1958). Used by permission of Florence Schulz.

You can improvise endlessly on this one. The third and fourth line could go:

And for all our friends here,
Tom and Jane and Mary Ann.

The names are of the children in the group. The rhyme does not matter; including every child is important. Maybe you will have to sing that line several times to get all the children's names in.

God, we thank you; God we thank you
For this day, for this day,
And for all the sunshine [white snow],
All the bright warm sunshine [that is fun to play in].
Thank you, God; thank you, God.

This Is the Way

Words and tune traditional

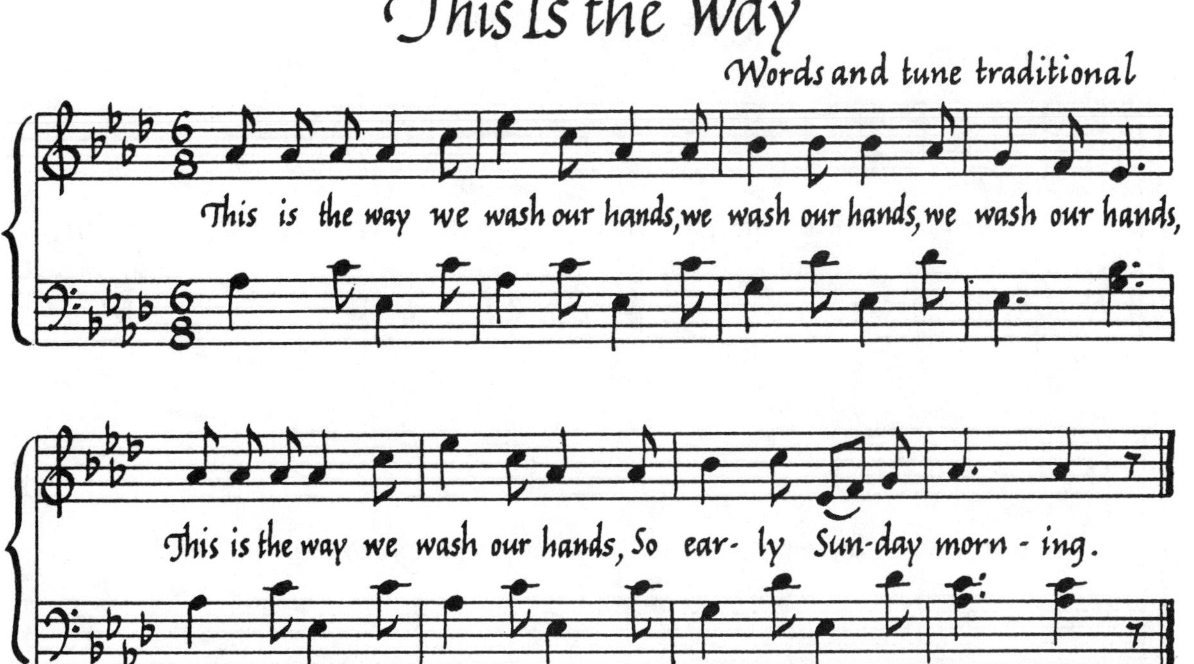

Use motion of washing hands as you sing.

Change the words and motions to describe several parts of the process of getting ready for church: comb our hair, put on our clothes, tie our shoes, walk to church.

Different words and motions will make this song a good activity for other occasions.

This is the way we dig the ground,
[plant the bulbs, water the flowers],
So early in the morning.

Creep them, creep them, creep them, creep them,
Right up to your chin,

Open wide your little mouth,
But do not let them in!

Today Is Sunday

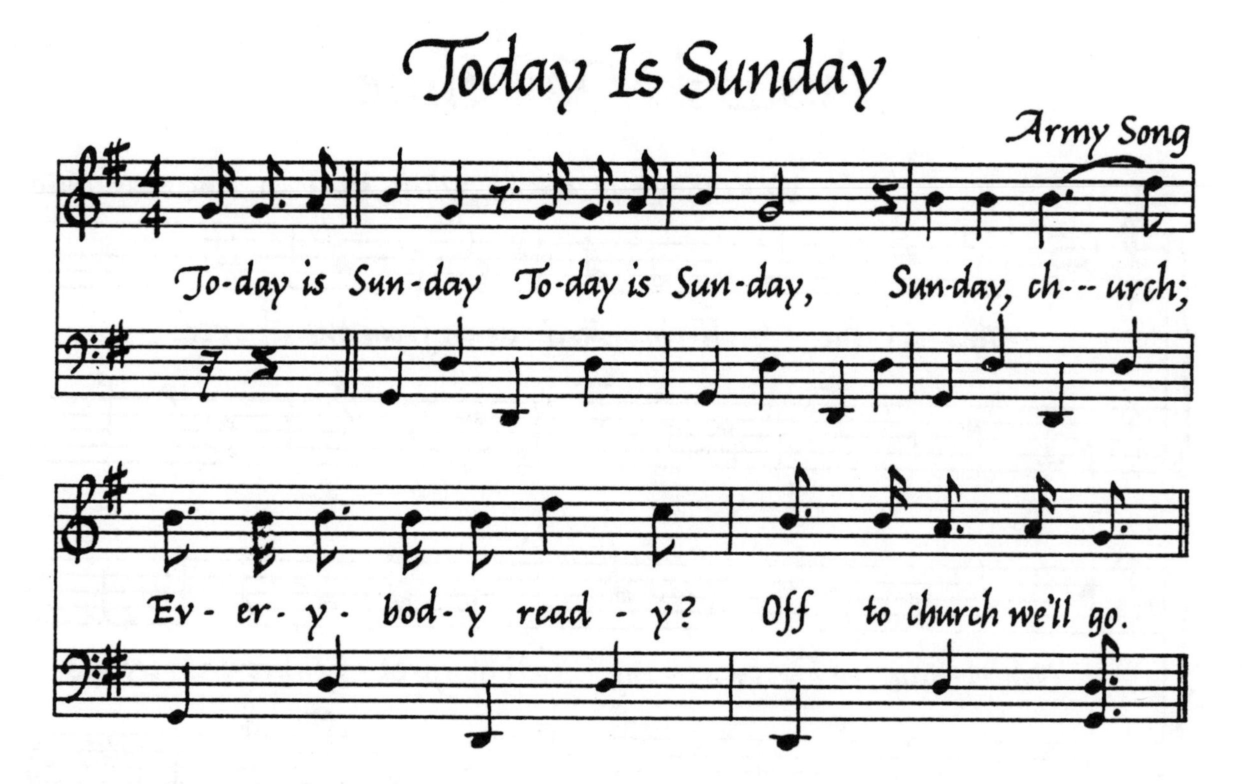

Today is Sunday, today is Sunday,
Sunday, ch—-urch;
Ronnie, if you're ready,
Off to church we'll go.

Today is Sunday, today is Sunday,
Sunday, ch—-urch;
If you'll tie my sho-o-oes,
Off to church we'll go.

This Is the Fall-time

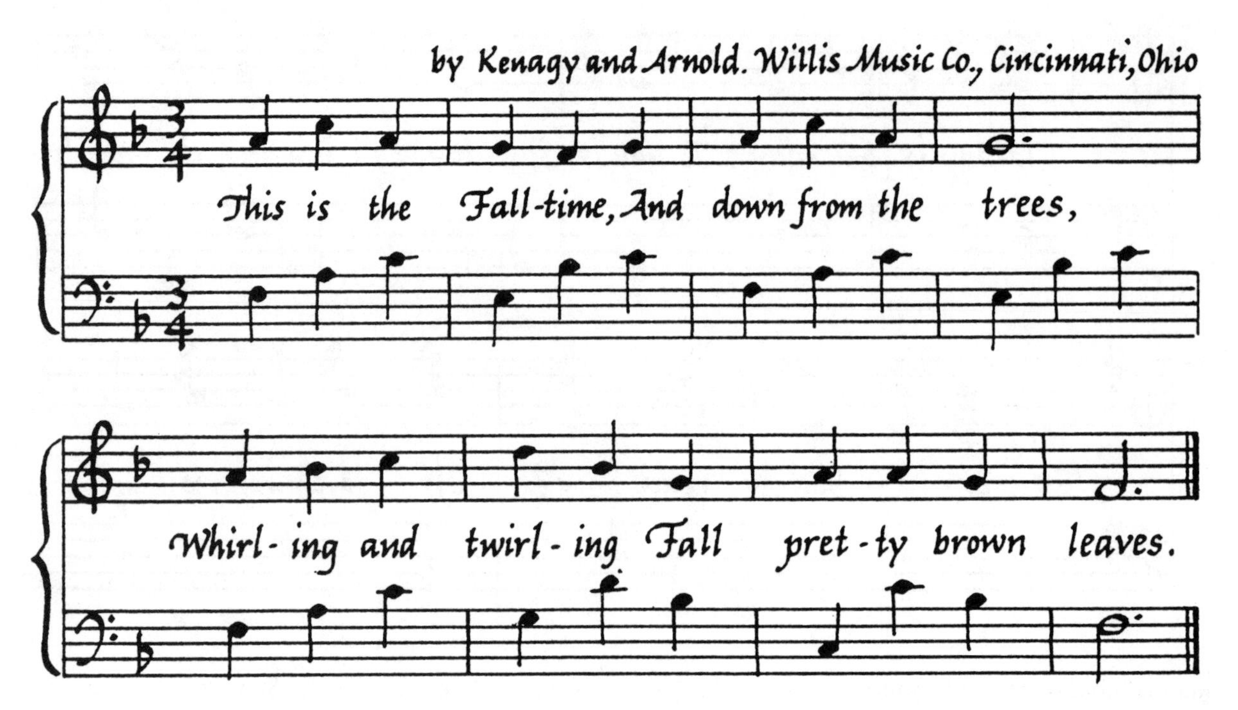

This is the Fall-time,
The old apple tree
Gives us ripe apples
As red as can be.

This is the Fall-time,
And pumpkins so gay
Come from the country
For Thanksgiving Day.

From *Songs for Early Childhood*. Music arranged by James R. Murray. Philadelphia: Westminster Press, 1958.

Bye-low, My Baby

Part II

Hearing the Children

"That they may have life . . . abundantly."
—John 10:10b

Letter 11 How to Teach When You're Not Talking—and When You Are

Remember the teachers who turned into spectators right there in the preschool? They really were baby-sitters, not teachers. They acted only when some crisis or near-crisis demanded something of them. They saw to it that the children did not get hurt or hurt others, and then they sat down again. The children were left to their own devices. This method results in a child-directed preschool. The children set the pace and are left almost on their own to do as they please. The teachers function only when matters in the young society get out of hand.

There are teachers, too, who "run the show." The preschool program is almost entirely teacher-directed from beginning to end, often subtly and skillfully done. The children who cause the crises for the "spectator teachers" are held in check so that matters rarely approach crisis stage. These teachers put words in children's mouths and prescribe the feelings, the responses, and the attitudes which children should have in every situation that comes up. On the surface this teacher-directed preschool program appears to be nice and orderly.

Neither one of these situations portrays good educational methods, for the methods used do not take into account the child's needs, feelings, or "growing edges." It could seem to children in either group (the "wild and free" and the "subtly controlled") that the teachers do not care about *them.*

PERSON-TO-PERSON TEACHING

There is a better way to teach than either of these two ways; it requires more effort, more understanding, and more decisions on the spot. But I believe it is the only way of teaching that reflects our faith and justifies a church's expenditure of money, space, and leadership for preschoolers.

I call this way "person-to-person" teaching. It is a *relationship* between teacher and child in which each treats the other as a worthy, significant person. Neither one has special privileges; neither one directs or controls the activity of the other. Both share in the responsibility of caring for the persons and the things in the room, teachers and children in proportion to their understanding and maturity.

It is person-to-person teaching that really communicates the gospel, the good news.

WHAT IS THE GOOD NEWS?

It is that God loves you. God knows you, accepts you as you are (mean or fearful, glib or quiet, neat or messy), and understands and forgives your unkindnesses and your mistakes. Throughout this relationship God offers you, again, new opportunities to grow, to learn, to love, and to forgive. The good news is that God is love—greater than any one of us can know; that God is within you and me; and that wherever two or three—or fifteen and three—are gathered together in God's name, there is God in the midst of them.

How does person-to-person teaching communicate the gospel to children? Two ways: *By living* this kind of relationship with children, and *by talking* with them about it. First, and most important by far, is the living of the good news; telling about it comes second. But both must be done.

LIVING THE GOOD NEWS

How can preschoolers have an experience of God-is-love and God-is-here-now? By the way they find themselves treated, cared for, helped, enjoyed. These children are the most precious beings in the universe. (Who has greater worth?) We, their teachers, have been entrusted by God and by their parents to help them grow in love and understanding. To do this we treat them with respect and concern. We observe them, listen to them, think about them, try to do for all what each one most needs to have done. We pray for them and for wisdom and understanding to do God's will with them.

To do this job of person-to-person teaching you have to care deeply for children. You have to use every talent you have. Listening to a child requires more than your ears. You must use your eyes, your intelligence, and your feelings as well. You try to understand what a child's behavior means to that child and help that child find opportunities for self-expression. You respond to the children according to your best understanding. You may help children with what they are trying to do or remind them of the rules or the limits, make a suggestion, or laugh with them; you may play with them, deny them, or hold them in your lap. However, there is no precise pattern or formula that you can follow with each child. You have to decide on the spot with the best insights you have.

HELPFUL RULES OF THUMB

There are, however, some general rules of thumb about *how* to respond so that your attitude of respect and concern for the child is evident.

1. When you make a suggestion or give a direction, help *clarify issues* so that a child may learn from the experience. "If we put clay in the doll dishes, there will not be any dishes to play with in the doll center," instead of "Don't put clay in the doll dishes."

2. *If you give a child a choice,* be sure you can *accept the answer.* "Would you like to learn a new song about church bells?" "No." You've had it.

3. Be sure that what you say and how you say it to a child will *help that child feel reassured and good,* not guilty or afraid or ashamed. This rule eliminates comments such as "That's naughty." "You're bad." "You're not acting nice." "Shall I tell your mommy or daddy on you?" Unskilled, clumsy, aggressive behavior should not be branded. The child should be helped to change behavior so that it becomes acceptable.

4. *Avoid comparison and competition* in the preschool as a means for making a child do, or not do, something. Trying to get something done first before the other children or playing "nicely with the blocks the way Winoa does" results in bad feelings and rivalry between children. Christians help people; they do not try to beat people or be better than other people. You can help children toward finding more acceptable ways of behaving by saying such a thing as: "How can we sit so that everyone will be able to see? Let's try sitting on the rug the way Lisa and Arnie are; then we'll see if everyone can see."

5. *Your voice teaches.* Keep the tones quiet, the pace slow, and the words clear. Children behave and understand better if you speak to them directly, face to face, rather than calling out across the room. And if you are uneasy, annoyed, tired, or alarmed, your voice may give you away in spite of your words. *Listen to your voice* with your preschoolers' ears and experience.

6. If you are trying to redirect a child's activity into something more acceptable to others and more satisfying to the child, *try to understand first what the child is trying to accomplish.* What are the child's motives and needs? If you understand these, your suggestion is more likely to be accepted.

FOR EXAMPLE

If Dominic is punching everyone who comes near him, he needs to work off some angry, uncomfortable feelings. Provide him with a pounding board or a large stuffed animal to punch. Trying to divert him by suggesting that he build with blocks or come hear a story may not help because these activities do not help him release his feelings. If these are the best activities you can offer him, however, stay with him as he begins his play until you feel that the bad feeling is gone and he is absorbed in the new activity.

Many times a child will appreciate being invited by one teacher to go for a walk, outside if possible. The outdoors with no shrill voices ringing in the child's ears and no busy children to contend with on every hand is often the best help a tense, excited, or unhappy child can have. Walk and talk—about anything. Listen. Try to find clues about how the world looks to the child. Don't scold. Don't moralize. Get to know the child. Become a good friend. Take your time.

The preceding example underscores the importance of having several teachers in the preschool. There should be enough teachers so that each child can experience understanding and acceptance—so that each child can be given repeated chances to learn, to love, and to grow "in favor." This is teaching and living God's love without talking about it.

Seems like a lot to remember, doesn't it? But do not be anxious about it, for there is a saving grace at work in the preschool, as there is elsewhere. If you really do love each child and intend for all children the best experiences they can have, whatever errors you make will likely have no devastating consequences. Children know how we feel abut them. They are most remarkably mature in accepting our sincere intentions and in forgiving an error or an injury, if they feel we are really *for* them.

TELLING THE GOOD NEWS

Now let's think about the teaching that *is* talking, the words of your stories and prayers. Here, too, do not be overconcerned about what you tell the children about God. If you make an error, seem uncertain about what to say or how much to say, or fumble around for an answer that you cannot clearly make, remember that what the child will sense and remember is the sincerity of your effort and the greatness and importance of God to you. The children may not remember your words. They must eventually find their own words to express that faith. But they will remember your earnestness, and they will feel the strength of your conviction.

I know a lovely, lively grandmother who was teaching preschool children. One day in the spring of the year I visited her preschool, and she permitted me to record this conversation (see "Jesus," page 89).

"Boys and girls, I'm going to tell you a story today about Jesus and the children. See, here is a picture some person made about the story. There are many pictures about this story, for it is a story that people like very much."

"This man is Jesus." *(She pointed to a picture of Jesus with adults and children.)* "Do you know who Jesus is?"

(Here there was a great response from the children. They knew. He was "the baby who was born at Christmas.")

"You're right. And you know he grew up to be a good, strong, kind man whom the people loved. He was a teacher and he taught people wherever he was: sometimes in church, sometimes along the seashore where the daddies were working with their fishing boats, sometimes in the market place where people were buying and selling their goods, sometimes on the side of a hill where the people all sat down on the grass and listened."

"One day Jesus came to a town where he had not been for a long time. Everyone wanted to see him and to hear him talk about God. Do you know what he told people about God?" *(Not really.)*

"He told them the most wonderful good news they had ever heard. He said, 'God loves you. God knows you and cares for you, always, all the time, day and night, year in and year out.'

"You know, boys and girls, that's true. God does love you, each of you, and me, too—all of us. When we are sad, or feeling bad, or are afraid, or have made some mistake, God still loves us, and God is ready to help us. That's a pretty good thing to know about God, I think, don't you?" *(Some nodded their heads.)*

"The people wanted to hear about God and how God loved them. They crowded around Jesus. They even brought their children to see Jesus.

"Then something happened that was almost unhappy. The men who were with Jesus thought he was too tired to have children around. So they told the mommies and daddies to take them away. I think the children must have felt pretty bad about that, being told to go away, don't you think so?" *(The children agreed.)*

"What do you think Jesus did? He stopped the men from sending the children away. He said, 'No, no. Do not send the children away. Let them come and sit here with us and hear about God too. God loves children even though they are not big and strong. God loves children just as much as God loves everybody else.'

"So the children gathered around. Jesus held some of them while he talked, and he told them to come back as often as they could.

"The children loved Jesus, for he was their grown-up friend who really, truly loved them."

This may not be a perfect story, but perhaps the children listening understood what it meant. If the children have had experiences at home and in the church school of being truly loved, they may have some understanding of what it means to say that Jesus loved the children. They knew how the children felt when Jesus welcomed and loved them. Every Sunday they had the same experience with *their* grown-up friends, their teachers, who really, truly loved them.

Letter 12 Every Child Asks: "Who Am I?"

Making the Christian faith real to a preschooler is a big order. As I wrote in my last letter, there is only one way to do it. That way is to live the faith in our everyday lives.

I once heard Dr. Daniel Williams of Union Theological Seminary speak on the subject of living our faith. He said that the Christian faith becomes a real part of a person's life only when it provides an answer to a deep or real question which the person is asking.

"Here is a clue," I thought. "What are the real questions children are asking? If we can discover the questions and work out some ways by which children can find their own answers, they will be able to take their first steps in Christian growth."

It was an exciting idea for me and not as difficult to work out as it might seem. Many people—teachers, preachers, psychologists, social workers, to name a few—have been working to discover these questions. A good start has been made.

I found that three questions seem to be fundamental, whether a person is three or thirty-three or sixty-three. They are: "Who am I? Who are you? What is the world like?" Every age and every stage of life from birth to death bring these same questions. The answers are personal and specific, different for each person. No person can give the correct answers for anyone else. The task of Christian teachers is to help each child in their search for a full, creative, abundant life. One day it dawned on me that while helping children find their answers, I had found some important answers for myself. I found I was experiencing the truth which Jesus told his listeners, that "anyone who loses their life for my sake will find it."

THE FIRST QUESTION: "WHO AM I?"

It is the lifelong quest of each of us to discover an acceptable answer to the question "Who am I?" This question has other forms: What kind of person am I? Where do I belong and not belong? Am I acceptable, worth something, important to someone?

Behind the question there is a need. It is the need to feel worthy, to feel competent and useful, to be respected, accepted, loved. You as a teacher have these needs. The fathers and mothers of your children have these needs. The children themselves have these needs.

We find answers to the question "Who am I?" in every experience we have. For example, Chano sees the floor train and wants it. He takes it from Kendra, who protests. What is done then provides some answers for both children. Chano may feel: "I am wanted here. I belong here. The teacher will help me have a turn with the train. It's all right to make mistakes." Or he may feel: "They don't want me here. They say: Do this. Don't do that. They scold, but they don't really help me. I am not cared for; they don't want me. I'm not important."

Photo by Rohn Engh

Kendra would find two corresponding answers. "The teacher will not let Chano hit me or take things from me. I belong here, and I will be helped when I am in trouble." Or she could feel: "I'm very important here. No one can take my things. The teacher said so. The train is mine."

Some time ago I made some careful observations of Ned's first three Sundays. The records seemed to show clearly that one of Ned's real and important questions was "Who am I?" He was seeking an answer to all the forms of that question.

I have condensed the observations here. As you read them, see if you can imagine what answers Ned was finding. Think, too, if you had been his teacher, how you would have helped him. I have purposely omitted some of the teacher's actions so that you will not be influenced in your thinking.

Keep in mind that most preschoolers are not very fluent about matters of deep concern to them. The child's behavior and play are the way the child tells you about himself or herself. If you can understand what the child is "saying," perhaps you can be of help.

NED'S FIRST SUNDAY

It was the first Sunday of December. Ned and his mother were sitting at the edge of the block center in the preschool room when I arrived. Ned's mother was trying, quite unsuccessfully, to get him to build with the blocks. Then she got up, saying she had to go to church. Ned got up too, grabbed her hand tightly, and whimpered. She walked with him to the record player, stood a minute listening and watching Kathy play a record. Again, his mother tried to leave, and again, he whimpered.

Finally, she got him to sit on a large metal train that he could ride. Then she said, "Good-bye. Do what the teacher says," and she left.

Ned sat on the train tensely. He seemed to pull every bit of himself as deeply inside his skin as he could. He held a small green car in one hand. He watched two boys having great fun with the large building blocks, but his face showed no interest, enjoyment, fear, or curiosity. It was almost as though he wasn't really seeing them.

Once he turned to look out the window of the door by which his mother left, and he saw her watching him. She waved quickly and disappeared. He smiled slightly and turned to watch two girls playing with a doll buggy. His mother continued to watch from outside, concern showing on her face. He continued to sit tight. Finally, his mother left at 11:10. (The preschool group met from 11:00 to 12:00, during the church service.)

Ned sat for twenty minutes, holding his little green car tightly and picking at his lower lip. Then he got off the train and stood beside it.

He watched the children who were playing in the housekeeping center with the doll dishes. He ventured two steps toward some lively activity in the rocking boat but quickly returned to his train again.

He watched the block activity, was clipped on the heels by two "mothers" pushing the doll buggy, and seemed pained at the crying of a baby outside the room. He took two steps from the train toward the door. There he stood, listening to the baby's crying, picking his lip, and holding the little green car.

Near the end of the hour he responded to the teacher's invitation to have a cracker at the table. He ate his cracker and seemed to listen to a story. He said nothing, even when spoken to. He sat there with his car until his mother came.

She came before anyone else, at 11:55. They both seemed very glad and considerably relieved to be together again.

What answers did Ned find to his questions today? Think and feel with him. "Who am I? Am I valuable to someone?" What would you have done if you had been his teacher?

NED'S SECOND SUNDAY

Ned and his mother arrived and walked straight up to the teacher. Both of them seemed tense. Ned's mother was holding his hand firmly, pushing him a little in front of her. She said to him, "Say 'Good morning' to your teacher."

"No!" he said, with great feeling.

"Oh!" she said exasperated, embarrassed. "He was all ready to say it when we got here."

"Good morning, Ned," said his teacher. "Would you like a little bell today?" She extended a small bell to him. He looked pleased and took it. His mother shook off his hand, said good-bye, and left. He sat down at the table which was right beside him.

Ned sat there for forty minutes, holding his little bell and watching the bustling activity in the room.

One teacher read him a story which he listened to and seemed to enjoy.

Later another teacher invited five or six children to the table where Ned was sitting to make "Christmas napkins." The children stuck Christmas stickers on the napkins. Ned did one, then left the table and walked a few steps to an open shelf where he picked up another bell. He stood gently shaking the two bells that he now had. Then he watched, amused, while Alice loudly advertised from her "store."

"I got little orange scraps in my store. I got little orange scraps in my store. Anybody want any?" Nobody did.

Judd came up to Ned, took both little bells right out of his hands. Ned looked half hurt, half bewildered, but said nothing. The teacher did not see Judd take the bells.

Ned joined the children for crackers but paid no attention to the story. His face lit up when the teacher passed around more little bells to all the children. They shook them while they sang "Jingle Bells" together. Ned, looking delighted, shook his ever so gently. The rest of the children shook theirs vigorously, as loudly as they could.

When the song was over, most of the children left the table and went to do something else. Ned remained, shaking his bell gently until his mother came. She came early again, and they left quickly.

Think with Ned again. "Do I matter? Am I important? Am I wanted? Do I belong here?" What would you have done today to help Ned find some answers to these questions?

NED'S THIRD SUNDAY

When I arrived, Ned was already there and his mother was gone. He was standing by the small worktable where he had put one sticker on one napkin last Sunday. He was holding a small red plastic airplane.

At 11:10 a teacher approached the worktable with scissors, paste, and construction paper for Christmas decorations. She invited Ned to make some. He shook his head, turned, and walked straight over to the rocking boat and climbed in. This was the first time he had crossed the room.

A teacher helped him rock by pushing the other side of the boat with her foot. She sang "Row, Row, Row Your Boat." He looked pleased. Neither one said anything. He left the boat.

Then he spoke for the first time. He asked the same teacher if he could load wooden beads into a dump truck. She said yes, and he played with that activity for ten minutes.

At this point I noticed that Ned did not have the red airplane with him. I later saw it in the rocking boat. He apparently did not need it any longer.

He did several things for the first time that morning. He tied a pull toy to the tender of the train and ran it around the room. He set and reset the table with the dishes and poured pretend coffee over and over. At one point Jan approached him, and he raised his hand threateningly. This was his first response to a child. I wondered if he thought she intended to take his dishes as Judd had taken his bells last week. Later Ina joined him and they played side by side for a few minutes, taking turns with the coffeepot, saying nothing.

After nearly twenty minutes of play with the dishes, Ned returned to the beads and the dump truck.

This entire morning Ned moved about the room quite freely, more relaxed and at home than I had yet seen him. He did not move quickly or vigorously. He made no noise, not even when he rode the metal train around. He spoke only once.

His mother came, and I observed for the third time that they seemed unusually glad to be together.

Here is a chance to try yourself out before you meet your own Ned. What can you guess, from these three records, about what Ned is feeling? How would you "teach" him? There are several things a teacher might do:

1. **Observe:** The teacher observes that Ned appears to be timid and shy. The teacher might decide that the best thing to do for him would be to invite

him to help do something, such as hanging pictures on the bulletin board. Or the teacher might encourage him to join in play by offering him a ball of clay or showing him a puzzle to work.

In other words, the teacher's treatment of Ned would be based on a label that describes how he looks and acts. This approach is not wrong, but if Ned does not respond to the teacher's invitations, what then? The teacher can only continue to be friendly toward him, hoping that he will overcome his "shyness." More than this can be done.

2. Understand: Instead of putting a label on Ned's outward behavior, the teacher might try to describe his inward feelings. She might say that Ned appears to feel insecure, alone, perhaps a little afraid. Why? Since this is his first experience in the preschool, he probably does not know what is going to happen to him, how the children and grown-ups will treat him, or what he can do there. He is not sure where his mother is or how long he will have to wait until she comes back.

If this had been the teacher's understanding of Ned's feelings, the teacher probably would have approached him soon after his mother left that first Sunday, squatted down so they could look in each other's eyes and talked with him a little, if he would talk. If he had listened but had not responded, the teacher might have told him something of what was going to happen the rest of the morning and what time his mother would return with all the other mothers. This might have taken a few seconds or a few minutes, depending on how comfortable he appeared to be with the teacher.

With this method, what the teacher says or does varies with each situation, but what the teacher is trying to do remains the same: that is, trying to lessen the child's feelings of insecurity, aloneness, and fear.

This way of thinking about Ned suggests many way of "teaching" him.

3. Get to know them: Teachers will teach best the children whom they know best. Fortunately for Ned, he had a teacher who was devoted to doing the best she could for and with each child in the room. She talked with Ned's mother after church the second Sunday for a few moments and then made an appointment to visit Ned at his home in the early evening. It had to be early evening because Ned's mother worked all day. His parents had separated. Ned and his mother were seeking to establish new roots, new friends, and a new life in a large impersonal city. His mother looked a little frightened and bewildered herself. It is not strange that Ned moved no farther than ten feet away from the spot where his mother left him that first Sunday. So much change and uncertainty and loneliness in a life only three years old would make one cautious and anxious and afraid.

Can you see how much better a teacher you could be for a Ned in your group if you had this understanding of his life and his experiences rather than if you proceeded on the basis of "He's just a little shy?" You would know not only that he is timid and feeling insecure but that underneath it all, he is hurt and bewildered. The experiences he has had are not understandable to him and no one can make them so. His whole world had become topsy-turvy; close relationships have been broken and familiar faces and places are gone. Experiences like these often seriously disturb adults; you can imagine how distressing a child would find them.

"Who am I?" Ned is asking. "Do I belong here? Am I of worth? Can these people be trusted?"

The Christian teacher reflects: "You are a child of God, Ned, created in God's image. You do belong here, for Jesus said, 'Let the children come . . . for to such belongs the kingdom of heaven.' We respect you, Ned, and cherish you. We offer you whatever you need—to the extent of our wisdom and understanding—to help you grow in trust and faith and freedom. We will not desert you."

You cannot say these words to a child any more than you can explain away hurts and confusions. But you can *think* these thoughts, and it might be very helpful to you in your teaching if you were to write them down and ponder them. You really become Ned's teacher when you help him experience these answers to his questions.

How will you do this? You will respect the child as a person, knowing that there are good reasons for behavior, even though certain behavior may not be acceptable. You will grant time, all the child needs, to get the feeling of the preschool, to decide about the trustworthiness of the people there, to make tentative and experimental approaches toward children and toys. You will give him opportunities for expressing hurt or hostile feelings through clay or finger paint or soapy water. Whenever a child expresses hostility toward you or other children you will not judge, condemn, isolate, or reject that child. Instead you will use words to show how you think the child is feeling and try to help the child get rid of bad feelings in ways that do not hurt people. In this way you will help lay the foundations for the Christian faith.

Ned's questions are not his alone. They are the questions of every person: "Who am I? Do I belong here? Am I of worth and significance?" Each person, including you and me, becomes who we are in terms of the answers we discover to these questions.

It is a big job to help a child experience good answers, Christian answers, to these deeply significant questions, but you will never do a more important task.

Letter 13 And "Who Are You?"

This business of thinking about the significant basic questions that children are asking I find intriguing. Every session in the preschool where I am teaching now, I find myself observing the children and wondering, "What is the big question they are asking?"

"Who am I?" is clearly one question of every preschooler. The second big question concerns other people. "Who are you? What do I have to do with you? Do you like me? How will you treat me? How should I treat you?" The child has to find out about other people, big and little, old and young, teachers and friends, grandpas, grandmas, and new babies at home! As I mentioned to you several letters ago, the way a child feels about other people affects greatly their first contacts with the church preschool. Think of Ned in the last letter, for instance.

DEVELOPING ATTITUDES

The child's attitudes toward other people begin in the home. In most homes children have experienced love and trust before they get to the preschool. Unfortunately, there are exceptions, many of them. Ned's home was one of the exceptions. Ned's experiences in his family had made him unsure of himself and other people.

We often do not know when a child first comes into the preschool what experiences that child has had with other people. The child may have been disciplined by threats and scary stories. The child may have had to win adult approval by living up to rigid, perfectionist standards, or perhaps has been criticized and nagged by one parent and indulged by the other. The child may have been abused.

The child might have had a long illness or hospitalization that caused separation from home and parents; or there may be a new baby at home who gets lots of attention, and it seems to the child that mommy and daddy think this is all right. The child feels displaced.

The child may have recently moved to your town, and finds the whole world changed and strange. Some children may have lost one parent or both and find themselves with a stepparent or grandparents.

The child may have working parents who have little time at home. The child may be in a day-care program or cared for by someone in her or his home or in another home. Many parents may provide for physical needs and may even oversupply their child with toys and clothes, but basically reject their child. They wish the child were a different sex or did not exist.

Good experiences or negative experiences may lie behind every preschooler's question, "Who are you?" In fact, the experiences of the early years have already provided some answers to this question. You can do a lot to strengthen or to help the child find other answers.

Photo © Kathryn Abbe

KNOW YOUR CHILDREN

Knowing a child's past experiences should make you more patient and sensitive, especially if you are just learning to teach. Such knowledge should provide you with some clues about what to say or do. For example, in one school there is a child who lives with the mother and the mother's parents. During any conversation about fathers the teacher always says "fathers and grandfathers" or "daddies and grandpas" so that all the children listening are included in the talk or the story.

Even when we do not know and cannot discover the reasons for a child's fears, distrust, aggression, showing off, or constant demands, we still have a fundamental principle to guide us: All children need a teacher who will love, who will understand, and who will accept them as persons of worth.

If your children have already experienced love and trust in their homes, it will be both natural and good for them to have the same kind of experiences with new adults—their teachers—in the church. On the other hand, if any of your children have known little love and trust and security, it is tremendously important that they find it at church. I almost wrote that it is a matter of life and death. In a sense it is. A life of love and trust and faith leads to an abundant life. A life of strife, distrust, and fear seems to me to be the death of the human spirit. But we can make a difference by providing new and loving experiences.

DOUBLE ANSWERS

Every child finds answers to "Who am I?" and "Who are you?" at the same time. Do you see how that is? If children experience acceptance, help, and trust as members of the preschool, the children come to believe that they are important, significant, and all right as they are. At the same time, they find that you are a wonderful grown-up friend whom they can love and trust.

So it happened with Ned. So it can happen with your preschool children and you. With trustworthy teachers, children begin to trust. With understanding teachers, they grow in an understanding of themselves. With loving teachers, they become more and more able to love. The Bible says, "We love, because God first loved us." It is true. This is the way we learn to love. Love helps the child discover who you are. And to the child you represent more than yourself. First, you represent new grown-ups. Second, you represent the Christian church. Third, and most important, you represent the love of God expressed toward children. You are the channel.

Photo © Kathryn Abbe

Letter 14 And "What Is the World Like?"

Can you imagine what it would be like to be three years old? How much would you know, and how little too?

You would have almost no comprehension of time and, therefore, have little regard for it. Most preschoolers have difficulty at bedtime recalling even outstanding events that preceded their nap time. One day broken by a nap is like two days to a preschool child.

Places you know would be places you go—the grocery store, the shopping mall, day-care, the church, grandpa's and grandma's house, your friend's house, and your own yard or the park near your home.

You would know that water is for washing your hands and for getting a big drink. You would probably not know of any relationship between that water and the rain.

You would know that leaves are parts of trees, but you would probably not know of the yearly cycle of leaves and trees.

You would know a bird when you saw it and you would know it goes, "Tweet, tweet"; but you would probably not know of birds' nests or eggs that hatch or babies that have to be fed and cared for.

"What is the world like?" The preschooler, like Kipling's Elephant-child, has a " 'satiable curiosity." Things keep happening, sometimes to, sometimes because of the child. Often children do not know how or why, but they want to know. They are eager to learn. For many, television is the most constant and reliable source of information and knowledge, but they do not separate truth from fantasy yet.

THEY WANT TO KNOW

Do burrs bite? Why do they have so many legs? Do they crawl? Are they dead?

Do adults grow little while children grow big? Will the children be the mommies and daddies someday and the mommies and daddies be the children?

Before I was me, did I used to be a frog?

Where did my sandwich go when I ate it? If it isn't gone away, why can't I see it?

I'm awake so early because Laddie Dog (stuffed animal) in my bed woke me up. He barked and barked. And my Pink (blanket) talked at me.

Once, when I was a big bird, I flew high up to my nest on the mountain, and there was my mommy and my daddy.

They yelled at me. Why did they yell at me? But I *wanted* to knock over their dominoes.

The children won't let me play in the box house. Why won't they?

I'm not sleepy. It's just my eyes.

What is this soapsuds made of? It cleans like a big, white cloud.

Mommy, teach me to fly. I want to fly, like the pigeons over there.

Why did my fish die? Will it not be dead after a little while?

And so it goes. Young children know little of cause and effect. Sometimes they truly cannot understand why another child hits them or why they cannot fly when they want to so much, why it rained on the picnic day, or why there is thunder.

Compared with the newborn infant, the preschooler is a mental giant. But compared with the vast understanding of the world which adults have, the preschooler is very inexperienced.

A FAIR LABEL

That word "inexperienced" is one label we could use fairly and profitably to describe young children. Nevertheless we must remember that they are not inexperienced in *all* things.

In any preschool group, several children may be inexperienced at getting along with new adults and new children—but several may not be. A few may be inexperienced in playing with clay or blocks or paint—and many may not be. Some may be inexperienced in the matter of pets and plants and their care—and one or two may not be. Some may be inexperienced in matters of wind and rain, birds and bugs, life and death. Some will not be. Some may watch television every day. Others may not.

Here I am saying it again: *Every child is different.* Every child's needs are different and experiences are different. Still, every child asks the same question, "What is the world like? Is the world hostile or friendly? Is it dependable or fickle?" The child is asking about both the world of people and the world of things, which are all around us.

THE RESOURCE SECTION

The resource section will help you plan some activities and experiences with your children through which they can learn more of what the world is like. There are suggestions about the seasons, a rainy day, the wind, growing things, and pets and animals. There are other materials about families, new babies, friends, and helpers.

It is our plan and our hope that these kinds of experiences will lead the children to feel that they are part of a world that is rich and alive and full, a world that moves and changes according to plan. They will discover some understanding of the plan and will find, to their great delight, that they can participate in it.

I hope that children will sense, through their relationship with you, that the miracles of life, growth, and change, though partly understood, are yet clothed in mystery. I hope, too, that they will begin to discover that the certainty and abundant goodness of the earth is a reason for continual thanksgiving. You will not, of course, say these words, nor will they be able to put in words even the least of these ideas. If you feel this way, the children will know it and may begin to feel this way.

Experiences such as these may provide the children with feelings of certainty and security regarding the world and God. They also provide occasional moments of awe and wonder which may become real prayer for some of the children. For these two reasons, activities and conversations concerning the people and the world about us form a large part of the preschool curriculum.

Letter 15 Listen: "What Are They *Really* Saying?"

Thinking of a child in terms of the three big questions is one of the best ways I know to try to understand the child. Take Tony for an example. I first met him on an Easter Sunday. That afternoon I wrote the following notes on our first day together:

> He is three-and-a-half years old, new to me and I to him. My brief conversations with him have been both puzzling and revealing. He rides a trike well and all the time, unless some teacher (that's me) insists he give someone else a turn. Ricky and Sue are the most persistent contenders for the trike. For the most part, he manages to ignore their pestiferous requests. He told me that he has a trike at home, it has three wheels, and he can ride it well.
>
> At another time, when I was helping him remove his paint apron, I asked how he managed not to get any paint on his hands. He said simply, "Because I'm Superman."
>
> When I think of this next note for this Sunday, I can still recall my flabbergasted feeling.
>
> Right in the middle of the traditional story of bulbs, he interrupted in a loud, clear voice, "Where do Easter eggs come from, and when do we get ours?" That really caught me short. I answered the question and put it aside, I thought. Not so. His wonderment was the concern of the whole rug full of children. That Sunday we talked about Easter eggs.

PUTTING THE OBSERVATIONS WITH THE QUESTIONS

Who am I? My guess, on just this little evidence, was that Tony felt himself to be quite a competent boy. "I can ride my trike well." Maybe he also wished he were bigger, stronger, more powerful than he was. "I'm Superman."

Who are you? He probably thought of the teacher as a police officer—albeit a rather pleasant one—and of other children as trike contenders. He got along with the trike contenders by ignoring them. He got along with the teacher by ignoring the teacher too, until the teacher became insistent. Then he gave in, with an air of resignation but no apparent anger.

What is the world like? Tony's angle of this question was, "Where do Easter eggs come from, and when do we get ours?"

In the following weeks I made many more notes about Tony and began to know him quite well. These three questions not only helped organize the observations I had made, but they also pointed out the questions I needed to be asking:

Who am I? Does Tony show competence in any activity other than tricycle riding? Maybe his Superman remark can be seen as an intense wish.

Who are you? Does Tony relate to anyone while he is on his trike? When he is not on it, what does he do? Does anything indicate how he feels about other children and the teachers?

Photo © Kathryn Abbe

What is the world like? It seems as though Tony's information about and observation of Easter, gained in his home, is egg-centered. As is typical of a preschool child, he makes no distinction between the real and the fanciful. He may believe in elves and fairies, Easter bunnies, and Santa Claus.

CONVERSATION CLUES

Think what a wealth of clues just one morning of observation will provide.

The following are isolated remarks, recorded by three teachers as they thought over one session's experience in the preschool.

JONAH: "Look, Teacher! Patty and I are driving this long train with this big load together!"

He is feeling pleased with himself and feeling good about Patty.

JILL: The conversation was about doctors as friends. Everyone talked at once. In a lull we heard Jill say, "I have a big sister, my mommy, and my daddy. They are *my* grown-up friends."

Jill might really be saying, "You can call the doctor your friend if you want to, but as for me . . ."

KEVIN: "Good-bye, Teacher."

"Good-bye, Kevin. I'll be looking for you next Sunday morning."

"OK."

This was the first time Kevin went home without tears. He loves the preschool and does not want to leave. Why does it mean so much to him? What is his home life like? Does he have friends in his neighborhood?

DAIKI: The teacher was playing a guessing game about what came down last night—all over town. (The rain.) Daiki's eyes were big, and he looked frightened: "Nothing came down in my room. It can't get in; there's a roof on."

JACK: "I have a new baby brother."

The teacher and Jack talked some. Then the teacher said, "You will have fun helping your mother take care of your baby brother. Have you thought about that?"

"No," he answered blankly. "I don't think I could do that."

ITO: As usual he played with boxes, calling them "pizzas," all morning for the third session in a row. Wordlessly, he picked up and delivered "pizza" to the children at the clay table. During the conversation time he delivered pizza to the teacher until she had a lap full of boxes, then he quietly came and collected them. For the first time this year he ate a cracker at cracker time. The teacher shared hers with him. Until now he had crawled under a table at this point in the morning.

CHANTEL: "I know the 'Eentsy, Weentsy Spider.' Could we do it?"

TED: "I won't wear an apron to paint. My daddy never wears an apron, and neither will I."

RACHEL: "I'm growing big, big up to the sky." She stretched high as she said this.

KEEPING NOTES

If you keep a loose-leaf notebook with a few pages for each child and enter jottings such as these after each session, before long you will begin to have quite a good understanding of many of your children. If you are in a preschool room with other teachers, all of you should spend some time sharing your notes at your teachers' meetings. Your skill and ability to work with children and your enjoyment and satisfaction in your task will increase as you begin to know your children.

IDENTIFYING WITH CHILDREN

I wish there were some magic way by which I could help you to identify with each of your children. To identify means not only to look at the world and the child but also to look at the world with the child. It means not only to think about the child's behavior and what you should do about it but also to feel with this behavior and how the child feels about it. It means to understand not only the words but also the feelings behind the words that are said.

Perhaps the reason we find the method of understanding children by identifying with them so difficult is that we are too conscious of our plan for the morning and are too busy with the sheer management of the room. We do not want to forget the story, we are short one teacher, someone has dumped all the food in the goldfish bowl, and Christie is surely coming down with a terrible cold.

The only advice I have for this is to be patient. Time is on your side. When living with preschool children, the unexpected becomes routine. After surprisingly few weeks, you find yourself carrying on a discussion that is more creative than the story you forgot to tell ever could have been. You gather the children around you who need direction while you bail out the fish. You tuck Christie in a corner and send someone to church after her mother. While the feeling, identifying part of yourself is not consciously working, you hear Chano saying, "My mommy goed away last night and a lady came and I cried." You *hear* the words, and you *feel* the fearful aloneness.

"You don't like it when your mommy goes away, do you?"

"No, I don't."

You do not tell him he should not cry, that all mommies go away sometime, and that sitters are our grown-up friends—not then. You understand, and let him know that you understand. You feel his feelings, and you learn much about how the world looks to this child, especially what he fears.

"I don't like anybody to put me to bed, only my own mommy."

"Bedtime is when you want your mommy most."

"That lady was mad when I cried. She told me that my mommy wouldn't come back if I didn't stop crying."

You look at Chano and forget the fish—they will just have to curb their appetites or burst. Here is a red flag of distress related as casually as "I had an egg for breakfast." But it is not casual, and you know it is not because you are feeling with this child. Children do not know that what "that lady" said is not true. Maybe someday it would happen. You are not listening to a story, you are feeling a child's panic. You do not add to the child's fear.

"Chano, did you tell your mommy about the lady this morning?"

"No."

"If you think of it today, tell her. She would like to know what your sitter said because that is not true, you know. When your mommy goes away, she always comes back. If you are asleep when she comes home, she tiptoes into your room and covers you up and gives you a little soft kiss on the cheek. Did you know that?"

You have Chano on your lap, and four children are gathered around telling Chano and you about the times their mommies "goed" away, and what happened, and then they "comed" back. They all talk at once, of course, but it does not matter. There seems to be a kind of joyous relief in the air: "Your mommies came back after she left."

And they do come back. Church is over, and here are the parents. You never got to the conversation and prayer about friends that you had planned. Can you see that it does not matter, that you have done a far better thing? You have listened and felt and understood. You have loved a child by doing for the child what that child most needed to have done. I think all the children learned a great deal about friends without your having used the word. The experience of trying to help Chano was prayer in action.

Note: Some children may have experienced a parent who left and did not return. Only when you know the home circumstances will you be able to offer secure and truthful assurances.

Letter 16 Dealing with Fears and Feelings

Have we depended too heavily in the past upon the forms of worship, the prayers and hymns and reading from the Bible, to transmit the good news? The early Christian community had few forms, but it was not difficult for them to spread the word. One historian wrote of them, "Behold how these Christians love each other!" They *lived* the good news.

Maybe too much of our educational effort in our church schools, large and small, has been spent introducing children to the ideas and the forms of the Christian church, and not enough attention has been given to experiencing love and accepting and trusting within the Christian church.

Wherever the good news is not *lived,* the church is weak. And that is too bad, for we need to know the strength of the gathered community, the body of Christ, witnessing to God's love and grace. The truth is that every single one of us at one time or another needs some help from another human being. In time of sorrow, in crucial decisions, when things go wrong in our closest relationships, when the future looks dark and uncertain, when our mistakes seem unforgivable, and when we cannot understand ourselves, the battle is half won if we know where and how help can be found. From the beginning of the Christian church, the worshipping Christian community at its best has provided a loving, sustaining fellowship for its members. I fear that too few people in the church pews have ever experienced such a fellowship with other Christians.

EVERY YOUNG CHILD HAS PROBLEMS TOO

All young children have problems, although many grown-ups do not think so. A child's life appears to be so protected, cared for, and free from responsibility that sometimes we feel we would like to trade places for a while.

When we yearn so, we are looking at the child's life from our vantage point, with our knowledge and experience. For example, a young boy has a new baby sister, and he is not sure that he is still wanted. Maybe he has a big sister who gets to do all the new things first, and she can run faster, talk faster, and bargain better than he can. He is a "big boy" who is expected to toilet himself and wash his hands himself but is too little to cross the street by himself. He skins his knee, and it hurts and hurts; he doesn't know if the hurting will ever stop. His mommy goes away and leaves him with a strange lady, and he doesn't know for sure that mommy will come back. He wakes up crying at night, quivering from a bad dream, and he does not know it isn't real.

All children have the same problems. For example, a young girl lives in a world not made for her. She has to climb up on every chair to sit down. She cannot see what is on top of the dresser, the table, the desk, or the television set. Nothing fits: the silverware, the bathroom facilities, nor, sometimes, her clothes. Every day has its perils, and sometimes they pile up overwhelmingly. She goes to the doctor

Photo © Kathryn Abbe

for a checkup and gets a shot; meets a big friendly dog that knocks her down; sees and hears a screaming fire truck come down the street right past her. Her daddy packs a suitcase and goes away.

Some things she just cannot understand. She brings mommy a pretty yellow dandelion and mommy kisses her; she brings mommy the first pretty tulip and mommy scolds her. Her old blanket wore out. Her mommy threw it away and got her a "bran' new" one, but she wishes she had the old ragged one instead. It isn't particularly easy to be a young child. It isn't even always fun.

The child doesn't always see life as protected and cared for and free from responsibility. The child feels the power of grown-ups who many times do not understand. In fact, they cause much confusion and heartache for the child.

DISCOVERING AND WORKING WITH FEARS AND FEELINGS

Frequently in your teaching you will be told, by word or by behavior, of a child's fear or of a strong feeling that the child cannot handle. How will you respond to the child's problem?

First, do not deny its existence, either to yourself or to the child. If you do not recognize and accept a strong feeling, such as hostility, how can the child be helped to understand and to handle it?

SALLY: "I don't like babies."

FIRST TEACHER *with disapproval in her voice:* "You shouldn't say a thing like that. You have a sweet little sister, and I know she loves you."

SALLY: "Oh, no, she doesn't. She cries, and my mother has to take care of her all the time. I don't like babies."

SECOND TEACHER: "Babies are a bother sometimes."

SALLY: "Yes, my baby sister bothers me all the time."

TEACHER: "Sometimes you would like her not to be around."

SALLY: "Yes, *sometimes* I would."

TEACHER: "Other times you have fun with your baby."

SALLY: "Yes, mommy lets me help give her a bath, and that's fun."

The First Teacher did not understand or accept Sally's feelings. This teacher did not "become as a child" and "put on" Sally. The teacher passed judgment on Sally, calling a feeling bad and almost calling Sally bad. This made Sally feel guilty and showed her that the teacher did not understand.

The Second Teacher accepted Sally's feeling. Sally accepted the feeling, then herself, and discovered that she had other feelings, pleasant feelings. Accepting a child's feelings does not mean that you approve of them or that you disapprove of them. In fact, there is no judgment in acceptance. There is only recognition and understanding of the feeling. It should also be said that accepting a feeling does not intensify it, as grown-ups seem to fear. Perhaps *our* fear is the reason we so quickly deny the existence of hate, anger, jealousy, and fear in the child.

How do you accept a child's fears or feelings? Listen to the words, think quickly of the child and all you know about the child, and then try to imagine how the child must be feeling. Express the feeling as well as you can. If you make a mistake, the child will correct you. A mistake on your part is not as serious as rejecting the feeling. For even as you are making the mistake, you are saying to the child, "I want to understand." The child will know that.

DICKIE: "Last night there were dragons in my room, and they scared me."

FIRST TEACHER: "They weren't really dragons, Dickie. They probably were shadows. There aren't any dragons, you know.

DICKIE: "Last night there were dragons in my room, and they scared me."

SECOND TEACHER: "Tell me about them, Dickie."

He has expressed the fear already. The teacher expresses interest and gives him her undivided attention. She may learn a great deal about dragons—and Dickie.

KENNY: "I'm mad at you, and I'm not going to come back to this dumb church any more."

TEACHER: "You feel pretty bad about the whole place." (This is not a question; it is acceptance.)

KENNY: "Yes, I do. Nobody likes me here."

Take the child by the hand or offer your lap. The child very likely will respond. Powerless in the grip of a strong emotion, the child is fighting and afraid. Sometimes this physical expression of your love will dissipate the feeling of aloneness and of being unwanted, and after a few seconds the child will return to the activity of the room.

Other times, with older preschoolers, you may talk the feeling out. The teacher's next remark might be, "Tell me about it." This is an invitation, not a command. If it seems possible for the child to understand the meaning of your words, you might say—*after* the child has expressed feelings and you have accepted them and the child—"I am sorry you have had such bad feelings, and I am glad you told me about them. I care about you very much, and I want to help you. That's what teachers do." Some children will understand these words. Others will know by your behavior that you understand and that you care.

HOW NOT TO DEAL WITH FEARS AND FEELINGS

There are some common ways of dealing with children, especially young children, that are the exact opposite of what I have been writing. One child (1) is afraid to go into the water to "swim." Another child (2) is frustrated because the shoelaces do not go into the holes, and so the shoe is thrown across the room—the child has not read the books that say fives are supposed to lace shoes. Still another child (3) falls down on the sidewalk and skins a knee.

1. "Oh, come on, be a big boy. Look at your brother. The water won't bite you. Don't be a baby. The fish like the water. Come on, you be a big fish." (Here daddy takes the screaming child into deep water and douses him up and down. I can't stand the frightened cries any longer and I leave.)
2. "What are you so mad about?" (Said brightly.) "Is it a dumb old shoe?" (Adult tickles child in the ribs.) "The dumb old shoe, the dumb old shoe, high-o the derry-o, the dumb old shoe," the adult sings while laughing and tickling the child.
3. "Oh, my goodness! What happened? You hurt your knee? What happened to the sidewalk? Did it get hurt too? Let's go see. Maybe it got a big crack in it."

Jollying, cajoling, ridiculing, and coercing children out of their feelings may be effective at the moment, in the sense that the child may be more pleasant to have around, but these methods are not at all helpful to the child nor do they strengthen the relationship between the child and you.

ACCEPT AND UNDERSTAND

Accepting and understanding a child's feelings, on the other hand, are very helpful. When any child discovers saying a bad thing or acting in a bad way does not make the child bad—although the teacher may have to limit the child's behavior—several things begin to happen.

1. Some of the steam is taken out of the feeling. The child does not have to defend the behavior or bolster up the bad remark with additional strong words or worse behavior.
2. The child is greatly relieved.
3. Having expressed the feeling and found it not so horrible, the child may find other feelings of just the opposite kind. The original bad feeling may leave unnoticed.
4. The child grows more and more to trust you.

Learning to understand and to handle one's feelings is necessary for the development of a healthy personality. Hospital beds are occupied by persons suffering from disorders that have their roots in fear, anxiety, hostility, and feelings of rejection and worthlessness. Mental institutions have many patients who never understood to any degree—or worse, who denied—their feelings about themselves and other people and the world they lived in. Sadly, their numbers are increasing. Many walk our streets today.

BEHAVIOR PROBLEMS

You will have children from time to time who do not, or cannot, or are afraid to express their feelings in words. They give clear indications, however, that all is not well with them. Juan, in my letter "Teachers Are Dependable: All Children Have Rights" (page 39), is a good example of this. These children have been called problem children because through their actions, they make it hard on the teacher.

One thing to remember is that these children are suffering children. In all likelihood you will not know why or what or how they are suffering. You will not know at first what to do. You should not, of course, permit any child to attack another child or you, nor should you permit a child to be destructive. These are necessary limits. But you can recognize how the child feels and offer a more acceptable way to work out the feeling. A child can wrestle and punch a big inflated toy or pillow or even a teddy bear, or he can pound a pounding board or a ball of clay. If your space is small, and hopefully your group is too, one teacher ought to be free to take the child who is upset for a walk, indoors or out of doors. Often a teacher who spends this time with a child can really begin to understand who the child is, who the child wants to be, and what the pressures on the child are.

I have no easy formula for dealing with your lively, rambunctious children or your timid and fearful children. Each one is different, with a unique set of circumstances, as I have already said. If you can remember that each child desperately wants to feel adequate and competent, to feel wanted and belonging, to feel trusted and understood and loved, you will have some pretty clear ideas of what to do and what not to do. Remember, too, that discipline should be helpful, not hurtful. It should strengthen the relationships between one child and the others in the group—including you—not weaken relationships; it should grow out of the situation and not out of your annoyance. Discipline, if it is helpful, is educational; it becomes a process of problem solving for the child. It helps the child begin to understand the problem and to discover possible ways of handling it. Some of the "whys" and "why nots" should begin to make sense to the child, as good discipline equips the child to begin to handle bad feelings or unacceptable behavior more satisfactorily the next time.

If you find toward the spring of the year that the children's mischief is more mischievous and the expression of strong feelings more frequent, rejoice and blessings on you! You are succeeding. I am not being facetious. As children grow increasingly to trust you and to accept you as their friend and helper, they will increasingly be free to try to solve their own problems and to express their joys and hurts and anger. In a sense, you and the children are becoming a Christian fellowship, a redemptive community—the church. To this end we have been called.

Photo from Sunrise/Trinity Photos

Resource Section II *Contents*

TEACHING PLANS 130
Theme: Wintertime 131
A Sample Teaching Plan for *Wintertime* 133
Theme: Pets and Animals 135
A Sample Teaching Plan for *Pets and Animals* 137
Theme: Springtime and Easter 138
A Sample Teaching Plan for *Springtime and Easter* 142
Theme: Friends and Helpers 144
A Sample Teaching Plan for *Friends and Helpers* 145

PICTURES 147

ACTIVITIES 147
General Activities 147
- Box Play 147
- Dramatic Play 147
- Water Play 147
- Looking Walks 147
- Visiting Walks 148
- Visitors Come to the Preschool 148
- Rainy Day Play 148
- Wind Play 148
- Making Valentines 148

Wintertime Activities 148
- Icicles 148
- Snow 149
- A Bird-feeding Station 149

Springtime Activities 149
- Planting Seeds 149
- Other Springtime Activities 149

Activities Related to Pets and Animals 149
- Animal Babies 149
- Caring for Pets 150

Friendship Activities 150
- Guess Who 150
- Match Colors 150

STORIES 150
- *Four Looking Walks* 150
- *More Fun for Joey* 152
- *The Storm* 153
- *Ms. Puff* 154
- *The Ladybug Helps Kendra* 155
- *A Little Boy Wonders* 156
- *When Mother Goes Away* 157
- *Baby Bear's Adventure* 158
- *People Are Friends* 159
- *Mr. Red Ears* 160

FINGER PLAYS 161
- *Little Chickadees* 161
- *Wee White Rabbit* 161
- *Two Funny People* 161

POEMS 162
- *Rain* 162
- *Who Has Seen the Wind?* 162

PRAYERS 162

SONGS 163
- *It's Snowing* 163
- *Thank You, God* 164
- *High Stepping Horses* 164
- *All the Birds Are Singing Again* 165
- *Easter Day* 166
- *We're Going on the Train* 167

TEACHING PLANS

There are many themes you can use during January, February, March, and April. What you choose will depend a great deal upon the climate in which you live and on the experiences of the children from session to session. You may spend four, five, or even six sessions on a theme that is particularly significant and only two or three on some of the others. Preschoolers do not remember much in the way of ideas from one session to the next. Therefore, if it rains on the second session of your theme on friends, change your plans and make use of the rain. You can pick up the friends theme later. Nothing will be lost.

THEMES

Suggested themes for these months are:

Wintertime (adapt to fit the seasonal changes in your part of the country or to introduce new experiences) ("Big Tree," page 214)
Pets and Animals ("Mr. Red Ears," page 160)
Springtime and Easter ("Jesus," page 89)
Friends and Helpers ("People Are Friends," page 159)

Use these themes to fit your situation. In the southern part of the country you will probably want to adapt the theme "Wintertime" or combine one or two sessions from it with the "Springtime and Easter" theme.

EASTER

If possible, use the theme "Pets and Animals" sometime before Easter. "Mr. Red Ears" (page 160) is the story of a pet, but it is also a story about death. You may want to recall this story at Easter time if children ask questions about death.

If you use the themes "Wintertime" and "Springtime" in January or February (or if Easter is early and spring is late in your part of the country), you may want to plan your sessions just before and after Easter around the theme "Friends and Helpers." The story "Jesus" could be used the Sunday before Easter as well as on Easter Day.

HOW TO PLAN

To prepare a plan for a session, first decide which of the experiences the children are having need further development for better understanding. For instance, are there three or four children with new babies in their families, and do a good percentage of all your children have younger brothers and sisters? Perhaps one or two sessions on babies would be a good experience for all.

Another way to plan is to read over the suggested activities for ideas. You may be able to use some of them, or they may suggest other ideas to you.

Once you decide upon your theme, do all you can with it. Look for pictures for your walls or bulletin board or interest centers. Look up suggested library books. Adapt the suggested activities to the interests and abilities of the children in your group and to the opportunities for the varied experiences which your community offers. Look through all three resource sections to see if there is a song, story, or finger play that fits your theme. If there is none, perhaps you can create one. Make plans for the group time conversation period and the possible prayer ideas. Jot down a few notes, and there is your plan.

CHANGING NEEDS

The children in your preschool are growing and starting to develop some feeling of being a group. You will want to plan your sessions to meet the changing abilities and needs of the children. Their interest spans are longer. Three or four children may become involved in dramatic play in the interest centers, whereas at the beginning of the church school year each child played alone or alongside another child. The children may spend more time painting at the easel or coloring. Read the letter "They Are All Growing Older" (page 195).

PROMOTION

Children who are just having their third birthdays should not be brought into the preschool group in the middle of the church school year. Their interests and needs will be quite different from those of children who have been together for several months and who are nearly a year older. Promotion should be held in all departments of the church school at the same time, either at the end of the spring term in June or at the beginning of the fall term in September.

Theme: Wintertime

Cold weather, winter rain or snow and ice, bare trees, warm clothes—all these and other indications of winter have a quality of newness to the preschooler. They are too young to remember their first two winters. Try to look at the world with "preschool eyes" as you plan experiences which will help the children become increasingly aware of the world about them and of the goodness of God's "plan" for plants and animals in wintertime.

PURPOSE

Your purposes for the sessions planned around the theme "Wintertime" might be stated this way: *To help the children discover more about what the world is like as they have experiences with the wintertime world; to help the children begin to relate the events and wonders of nature to God's creative activity* (a very beginning concept of God as creator and sustainer).

To help accomplish these purposes, plan your sessions around the kinds of experiences your children are apt to have. If you have the good fortune of having a soft, fluffy snowfall during a session, be prepared to catch some snowflakes (see page 149) for the children to examine. You might bundle the children up a few minutes before the close of the session and go outdoors. Children will have a wonderful time catching snowflakes on their tongues, trying to catch individual flakes with their hands, or just whirling and twirling with the snow. In other sessions you might use some of the following suggestions for original stories or group time conversations:

- What is happening to the seeds, bushes, and bulbs under the snow? Or: What is the cold rain doing to the seeds and bulbs?
- Where are the woods creatures, the rabbits, squirrels, chipmunks, deer? What do they eat? Are they warm?
- What happens to the birds in wintertime?
- Discuss the wonder of snowflakes, ice, or frosted windowpanes.
- Discuss the fun of play in the clean, white snow.

THE ROOM

Remove the Christmas decorations and the special materials you had for Christmas activities. Pack away items to be saved for next year and dispose of the rest. Ready your interest centers—housekeeping center, block center, art activity tables and easels, and book center—for the free play activities.

Make a New Year's resolution to provide interest centers for the children in spite of any shortcomings in your preschool space or facilities. Read again the letter "Doing Big Things in Little Space" (page 11).

Suppose you share a room with three or four other groups and the room is used for church dinners and other purposes during the week. How can you have interest centers? First of all, you need help. You need to get together with the other groups that use the room and talk over the use of cupboards and the storage of materials. You may need to get the help of the Christian education committee and the parents of the children in your group to buy or make necessary equipment.

A carpenter in your church, or some parents who are handy with tools, might make a couple of deep cupboards set on casters. These could be used to store your supplies during the week. On Sunday they could be rolled out to form two walls to separate your preschool corner from the other groups meeting in the room. Housekeeping equipment, blocks, toys, art materials, puzzles, books, and pictures could be stored in the cupboards for quick setting up of interest centers. See Appendix (page 221–34) for sample room arrangements and for instructions for making equipment.

In particular, you may wish to use the following books from the Bibliography (page 238) in your center:

White Snow, Bright Snow
The Snowy Day

Add other books from the Bibliography as well. Keep a Christmas book on the book table. Children will continue to enjoy "reading" and playing this story throughout the rest of the church school year.

Make your room bright with pictures. Magazine pictures that show a variety of families having fun indoors on cold wintry days are especially good. Use snow pictures that show children or animals playing in the snow or snowplows clearing the roads, *if your children have had experiences with snow.* If you showed a snow picture to preschool children in Florida, for instance, they would learn just one thing about snow—it is white. They would have no basis for knowing that it is cold or wet or slippery, that it sticks together so that you can make snowballs or snowmen, or that it stays on the ground for many days or weeks, unless they had seen, tasted, and held snow.

You might place a winter picture on the table with the Bible and the offering basket.

If rain is usual in your part of the country in wintertime, you may wish to use the story "The Storm" (page 153) during this theme.

ACTIVITIES

Use any of the following activities or adapt activities suggested under other themes to give your children good experiences with the winter world. The activity of feeding the birds is particularly good if the feeding station can be placed so that the children can watch the birds from the nursery windows.

Looking Walks, page 147
Icicles, page 148
Snow, page 149
A Bird-feeding Station, page 149

Art activities

Continue to use the art activities the children have enjoyed in the previous units. If there are some art activities you have not tried to use, include these in your New Year's resolution to provide as many good experiences as possible for the children in your group. See pages 221–24 in the Appendix for recipes and instructions.

GROUP TIME

The activities suggested for this theme may become the basis for your group-time conversation, songs, and prayers. It is not necessary to use a story each time to stimulate the children's thinking during this part of your session. If the children have enjoyed the stories in the books in the book center, you might reread some of these during group time. Part of the fun of wintertime is to sit close together to look at pictures in a book and hear a familiar story.

The song "It's Snowing" suggests rhythmic play. The children may want to pretend to be snowflakes whirling and twirling all about the room.

Finger plays

Little Chickadees, page 161
A Bedtime Story, page 90
Here's the Church, page 91

Stories

A Looking Walk in Winter, page 152
Four Looking Walks, page 150
Joey Feeds the Birds, page 152
Joey Plays in the Snow, page 153
Big Tree, page 214

Songs

Thank You, God, page 164
It's Snowing, page 163
This Is the Way, page 95

Prayers

Prayers of wonder, gladness, and thanks to God should grow out of wintertime conversations. If you have been talking about the rabbit in the story, "A Looking Walk in Winter," your prayer might include wonder that the bunny knew how to find its home and how to keep warm in the winter. Conversation about snow might lead into a prayer telling God about the ways we like to play in the snow. See page 162 for sample prayers.

You may want to use the suggestions for wintertime at various times throughout the winter months rather than to concentrate on the theme for several sessions in succession. That's fine. Never lose sight of your basic purpose in the preschool—to help children find answers to their three big questions as they live together in the Christian fellowship of the church preschool.

A Sample Teaching Plan for *Wintertime*

In every part of the country there are birds to be enjoyed by preschoolers. They are as interested in the sparrows and pigeons as they are in robins or mockingbirds. Children like to watch the birds, to listen to their twittering, to help feed them. Learning to care for birds by providing food for bird-feeding stations or by putting water in birdbaths is a first lesson in stewardship—the meaning of having "dominion over . . . the birds of the air and over every living thing that moves upon the earth" (Genesis 1:28b).

As you plan for the special activities and conversation you will use with this session, you may have these purposes in mind: *To help the children discover that God "planned" for birds and animals to have food in wintertime; to learn ways in which we can share in caring for the wild creatures, particularly the birds; to share with the children the joy of watching and listening to birds.*

If you do not have a bird feeder in a place where your children can watch the birds from a window, you might plan your session to refer to the birds the children see around their homes.

PREPARATION

The Room

- The interest centers will be the same as for other sessions.
- Place pictures of birds, especially birds eating in feeders or gathering seeds from bushes or trees covered with snow (if your part of the country has snow), in the interest centers as well as on the bulletin board or picture rail.
- If you can obtain some picture books of birds, have these in the book center.

Special Equipment

- Bring bread crumbs, seeds, suet, popcorn, or other food to put in the bird feeder.
- If you put out the preschool Christmas tree for the birds, you might string some of the food on heavy thread for the children to hang on the tree.
- If you do not have a feeder at the church, prepare small sacks or envelopes of the food for the children to take home to feed the birds.

SESSION TIME

Greet Children

Take time to listen to and talk with the children as they arrive. If heavy winter clothing is the order of the day, you will have plenty of opportunity to chat as you help take off boots and snow pants.

Free Play (about 25 to 30 minutes this morning)

Remember that this period is exactly what it is called—free play. This period is especially important to the big purpose of learning Christian answers to the questions: "Who am I?" (Am I able to build a road or a high tower with the blocks? Can I be a parent to the doll and fix breakfast or help the doll be good?) "Who are you?" (Are you a friend who likes to play in the rocking boat with me? Are you, the teacher, a police officer who will not let me race around the room when I feel like running; or will you understand my need for working off steam and give me some clay to pound?) "What is the world like?" (Is the preschool world a safe place where I can put my puzzle together in peace; or is this world a dark, noisy place where I have to stay while mother and father go to church?) Reread the letter "How to Teach When You're Not Talking—and When You Are" (page 103).

The children may also be interested, during the free play period, in watching the birds that come to the feeder. Their questions and conversation cannot be put off until group time. Adapt your plans to the experiences and interests of the children you teach.

Group Time (about 10 to 15 minutes)
The experiences of the children during the free play time or the concerns and interests they brought from home may take up most of the group time. In this case, you might just sing a song with the group, perhaps do a finger play, and bring some of their thoughts together in a prayer before helping the children into their coats and saying good-bye. There is a good chance that you can introduce a conversation about birds and how we can help take care of them by putting out food. Your group-time plan might be something like this:

Finger Play: "Little Chickadees" (page 161)

Song: "Thank You, God" (page 164)
Substitute "birds" for "snow."

Conversation: Show any pictures you have of birds eating. Let the children tell you about times they have put out crumbs for the birds or have seen birds pecking for bugs in trees or eating seeds. Children may have parakeets or canaries at home and will want to tell about feeding them and giving them water to drink.

Do the children wonder how birds know where to find seeds and bugs to eat? We don't know how birds and animals know what is good for them to eat and how to find it, but we believe God planned that they should know. This is wonderful.

Story: If you told the story of "Marc's Sunflowers" earlier in the year, you might retell it with the emphasis on the birds eating some of the seeds and Marc and his mother saving the rest of the seeds to feed the birds in winter.

Prayer: The prayer might more naturally come as part of the conversation rather than following the story. If the children seem to be really wondering about the birds' ability to find food, express this wonder in your prayer. See page 162 for sample prayers.

Activity: Plan to share with the birds the crumbs and other food you have brought. If you have a feeding station, some of the children might put on their coats and go out with one teacher to put the food in the feeder or on the Christmas tree. The other children and teachers can watch from the window.

Free Play, Going Home Time, Cleanup, Pick up, Saying Good-bye (about 20 minutes)
This will give the children an opportunity to watch the birds come to the feeder or to play with some of the equipment or art materials they did not have a chance to use during the shortened free play period at the beginning of the session.

If the children are wearing snow pants and boots, begin the pick-up time a little sooner than usual and allow more time for the children to get into their coats. If they are to take home packets of bird food, be sure each child gets a packet and knows what it is for. Suggest to the children that they can tell you the next time how the birds around their homes enjoyed the food.

AFTER THE SESSION

As you do your final picking up and putting away, evaluate the morning. Think about the individual children. What clues did their conversation or play this morning give you for planning future sessions?

The children will probably still be interested in the birds next time. You can insure having birds at your feeder if you can arrange to keep food on it throughout the week.

Theme: Pets and Animals

The song "Happy Thought" reminds us that the world is full of exciting things. To a preschooler the things that live and move are probably the most fascinating. A bug, a worm, and a caterpillar may be on your list of "things you can do without"; but to the young child, they are wonderful. Fish are fun to watch and so are snails. Pets that can be played with are the best of all—turtles, parakeets, hamsters, cats, dogs, and all the rest.

PURPOSES

As in all the preschool units, your purposes for the sessions on the theme "Pets and Animals" will be *to help children have good feelings about themselves, to develop trustful relations with other people, and to learn about God's wonderful world around them.*

Children will have good feelings about themselves as they discover that they have the ability to care for pets and as they are helped to overcome any fears they may have of animals. Plan to have pets in the preschool. Let the children care for them. If other animals "come to visit," try to provide opportunities for the children to make friends with these visitors. Talk about the animals, what they do, and how people take care of them. If some children are afraid of a particular kind of animal, try to find out what may have caused the fear. Do not force a child to pat a dog or cat if the child is afraid of the animal. Let the child watch from a safe distance and discover that the animal is friendly with the other children when it is treated well.

Children will come to think of the other members of the preschool group and the grown-ups in the church as friends as they have good times together and share the enjoyment of pets and animals. Big brothers and sisters, deacons, choir members—all sorts of people in your church have pets. Many of these pet owners would be happy to bring their pets to visit the preschool group or to have the children come to visit the animals. (See pages 148 and 149 for suggestions about a trip to a farm, visiting walks, and having animal visitors.)

As children have actual experiences with animals and pets, they will discover many things about the miracles of birth and growth and change. In later years, when they read the story of creation in their Bibles, the children may be more fully aware of the miracles and mystery of creation because of the experiences you provide for them in the preschool. Reread "And 'What Is the World Like?' " (page 117) and "The Use of the Bible with Preschool Children" (page 175).

STORY

"Mr. Red Ears" should be read to the children during this unit. This is a story about the death of a pet—an experience frequently encountered by children. It is an appropriate subject in a theme which deals with birth and life in terms of living beings. You will want to be familiar with the story before you use it. Be sure to read the introduction at the beginning of the story. Children may ask many questions about death.

The parents of your preschool children will be glad to have the story of Mr. Red Ears to use with their children. This would be a good time to have a parents' meeting. You could read the story and the introduction and discuss the ways of interpreting death to young children. Part of the meeting might be spent in telling the parents about your plans for celebrating Easter in the church preschool and the various themes you expect to use in the next month or two. Suggest ways in which the parents can help either at home or in the church school to make the experiences children have with animals, friends, and the world of nature in spring vital and joyous. You will find help in answering questions parents ask about the preschool program if you review the letter "Lynn's Father Asks: 'Is This *Christian* Education?' " (page 117).

If you cannot have a parents' meeting, call in the homes or at least send a letter to the parents the week before you plan to read "Mr. Red Ears" to the children. Your letter could include the story and the following ideas:

Dear Friends:

Next Sunday (or whenever the group meets) your child will hear a story, "Mr. Red Ears," in the church preschool. This is an important story. At first glance it is the story of a little girl, Amy, and her pet turtle, Mr. Red Ears. It is this, but it is also a story about death.

Children discover dead bugs, dead birds, and dead small animals frequently. Like Amy in the story, they want to know: "What is dead? What made it dead?"

A preschooler cannot understand very much about death, but the child does want to know about it. If we can answer his or her present questions in matter-of-fact terms, as Amy's mother does in the story, we will have taken a first step in helping our children understand death as a part of life. We hope the children will, as they grow older, come to associate all of life, including death, with God's goodness and love and care.

You will find Phoebe Anderson's introduction to and story about "Mr. Red Ears" very helpful. I have enclosed a copy of it for you.

Sincerely yours,
(Teacher's name)

THE ROOM

To get the most value from sessions centered around pets and animals, you need to give the children experiences with live animals. Look over your preschool room or space. Where could you put a parakeet or hamster cage? It would need to be in a place where children could see it well—perhaps on a low table. Children could walk all the way around the cage to see from every angle. It should be in a place where the pet would not be in a draft. You may need to eliminate one of your interest centers for a few sessions to have room for your visitors.

Try to have toy animals in the block center during this unit.

Place a bowl of goldfish or a pan with turtles on a small table. Let the children be responsible for feeding them.

There are many excellent animal picture books available in public libraries. Borrow some for your book center for a week or two. From the books in the Bibliography (page 235) you might select:

Pet Show!
Big Red Barn
Baby Animals

Other animal pictures, especially pictures that show animal parents with their babies, may be placed on the bulletin board or in the interest centers. Always place the pictures at the children's eye level if you want them to see the pictures.

ACTIVITIES

Choose from the activities suggested the ones that will give your children the best experiences with pets and animals. Visiting animals or having them come to visit the preschool is not as difficult as it may sound and is well worth the planning and effort. One group of city children visited a farm on a Saturday morning. All the rest of the year one of the little girls talked about petting the "cow." "I petted him and he was all bristly," she told her mother and her teachers over and over again. "He was a meat cow, not a milk cow."

Visiting Walks, page 148
A Bird-Feeding Station, page 149
Animal Babies, pages 149
Caring for Pets, page 150

You may want to use several other activities not directly related to the theme of "Pets and Animals." For instance, if you are using this theme in February, you may want to make valentines one session (page 148). Be familiar with the activities in all three resources.

Art activities: Provide paper, paint or crayons, paste, or clay for art activities. If you have old farm journals or other magazines that have pictures of animals, the children will enjoy cutting these up (not *out*) and pasting what they have cut on sheets of paper to make "pictures."

Group time: Use stories, songs, finger plays, and other quiet activities that fit the needs and interests of the children in your group. This may mean telling a story about taking care of pets ("Ms. Puff," page 154) if the children have been particularly interested in pets that have come to visit them some morning. Or they may have satisfied their curiosity and talked about pets all they wanted to during the free play time. In group time it may be much more important to listen to a child's tales of being lost yesterday. Other children may have had the experience of being lost. Tell the story "Baby Bear's Adventure" (page 158) to reassure the children.

The following materials help to enhance the experiences children may have during this unit.

Finger plays

Wee White Rabbit, page 161

Stories

Mr. Red Ears, page 160
Ms. Puff, page 154
Four Looking Walks, page 150
Marc's Sunflowers, page 85

Songs

Thank You, God, page 164
High Stepping Horses, page 164

Prayers

These grow out of the experiences and conversations of the morning. "We are glad we can feed our goldfish; they are so pretty" may express the children's own feelings of joy. See page 162 for sample prayers.

A Sample Teaching Plan for *Pets and Animals*

Do you know which of your children have pets at home? Have the children indicated, in their conversation or play, an interest in animals or any fear of them? Probably all of the children have played or talked about mothers, fathers, and babies. One or more sessions might be planned *to help children discover that many animals take care of their babies just as the boys' and girls' parents take care of their children.*

Preschool children do not know a great deal about the planning and order of the universe, but they can begin to sense that there is a pattern to all life. It is wonderful that God created animals with the ability to reproduce "according to their kinds" and with the ability to care for their young.

PREPARATION

The Room

- Interest centers should be in order, with a few toys set out in a way that suggests interesting play to the children.
- You might set a doll in a chair at the table with a cup and plate on the table before it.
- Several blocks might be arranged to form a rectangle with an opening on one side. A toy animal could be placed to be coming through this "door."
- The focus of interest (if at all possible) should be a box or basket with a mother animal and her babies. If the visitors are a mother hen and her chicks, have some grain or mash and a small dish of water for the children to give them.
- One session, try to have animals that nurse—kittens, gerbils, puppies, bunnies. Protect the rights of both the animals and the children. Most mother animals dislike having human hands touch their small babies. If the mother is gentle, the children might take turns stroking her. Otherwise, ask the children to do all their looking with their eyes. One more caution: Be

sure to check on the health of the animals before they are brought to the preschool.

SESSION TIME

Greet Children
If you have animal visitors, most of the children will want to rush right over to play with the visitors. Explain to each child as you greet him or her whatever rules you think are necessary to make this visit a happy one for both children and animals.

Free Play (about 30 to 35 minutes)
One teacher should stay near the animal box or basket to talk with the children as they come to look at the mother and her babies. Be ready to talk with the children about their own pets, to answer questions they may have, and to help children pat the mother animal if this is all right to do. If the babies are old enough, the children may hold them.

Other teachers may move about the room, keeping an eye on the interest centers which are their special responsibility, giving a helping hand here, an approving smile or word there, as needed.

Group Time (about 10 to 15 minutes)
The children will probably want to talk about the mother and babies. If you have pictures of other kinds of animals with their young, show these and talk about some of the different ways animals take care of their babies. Father birds often help with food gathering for their young. It is a good conversation if the children are joining in, not just answering yes or no to the teacher's questions or comments.

Prayer: A prayer of genuine thanksgiving may grow out of this conversation. You might want to phrase your prayer something like this: "Thank you, God, for helping animals care for their babies. We love our pets. Amen."

Song: "Thank You, God" (page 164)
Substitute name of animal for "snow."

Free Play, Going Home Time, Cleanup, Pick up, Saying Good-bye (about 10 minutes)
Encourage the children to help pick up and put away toys and supplies that were not put away before group time. Conversation about the animals may continue during this period and as the children put on their coats. If children offer to bring their pet for the next session, follow through on the suggestion. Talk to their parents about any arrangements that need to be made.

AFTER THE SESSION

Take care of your visitors according to the arrangement made ahead of time with the owner. What were the high points of the morning? Perhaps a child who has a new baby brother or sister at home seemed to be more relaxed after watching the animal mother and talking about the ways parents care for babies.

Theme: Springtime and Easter

SOME THOUGHTS ON EASTER

If your preschool children could put together a definition of Easter, it would go something like this (understand, this is *after* they have experienced their third Easter, not before): "Easter is to hunt Easter eggs which the Easter Bunny left and to put on your new clothes and go to church." Children understand events in terms of what they did or what happened, not in terms of the idea or history or reason for the event. Thanksgiving means a big dinner with grandma and grandpa or aunts or uncles or cousins or somebody else. Christmas means a Christmas tree and presents.

These are the meanings that the child can talk about because they were what the child did, *chewing on the turkey drumstick* and *taking a walk* with grandpa, helping *trim the Christmas tree* and *opening the presents.* The child may have felt especially glad and happy, particularly loved and at peace with the world on each of these occasions; but it is unlikely that the child would have told you about that. Whether the child mentions it or not, the meaning of any experience includes the feeling that was part of it.

Think of your last Christmas. How do you feel inside? Whatever feelings you have in connection with Christmas soon come to you. Yet when you first speak of Christmas or plan for Christmas you probably do so in terms of getting the house ready, the presents, the food preparation. You do not think of the feeling. But getting ready for Christmas recalls the feeling of Christmas, and the feeling you have about Christmas determines what you do to get ready.

HOW TO OBSERVE SPECIAL DAYS

The best way to observe special days in the preschool is to try to make the meaning of the day part of the experience of the child. We participate in the special day customs in such a way that the child will experience some of the feeling behind the celebration. Think with me for a moment about how we celebrate Thanksgiving and Christmas. We try to experience the feeling of Thanksgiving (joy and gladness) over a period of several sessions with our falltime activities. We look at, taste, feel, and enjoy the beautiful, changing world about us. Christmas has a particular story, and we talk of love and making surprises for persons in our family whom we love. And the whole time we are trying to be loving persons to one another.

MEANING OF EASTER

The story of Jesus' death and resurrection, which is the adult story of Easter, is not suitable for young children. However, a meaning of Easter—love never dies is not entirely beyond their experience. I do not mean for you to use these words, of course. Use instead the tangible, touchable, seeable, smellable events of the world about you.

A SPRINGTIME FESTIVAL

Easter comes in the springtime in many parts of the country. (If you have little seasonal change in your area, see page 144 for alternative suggestions.) The whole world is being made new. What seemed dead is coming to life. Preschool children can become aware of this and will rejoice in it.

"Look out the window. See the trees with their little baby green leaves and the grass turning green? The flowers are beginning to bloom. The world is getting out its spring clothes, and so are you. It's springtime, it's Easter time. It's getting warm outdoors, and the winter is going away. We knew this would happen. It always does. First winter, then spring. God planned it that way."

It always seems to me that children respond to the warm, pale spring sun and the moist, earthy-smelling outdoors as much as the flowers and trees do. They race about shouting, laughing, jumping, and tumbling as though they had been set free from a prison which had held them too long. They have burst the bonds that bound them, and, as every parent knows, weeks before the weather is really warm and dry, they even burst out of spring jackets and sweaters. The feeling of Easter and springtime is joy—laughing, unrestrained joy.

Easter comes at such various times in the spring that the meaning, the experiencing of life and growth and loveliness coming from brown seeds, may not coincide with Easter Day itself. That does not matter. The meaning of Easter does not pass away with the day itself. Some years will find Easter in the midst of winter's last clutches. That day may be the first Sunday of your spring activities. Other years, when Easter is late, you may well have had three or four spring activities, and the world outside might be green and new.

You may plan something special for Easter Sunday, a tangible something such as a sprouting seed to take home. But do not be surprised if you are not very successful with a story or a talking time on the rug. Your preschoolers will *all* be there, and you will probably have visitors whom you do not know. Everyone will be keyed up. Your well-patterned morning may be somewhat hectic.

NEW CLOTHES

The high-pressure advertising of our day more and more is making Easter a time of fancy baskets, soft and expensive plush bunnies, new clothes, and presents. You will see much evidence of this in the preschool. If you talk with the children about their pretty new clothes, do not neglect anyone. If some have no new clothes, you can admire the color that is like the tulip or the shirt that is like daddy's. It does not matter how you deal with the subject of clothes as long as no child feels left out.

EASTER EGGS

Concerning Easter eggs, Easter bunnies, and presents, I would ask no questions. Let the children tell you what is on their minds. Listen (you may learn a lot), accept, and be genuinely interested in their Easter experiences. But I would not introduce any stories or conversations about egg hunts or Easter bunnies. I would check all books before placing them in the book corner to see that they do not have Easter bunny or Easter egg illustrations. Your talking with the children might better be about going to church on Easter, or growing things, or friends—especially Jesus, the friend of little children.

A VISIT TO THE SANCTUARY

If you can arrange it, the children may be interested in visiting the sanctuary on Easter morning. If they could sit with you and the other teachers in the front, where they can hear and see and have an easy exit, this could be a valuable Easter experience. To see the minister, the choir, the lighted candles, the lovely lilies, and to hear the prelude, invocation, and one congregational hymn would be enough to do. It could highlight Easter Day as nothing else could quite do.

Perhaps the total group should not go. The visiting children particularly might find the experience of moving about in a new church with new people frightening. But two teachers could go with a group of your regular, more mature children for the first ten minutes of the service.

PALM SUNDAY

Palm Sunday will not be particularly significant to your preschoolers. If your church gives all the children of the church school palm leaves to take home, the children might do a waving, swaying, twirling, dance with them immediately before they go home.

You are apt to have a longer and more satisfying group time on Palm Sunday than on Easter, when you may have a number of new children. Palm Sunday might be a good time to read the story, "Jesus," from the Resource Section and to relate this story to the Christmas story.

PURPOSE

Whenever spring comes to your locality you will want to spend several sessions *helping the children in your group to feel themselves part of a world that is rich and alive and full.* They can begin to understand that the world changes according to plan and that they can participate in this plan. As the children develop a sense of certainty and security in the world, they may be growing toward a sense of trust and faith in God. As you and your children have experiences with the springtime world, there may be moments of awe and wonder which become real worship for the child.

THE ROOM

Bring something green and growing into your room. Make it bright with flowers. Add colorful pictures of birds, flowers, children playing in the sunshine, or families planting gardens. Let your room speak to the children of new life, joy, the miracle of growing things.

Add a toy broom or other cleaning equipment to your housekeeping center. Be sure that the doll clothes, doll bed blankets and pillows, and dress-up clothes are clean and in good condition.

Remove any cars or trucks that need repairs from the block center. Some families living near rivers, lakes, or oceans buy or rent boats for family fun. A boat (preferably a sturdy one made from wood) would add to the possibilities of dramatic play. If you have farm children in your group, they could use toy tractors in many ways.

Change most of the books in the book center. Select spring books from the Bibliography (page 238) such as:

Home for a Bunny
Will Spring Be Early or Will Spring Be Late?
Ladybug, Ladybug

Have a large picture of the nativity and a large picture of Jesus and some children side by side on the special table.

ACTIVITIES

Select several activities according to the interests of the children and the opportunities for springtime experiences in your locality.

Planting Seeds, page 149
Rainy Day Play, page 148
Wind Play, page 148
Water Play, page 147
Looking Walks, page 147
Visiting Walks, page 148

Art activities: As children near their fourth birthday, you can begin to expect a little more skill in the use of art materials. They may begin to name the pictures they paint or color—after they have finished, not before. (See "They Are All Growing Older," page 195.) Provide easel painting if at all possible. You can make an easel from a cardboard carton and make brushes by tying wads of cloth to the end of fifteen-inch sticks if necessary.

Easel Painting, page 222
Clay, page 223
Crayoning, page 224
Cutting and Pasting, page 224

GROUP TIME

Spring may be "busting out all over" inside your preschool as well as out. It may be difficult to calm high spirits when *you* think it is time to gather together on the rug (or wherever you have group time) for a story and conversation. Watch for signs of fatigue or over excitement. One or two children may need to go for a walk outdoors with one of the teachers to use up excess energy. Read again "The Second Sunday" (page 31) and "Teachers Are Dependable: All Children Have Rights" (page 39) to see how other teachers worked with children who found it difficult to settle down to a happy, productive morning. It will also help to read the letter "They Are All Growing Older" (page 195) and books such as *Your-Four-Year-Old* and *Your-Five-Year-Old* (see page 235) to gain a better understanding as the children approach their next birthday.

About five minutes before group time, move quietly from child to child and tell each it is time to finish the picture or puzzle or block tower or whatever, to put the toys and equipment away, and to come to the rug. As soon as a few children gather, start a finger play. Others will soon join the group.

Finger plays

Use ones the children have enjoyed.

Stories

A Little Boy Wonders, page 156
The Storm, page 153
Four Looking Walks, page 150
Jesus, page 89
Big Tree, page 214

Songs

All the Birds Are Singing Again, page 165
Easter Day, page 166

Poems

Who Has Seen the Wind? page 162
Rain, page 162

Prayers

Joy and awe may be the keynotes in your prayers these sessions as you praise God for the miracle and mystery of life. "O God, it is fun to run in the wind. We wonder where it comes from and where it goes" might be your prayer on a windy day. (See page 162.)

Take time to marvel with the children when a tiny green shoot breaks through the soil. Enjoy spring. Do not plan too many activities.

A Sample Teaching Plan for *Springtime and Easter*

On Easter Sunday many new people come to church. A number of the people who make this yearly pilgrimage have three year olds (also twos, fours, and fives) to be taken care of during worship. Some will be brought to the preschool group before church starts. Others will go to the sanctuary with their parents but will be brought to the preschool room when they become restless after fifteen or twenty minutes.

Easter in the preschool can be joyous and meaningful if you take into account the many possible pitfalls and begin your plans and preparation early. Reread "Some Thoughts on Easter" at the beginning of this section. (See page 138.)

PURPOSE

On this day, of all days, you will want *to guide the children in experiences of joy and wonder at the mystery and miracle of life and growth and change.*

PREPARATION

Extra Helpers

Attendance in the preschool may begin to increase several sessions before Easter. If so, ask two or three mothers, fathers, or grandparents to join your teaching staff for these sessions, especially Easter. Their major responsibilities may be to sit in the book center reading or telling stories and to engage new children in quiet play with soft toys, "Ball Rolling" (page 75), or using art materials. Ask your helpers to read the letters "Love and Understanding" (page 35) and "How to Teach When You're Not Talking—and When You Are" (page 103). Include these helpers in your planning sessions or explain your plans to them before the sessions when they are to help so that they will know just what they are to do.

If you plan to have some of the children visit the sanctuary during the first part of the service of worship, make seating arrangements.

The Room

- Wherever possible, add duplicates of favorite toys and equipment. Perhaps you can borrow a couple of extra dolls to have in the housekeeping center for a few sessions. Remove all the dress-up clothes except scarves and perhaps an assortment of hats.
- Do you have several cars, trucks, and airplanes in the block center? I have not mentioned wooden trains, but these are popular play equipment with most young children.
- Have one or two plants—one might be an Easter lily—and some flowers or pussy willows wherever a spot of color will brighten the room and make it look more homey.
- Look at your room from the eye level of a preschooler. What do they see as they come into your room or corner? One group of teachers who made this check discovered that the children looked at a blank wall as they came through the door. They quickly put attractive, seasonal pictures on the wall and moved some of the play equipment so that children could see it as soon as they came to the door.
- Pictures of Jesus and some children and the nativity may be placed on the special table. If you have an Easter lily, it might stand on the floor beside this table.
- Have a variety of books in the book center to meet the interests of your children visitors as

well as your regular pupils. Do not include books about the Easter rabbit or Easter eggs, however. Books about birds, animals, flowers, bugs, trees, trucks, trains, farms, houses, babies, and families would all be appropriate.

Special Equipment
This may be the day you plan to use the planting activity (page 149). Put potting soil in the paper cups several days before you plan to use them so they will be ready for your session. (If you use this activity when you have a smaller group and fewer new clothes, the children will enjoy spooning the soil into the cups themselves.) In addition to the cups of soil, you will need:

- Newspapers (to cover the table)
- Aprons (to protect Easter clothes)
- Seeds (and pictures of the flower or whatever the seed will produce)
- Watering can
- Pan of water and paper towels (for washing hands)

SESSION TIME

Greet Children
Greet the children as they arrive. Listen to their excited conversation about new clothes, Easter presents, statements such as "Jesus got killed" (growing out of television programs or overheard conversations of older children or adults). Listen, accept, be interested in their questions and comments. Do not try to give adult answers to questions about Jesus' death and resurrection. Reassure the child with a statement such as, "Some people didn't understand that Jesus was trying to help them. They had him killed. But God's love is even stronger. That is why we are so happy on Easter." The children will not understand much of this, but they will catch your sense of all-rightness about it.

If the children ask questions about the Easter bunny, have fun wondering with them about how this could be. Do not try to explain the Easter bunny myth.

Learn the names of new children. It is a good idea to write the names down on a piece of paper. You may need to summon a parent from the worship service if a child becomes too upset in these strange surroundings. Show the new children the toys and other equipment with which they may work and play.

Free Play
If you have many visitors, most of your morning may be spent in free play. Be prepared with stories, songs, and finger plays to be used whenever one or more children need a few quiet minutes.

Some children may visit the sanctuary and stay for the first part of the service (see page 140). One or two teachers may take a small group of children for a "Looking Walk" (page 147).

Group Time
If you have only one or two visitors, the group time will follow the free play period as usual. If your regular routine is upset by visitors or a number of children who do not attend the preschool regularly, have group time whenever three or four children seem ready for it.

Story: "Jesus" (page 89) or "A Little Boy Wonders" (page 156)

Have several stories in mind so that you can use the one that will relate to the interests of the children.

Song: "Easter Day" (page 166)
Conversation: Talk with the children about the wonders of springtime, the fun of having friends, or whatever seems appropriate. All preschool sessions are "played by ear," but a special day such as Easter requires very sharp hearing.

Prayer: (See page 162.)

Free Play, Going Home Time, Cleanup, Pick up, Saying Good-bye
Keep this last portion of the morning relaxed. One or two teachers may help with picking up and putting away. Another can help children with their coats. The extra helpers can read to children who are ready to go.

If you have planted seeds or if you have provided small plants for the children, see that each child gets one to take home. Wish every child a happy Easter and tell them you are glad they were in your group today.

AFTER THE SESSION

There may be more picking up to do than usual, and you yourself probably have special plans for an Easter dinner. Yet try to take the extra minutes to finish the putting away and to schedule a time to make plans for the next session.

Theme: Friends and Helpers

You and the children will have been meeting together for six months or more by now. All of you have found many answers for the big questions that we spend our lives answering. Have you as a teacher been growing in your understanding of your own answers to these questions? Are you experiencing the reality of the Christian fellowship with not only your fellow teachers but the preschool children as well? Read again the letters "Every Child Asks: 'Who Am I?' " (page 107); "And 'Who Are You?' " (page 113); "And 'What Is the World Like?' " (page 117).

PURPOSE

Plan several sessions around the theme "Friends and Helpers" to guide the children in discovering further answers to their question, "Who are you?" Of course, this question cannot be separated from the other two, but the focus of the activities you plan, the stories, songs, prayers, and finger plays will be on *developing relationships of trust and love with other people.* Emphases for these sessions might be: friends in church school, grown-up friends, helpers, Jesus was everyone's friend.

ALTERNATIVE SUGGESTIONS

If you are using this theme for the sessions before and after Easter, you will want to read the suggestions for the celebration of Easter on pages 138–42. The story of Jesus, a helper, teacher, and friend of children, would be the central theme of your Easter sessions (Palm Sunday, Easter Day, and the Sunday after Easter).

THE ROOM

Provide hats (see "Dramatic Play," page 147) or other dress-up clothes which will suggest to the children playing the roles of various helpers and friends.

Pieces of old garden hose cut into two-or three-foot lengths may suggest playing fire fighter. A mailbag (made from a paper bag, with a long strap to go over the shoulder) and some old envelopes will set the stage for playing letter carrier. Rural route letter carriers use cars to deliver mail, so a large carton may need to be turned into a "car." Provide equipment that will suggest the kinds of helpers your children know—delivery people, store clerks, doctors, veterinarians, and others.

Do you have play equipment that children can use together or by taking turns? There is nothing like a seesaw to help children understand the value of working together! A workable seesaw can be made available in almost any preschool room or space by bringing in a small sawhorse and a six- to eight-foot plank. Have a parent nail a couple of cleats on one side of the board so that it will not slip off the sawhorse. If you cannot arrange to have a seesaw, a rocking boat, a slide, or other equipment of this kind in your room, plan to visit a nearby playground one session. Some families in your church may have excellent equipment and would be glad to invite the preschool children to spend warm mornings in their yards.

Pictures of friends and helpers placed around the room will remind the children of the great variety of friends and helpers upon whom we depend. Have them on the special table for use during group time on the morning you plan to use such stories.

Picture books about many different occupations may be found in the library. You may wish to use the following books from the Bibliography (page 235) in your book center:

Chester's Way
Curious George Takes a Job
Most Ministers Wear Sneakers
Make Way for Ducklings

ACTIVITIES

Select the activities that will give your children the best experiences. If possible, have the minister come to visit. One other visitor would be enough for the sessions in this unit. Choose someone who can talk and play with the children. Suggested activities related to this theme include:

Visitors Come to the Preschool, page 148
Dramatic Play, page 147
Visiting Walks, page 148
Guess Who, page 150
Match Colors, page 150

Art activities

Easel or Finger Painting, page 221–23
Crayoning, page 224
Dough Clay, page 223
Cutting and Pasting, page 224

Plan to have variety in the use of these art activities. Use only one or two each session. Mix spring colors for the painters. If you make a big poster with pictures of diverse children playing together (these may be cut from magazines, old pictures books, or calendars), the children may enjoy cutting out and pasting onto the poster bright colored shapes to represent flowers and trees. The object is to provide an activity that they may work on together.

GROUP TIME

If you have visitors for one or two sessions, they may play with the children a few minutes during the free play period; then during the group time tell the children about the kind of work they do.

Use the following resources or others that will give the children additional insights into the question "Who are you?"

Finger plays

Two Funny People, page 161

Stories

Jesus, page 89
When Mother Goes Away, page 157
Baby Bear's Adventure, page 158
People Are Friends, page 159

Songs

We're Going on the Train, page 167

Prayers

When the conversation is about friends who help us, mention these friends in your prayer. (See page 162.)

A Sample Teaching Plan for *Friends and Helpers*

Are there children in your group who do not know the minister? If so, invite the minister to visit. (The children in your group may be more interested in some other helper; *make your plans to fit your own group*. A pediatrician might also be a good visitor.)

PURPOSES

We assume that the children in our groups know the minister of the church and what his function is. Actually, many children (in a large church) many not even know the minister by sight, let alone have any feeling the minister is their friend. Other children have confused notions about the minister. They have heard that the church is "God's house" or that they go to church to "learn about Jesus." If these children associate the minister with the church, they may think that the minister is God or Jesus. Were you ever confused this way when you were young? Your purposes, then, for this session are *to give children an opportunity to get better acquainted with your minister and to help them know that the minister is their minister too.*

PREPARATION

Talk with the minister several weeks ahead of time to make plans for the visit. If the worship service and church school come at the same time, one of the elders or deacons might lead the first part of worship so that the minister can come to the preschool for fifteen or twenty minutes.

Suggest some things the children may be interested to hear about the minister's work—talking to their mothers and fathers during the service of worship while the children are in their church school room, baptizing babies, calling on sick people, and visiting people at home.

The Room

- Set up your room as on other days. Most of the morning will be spent in the interest centers as usual.
- It would be well for the minister to join in the play in the interest centers for a few minutes and visit informally with the children.
- You might suggest that the minister read the letter "Listen: What Are They *Really* Saying?" (page 119) before he comes to visit.
- If you have a picture of your church and one of the minister shaking hands with a young child, have these on the special table.

SESSION TIME

Greet Children

Greet the children and tell them you are going to have a special visitor today. If the minister is already there or is coming for the first part of the session, tell the children to go to the rug for group time first this morning so that they can talk with their visitor.

Free Play

Again, this period will be adjusted to fit the schedule of the minister. If group time comes first, spend about ten minutes in conversation with your guest. Then let the children go to the interest centers. The minister could move from group to group, joining informally in their play until she or he has to leave.

If the minister will be coming for the second part of the morning, you can prepare the group for the visit during the free play time. Talk with individual children or small groups about the visit. Tell them that the minister (give minister's name) will be coming soon to play with them for a few minutes, and then it will be time to come to the rug for a visit with their friend, the minister.

Group Time

Most of this period will be spent in conversation. Encourage the children to talk to the minister. See suggestions above under "Preparation." The children might sing one or two of their songs for their guest or do a finger play. Sing the songs they know and like (even if they choose "Away in a Manger"). If the group seems ready, the minister might tell a story or say a brief prayer about the fun of being friends in our church.

Free Play, Going Home Time, Cleanup, Pick up, Saying Good-bye

Close the period as usual by sharing in the task of putting away the equipment and toys. The children may want to tell you about other times they have talked with the minister or about guests they have had in their homes as you help them with their coats or pick up any art work they have made that they want to take home.

AFTER THE SESSION

Did you have a happy time with your visitor this morning? Do you want to plan another similar experience for the children and invite someone else? As you finish your pick-up chores, evaluate and make plans for future sessions.

PICTURES

Use pictures of familiar objects or people doing familiar things to stimulate conversation, focus attention, or identify people or animals in a story.

See suggestions on page 74 about the different ways to use teaching pictures and ways to build a picture file of pictures obtained from magazines or other sources.

ACTIVITIES

General Activities

BOX PLAY

Add variety to the equipment in the preschool room by bringing in some cartons, large and small. Large cartons can be obtained from furniture and department stores, smaller ones from grocery stores. Put rope handles through some of the cartons for "carrying boxes." Attach a length of rope to one side of a carton so that a child may pull it around like a wagon. Better make at least two of these. Two or three strong cartons might be roped together to make a train.

Other cartons could be used to crawl through as tunnels, to climb into (perhaps to play jack- or jane-in-the-box), to hide in, or to use as garages for cars or houses for dolls.

Reinforce the corners and edges of the boxes with tape, and paint them with bright colors to make longer-lasting equipment. Depending on your space, perhaps the children can paint the boxes. Replace limp or broken cartons with new ones.

DRAMATIC PLAY

If you do not already have dress-up clothes in the preschool, get some men's vests, ties, shoes; work or garden gloves, slippers; women's scarves, blouses, skirts, purses. The more elegant the style and fabric and trimming, the better. Children will have a wonderful time dressing up as adults.

You can have an interesting assortment of hats with the help of a discount store's supply of police officers' hats, fire fighters' hats, baseball hats, and others. A change of hat, and a young child becomes a different person! Have at least two items of each article.

WATER PLAY

Water play is not as difficult to handle as you might think. Put newspapers on the floor and plastic aprons on the children. Keep the water play in one place. Usually it is absorbing, quiet play for children rather than noisy and exciting (as block play sometimes becomes). Some children might enjoy just moving their hands through the water while pretending to be fish. If you use water play, plan for a variety of experiences that the children may enjoy.

The children might wash doll clothes, dishes, or bathe their dolls in soapy water in the housekeeping center. Another time have a large dishpan of water for sailing boats. Make the boats from thin pieces of wood or soap, sponges with a cloth sail stapled to a wooden skewer, small round aluminum or microwave pans in which prepared foods are packed, or buy inexpensive plastic boats. At another time children might try blowing bubbles. In spring or summer, children could blow bubbles outside.

Catch rainwater in a pail. Talk about the importance of rain to make plants, trees, bulbs, and seeds grow. Use some of the water to water the plants in the room or for sailing boats. Talk about why rainwater is not good to drink. Reread "A Change of Session Plans" (page 47).

LOOKING WALKS

If you can, take a looking walk several times during the year. To get the most from these walks you should try out the walk before you take the children in order to discover what is to be seen. In wintertime it might be a walk to see a building with lots of icicles or a bird-feeding station in a nearby yard.

In the springtime take looking walks to see tiny sprouts pushing up through the ground, leaves or buds coming out on trees, or to watch a bird build a nest. Perhaps later you can return to see the bird's eggs and the baby birds if this can be done without disturbing the mother. Certainly your children will want to make frequent trips to watch their bulbs come up if the group planted some in the fall. (As soon as there are enough blossoms for each child to have one, you may want to cut them for the children.)

VISITING WALKS

If you as the teacher can become acquainted with the friends who live near the church, you may find an interesting place to visit. A letter carrier I knew once had rabbit hutches and very tame rabbits that the children were always welcome to see and touch.

Children in city churches will enjoy seeing the pigeons that gather around the tall buildings or in the parks.

Depending upon your location, a visit to a greenhouse or a florist shop a week or two before Easter may prove valuable. Go first, yourself, to discover the values and hazards. If the flowers are all planted too high off the floor for preschoolers to see, it may be a frustrating experience. Be sure the owner understands the purpose of the children's visit and is willing to have them. You will need one adult to accompany every two or three children.

VISITORS COME TO THE PRESCHOOL

If you know a grown-up friend—a doctor, a nurse, a police officer, a letter carrier, a firefighter, a minister—or anyone who would be a good visitor, do invite that person for part of a session. These should be friends who will show the children their equipment, uniforms or robes, or whatever is related to their work and answer the children's questions without overwhelming them. Fifteen to twenty minutes is long enough for the visitor to stay. Find good picture books and pictures illustrating the visitor's work to use in the preschool room.

RAINY DAY PLAY

On a rainy day cut large, irregular shapes from brown wrapping paper to represent puddles. Place them about on the floor. The children can "take a walk" and jump over the make-believe puddles.

WIND PLAY

On a warm, windy day the children will enjoy going out-of-doors to play with scarves, with crepe-paper streamers (three to four feet long), or with "kites" made of diamond-shaped pieces of colored paper (about nine by twelve inches) tied to three-foot lengths of string. You will have to make the kites for the children. Use the poem "Who Has Seen the Wind?" (page 162) with this wind play.

MAKING VALENTINES

The session before Valentine's Day, have large hearts cut from nine-by-twelve-inch sheets of red or white paper. The children can decorate them with crayons or by pasting on bits of colored paper, foil, cloth, or little hearts which you have cut out ahead of time. You might even clip the large white hearts to the easel to be painted. These become valentines for people the children love.

Wintertime Activities

ICICLES

Some cold, winter day (if you ever have such a day), find a big, clear icicle. Place it in a pan or bowl. Let the children watch it melt. Talk about the cold turning water into ice and the warm air in the room melting the ice into water again. "It always works that way. Isn't that wonderful?"

SNOW

Try to catch a large snowflake on a piece of black velvet (any dark cloth or paper will do) for the children to examine closely. A magnifying glass or reading glass makes looking at snowflakes even more fun.

Bring in a bowlful of clean snow (or ice cubes). Watch it melt. Talk about the way in which the snow helps the earth prepare for spring, then melts to give the plants a drink when the weather becomes warm.

A BIRD-FEEDING STATION

If you have, or can set up, a bird-feeding station which the children can see from the preschool window, this is an excellent wintertime activity. A parent or older child would probably be glad to make a bird feeder for the children. Make arrangements to have food kept in or on the feeder throughout the week. The birds come to depend on it, and it will insure some "visitors." The children may bring crumbs and seeds from home to put on the feeder. A feeder will attract birds even in areas where winter is warm.

Springtime Activities

PLANTING SEEDS

Fill paper cups with potting soil. Let the children plant grass seed, corn, or beans in them. The children can take these "little gardens" home to tend.

Fill one or two flat pans with potting soil. Give the children a variety of seeds such as zinnia, marigold, or snapdragon to plant. Show the children how to plant their seeds by pushing them into the soil. Let the children water their seeds each week until they have grown large enough for transplanting. You may have to water them between sessions or arrange to have this done. Be sure the seeds and transplants have at least one-half day of sun. Then the children may help plant them in a little garden.

OTHER SPRINGTIME ACTIVITIES

"Looking Walks" (page 147); "Visiting Walks" (page 148); "Rainy Day Play" (page 148); "Wind Play" (page 148).

Activities Related to Pets and Animal

ANIMAL BABIES

Children love baby animals. Try to arrange for them to spend some time watching a mother and her babies. You may be near a farm where lambs or baby pigs or chicks could be seen.

Whenever you take such a trip, you should get permission in writing from the children's parents if you plan to transport the children in cars. Be sure you have one adult to every two or three children. There should be one adult, besides the driver, in each car. Be sure to check your church's policies about such trips. You may find it more satisfactory to make the trip on a Saturday morning when the parents can help. Have a picnic lunch afterward.

A mother dog and her puppies or a mother cat and her kittens might live within walking distance of the church. This could be the destination for a "Visiting Walk" (page 148). Talk over the visit before you go. Review the rules for taking a walk, and plan rules for visiting the animals.

- Be very quiet so as not to frighten the mother or babies.
- Stand in a circle so that everyone can see.
- Take turns to go up for a close look.
- Look with your eyes—do not touch the mother or babies.

Check with the owner of the animals to find out if this last rule is necessary. If it is safe for the children to pet the animals gently, plan with the children how to do this.

If you cannot go to the animals, perhaps they can come to you. A mother hen and her chicks could be brought in a large crate to visit the preschool. A mother cat with a small litter might be brought in a box or basket. A big brother or sister would be proud to show off their hamsters to the children. An older child or adult who has a parakeet would be delighted with an invitation to visit the preschool with the bird.

CARING FOR PETS

You might have turtles or goldfish in the preschool. The children could help care for the pets and will enjoy watching them. Someone will have to take care of the pets during the week, but they are very little trouble.

Friendship Activities

GUESS WHO

During group time, describe a child by some article of dress or color of hair or eyes, and ask for the name. "There is a boy here today with a handsome green shirt. Who can guess who he is?" Talk about being friends as you play this game.

MATCH COLORS

Point out a color in a mounted picture and ask the children to find the color in a friend's clothes. Tell the friends's name. Any of the colored pictures you have in the preschool will do for this purpose, but pictures which show children working and playing together would be especially good to use.

STORIES

Four Looking Walks

These four stories can be used separately to fit the season. Or, by omitting the introductory paragraphs in the story sections on summer, fall, and winter, all four stories could be used in a single story-conversation time to emphasize the year's cycle of the meadow and the trees.

You can adapt the story to have David and Grandpa see the kinds of things your children might see on their looking walks. What kinds of birds, other animals, and trees are common in your locality? If you live near a river, lake, or the seashore, you might tell about seeing such things as the wind ruffling the water, frogs and tadpoles, shells and the animals that live in them, fish, and water birds.

A single story might be used as an introduction to taking your own looking walk. See page 147 for suggestions about this activity.

If you cannot go on a looking walk outdoors, have a conversation about the birds, bugs, stones, dandelions, clouds, or whatever the children saw on their way to church this morning.

A LOOKING WALK IN SPRING

Did you ever take a looking walk? It is fun to do. All you need to do is find a big person to go with you to help explain things. Then you go walking to see what you can see.

David and his grandpa take looking walks quite often. One time in the spring they walked to the big pine tree at the edge of the meadow. They wanted to see if a mother bird had built a nest in the tree.

They stood very quietly. Soon they saw wings fluttering in the tree. There was a mother robin with a piece of broken shoelace in her bill.

David laughed. "Look, Grandpa, the robin has a shoelace! How can she use that in her nest?"

"I don't know how she will do it," Grandpa answered, "but she knows how. She will build a beautiful nest and have some baby birds."

"Who showed her how, Grandpa?" David wanted to know.

"No one did, David," said Grandpa. "She just knows how. I think God planned for her to know."

A LOOKING WALK IN SUMMER

One time in summer David and his grandpa took a looking walk. Do you know what that is? Well, you need to find a big person to go with you to help explain things. Then you go walking to see what you can see. It can be fun to take a walk.

David and Grandpa walked to the big pine tree at the edge of the meadow. David saw long green tips growing from the end of each branch of the big pine tree. New brown pine cones hung from the green tips. Some of the old pine cones had dropped to the ground. David filled his pockets full.

"Some people burn them in the fireplace in the winter," Grandpa told David. "Or you can paint them and hang them on the Christmas tree."

Then David and Grandpa walked through the meadow. The meadow was all yellow and white. It was full of dandelions. There were little tight folded-up dandelions. There were lovely long-stemmed yellow ones. And some had soft white tops. Grandpa showed David how to blow the tops. David watched the wind carry the fuzzy white dandelion parachutes with the little seeds across the green meadow.

Grandpa showed David how to make dandelion chains and belts.

Then Grandpa held a dandelion under David's chin to see if he liked butter. (That tickled.)

The meadow was full of grasshoppers. There were little green ones, big brown flying ones, and hundreds of in-between-sized ones. David and Grandpa tried and tried to catch a grasshopper.

Grandpa sat down in the meadow. He sat very still and waited. Sure enough, a grasshopper hopped right into his lap. Grandpa caught it. He gave it to David to hold. The grasshopper's feet felt so prickly, David let him go.

David liked the summertime looking walks with his grandpa.

A LOOKING WALK IN FALL

There are all kinds of walks: walks around the block; walks to the drugstore or the mailbox. There are walks to church and to the playground. Then there are looking walks. Do you know what a looking walk is? Well, I'll tell you.

When you take a looking walk, you need to have a big person go with you. It doesn't matter much where you go. But wherever you go, be sure you look and look and look. See what interesting things you can see.

David and his grandpa like to take looking walks. Their favorite looking walk is to the big pine tree at the edge of the meadow.

One day in the fall, David and Grandpa took their favorite looking walk. The meadow was turning brown. The flowers were gone. The long grass had gone to seed.

At the foot of the big pine tree a squirrel with a big bushy tail was burying a nut. The squirrel looked up as David and Grandpa came by. Then it scampered up the tree and chattered and scolded.

"Listen to the squirrel, Grandpa," David said.

"He's scolding us because we frightened him," Grandpa told David. "Perhaps the squirrel thinks we want his nut. Come back, Squirrel, we're going away."

David said it too. "Come back, Squirrel. We won't take your nut."

David and Grandpa walked on a little way. They stopped and turned around to look. Squirrel was back on the ground digging fast with tiny front paws.

"Why is he burying the nut, Grandpa?" David asked.

"He's hiding it for the winter, David."

"How does he know winter is coming?" David wanted to know.

"I don't know how he knows, but he does know," Grandpa answered. "I think God planned for him to know."

A LOOKING WALK IN WINTER

Did you ever take a looking walk? It can be fun. You need to have a big person go along with you to help explain things. Then you go for a walk to see what interesting things you can see.

In the wintertime David and his grandpa went for a looking walk. They walked to the big pine tree at the edge of the meadow. David looked and looked, but he couldn't see anything interesting.

He looked to see if Mrs. Robin was in her nest in the pine tree. She wasn't there. The wind and rain had broken her nest to pieces.

David and Grandpa looked over the meadow to see if there were any dandelions or grasshoppers. There wasn't one. The meadow was covered with thick white snow.

David looked and listened for Squirrel in the big pine tree. Squirrel wasn't there. There was not an animal to see anywhere.

"There's nothing to see today, Grandpa," David complained. "It is too cold and snowy for the birds and other animals. The grass is gone and all the flowers are dead."

Just then there was a rustle underneath the big pine tree. Something was making the snow fall off the branches of the tree.

"A little animal is caught here, David," said Grandpa. "Watch closely while I help it get out."

Grandpa gently lifted the lowest, largest branch of the pine tree. Out hopped—what do you think? A brown bunny with a big white cottony tail! It sat and looked at David and Grandpa for just a second. Then it ran and hopped and zigzagged across the meadow and into the woods.

"Where did it go, Grandpa? Won't it be cold? Why didn't we catch it?" David asked.

"I don't think it will be cold, David. It probably has a home in the woods in a warm hole under a tree or in the middle of some thick bushes," Grandpa said. "It knows where its home is and how to keep warm."

"How does it know?" David was curious.

"I don't know how it knows," Grandpa answered. "God must have planned it that way."

More Fun for Joey

Here are two more Joey stories that express some of the feelings of gladness for everyday living of preschoolers.

You may use the same paper doll or puppet you used when telling the other Joey stories. Or you may cut out and mount a figure of a child in winter outdoor clothes to make a new paper doll for these two stories.

JOEY FEEDS THE BIRDS

This is Joey. He has lots of friends. Do you? Some of his friends are people, like his friends Margaret and Timothy in the church preschool. Some of his friends are pets, like his little black kitty. And some of his friends are birds—sparrows, pigeons, a bright blue jay, and some little, black-capped chickadees.

On a cold winter day, Joey looked out the window and saw his friends, the birds, hopping about on the snow. They were looking for something to eat. But there was nothing to eat except the cold, wet snow.

"Mother," called Joey, "my bird friends are hungry. There's nothing for them to eat but snow. Can I give them some food?"

Mother helped Joey fill a little sack with bread crumbs and seeds they had saved for the birds.

Joey put on his warm jacket and cap and boots and mittens, and took the sack of food outdoors to give to the birds.

The birds saw Joey coming. They didn't know he was going to feed them. They chirped and chirped and flew away.

"Here, birdies; here, birdies," Joey called as he sprinkled crumbs on the back steps and in a little pan that sat on top of the snow.

Joey went back in the house and looked out the window. Sure enough, all his bird friends had come back and were eating the food Joey had given them. Then they chirped and twittered happily.

Joey liked his bird friends. Feeding birds is fun.

JOEY PLAYS IN THE SNOW

Playing in the snow is fun. Joey took big giant steps. His boots made deep holes in the snow.

Joey decided to make a snowball. He picked up some soft snow and patted it in his hands. His snowball wasn't round like his rubber ball, but Joey didn't care. He had fun making snowballs and tossing them in the air. One came down right on his nose! Joey laughed and laughed. Some of it got in his mouth. It tasted cold and wet.

Then Joey found a stick. He drew pictures in the snow with his stick.

Then Joey made a big pile of snow with his shovel. Joey jumped in the pile. The snow came way up to his knees. He put some more snow on the pile and jumped in it again and rolled over. Now Joey looked like a snowman himself, all covered with snow.

Joey liked to play games in the snow. Snow is lots of fun.

The Storm

The wonderful world in which we live is sometimes frightening to children (and to grown-ups too). Children do not know that the loud noise of thunder will not hurt them, that the rain and lightning or the strong wind or snow will stop.

The children in your group may remember times when they have been frightened, as Freddie was, by a storm. By identifying themselves with Freddie, the children may be helped to overcome some of their own fears.

Different parts of the country are subject to different kinds of storms. Adapt this story to fit the experiences of the children in your group.

If the children want to talk about the story or about their own fears or about storms they remember, help them to understand that it is all right to be a little afraid of storms, that the storms do not last long, and that storms are part of the world of nature.

Freddie hopped into bed. A big round moon shone in his window. The cool night wind blew the curtains back and forth.

Outside Freddie could hear the soft singing noises of the peepers and the crickets. He heard an airplane far, far away.

"The airplane is going home," thought Freddie. "The world is going to sleep." Freddie went to sleep too.

While Freddie slept, a big cloud came in the sky. Then another cloud came, and another. They covered the big round moon. The cool night wind became colder and stronger. The soft singing night noises stopped singing.

It began to rain. It pitter-pattered on the roof. Then it rained harder. Then the lightning flashed. The thunder rolled. Cr-r-r-ASH! Big thunder! Loud thunder!

It woke Freddie. His room was dark, and everything was still. "Mommie-e-e-e! Daddie-e- e!" he called.

"Here I am, Freddie," said his mother. "Did the thunder wake you?"

Then it came again. Lightning flashed. It made Freddie's whole room light. Then there came very loud thunder. Cr-r-r-ASH! Freddie jumped quickly into his mother's arms.

"It's so *loud*. When will it stop?" asked Freddie.
"Pretty soon," said his mother. "We'll sit here in the chair and wait until it's over. It is a good rain. We need it. The world needs a bath, and everything needs a big drink. Let's go out in the morning and see what the rain did. Shall we?"

"Okay," said Freddie. He sat on his mother's lap for a long time listening to the storm. He thought about his backyard getting a bath. He wondered if his swing would be all wet in the morning.

At last the thunder sounded far away. The wind died down. The rain pattered lightly against his windowpane. The storm was over. Freddie's mother tucked him back into bed.

In the morning Freddie woke up and saw the sun shining in his window.

Mother and Freddie went out into the yard to see what the big storm had done.

The garden looked washed and green. The earth was so soft and muddy they could not walk on it. The vegetables and flowers in the garden were getting a big drink from the wet earth.

Freddie looked at his swing. It was all dried off. But Freddie couldn't use it—not now, anyway.

Do you know why?

Underneath the swing was a big puddle. And in that puddle two little birds were taking a bath!

The big storm had given everything a big cool drink. It had given the world a bath, just as his mother had said it would.

Ms. Puff

"How did Ms. Puff know that she could keep warm by crawling under the big paper hat?" Enjoy wondering about this question with your children when you tell about Ms. Puff.

This story will help your children discover several answers to their question "What is the world like?" They may learn that pets need to be cared for by people, that boys and girls as well as adults are responsible for taking good care of their pets, and that somehow animals know about taking care of themselves too.

If someone in your church has rabbits, ask them to bring a rabbit to visit the preschool the day you plan to tell this story. Perhaps you can find a magazine picture that looks like Ms. Puff. There are many good picture books about rabbits (see page 235). You might show pictures from one of these books as you tell the story.

Roberta had a white rabbit. Her daddy got it for her. The rabbit was Roberta's pet. Roberta named the rabbit Ms. Puff. Can you guess why? That's right. Because its little white tail looked just like a puff.

Roberta took good care of Ms. Puff. Every day Roberta gave her fresh water to drink. She gave Ms. Puff carrots and lettuce to eat. Roberta put straw in the rabbit hutch for Ms. Puff to sleep in so she wouldn't get cold.

One day something happened to Ms. Puff. Roberta came to feed her, but Ms. Puff was gone. I don't know how it happened. I think probably Roberta forgot to shut the door to the rabbit hutch tightly. Sometimes people do forget.

Roberta looked everywhere. Roberta's daddy looked everywhere too. They looked under the back steps. They looked behind the garage. They looked all around last year's garden. But they could not find Ms. Puff.

Roberta called, "Here, Ms. Puff. Come, Ms. Puff." She didn't come.

Where had Ms. Puff gone? Do you know? No one knew. Where would Ms. Puff sleep all night? Do you know? [Allow conversation at these points.] No one knew. Would Roberta ever find her? No one knew.

"It is going to be a cold night," Roberta's daddy said. "We will have to put these big paper hats on our tulips to keep them warm tonight."

Roberta helped her daddy cover the tulips. Roberta thought about Ms. Puff. She might get cold.

The next morning the sun warmed the outdoors. Roberta and her daddy went out to take the big paper hats off the tulips. And there was a surprise! Can you guess?

Yes, there was Ms. Puff sitting next to a tulip plant, right under one of the big paper hats. She looked so funny!

Roberta was very glad to have Ms. Puff come back. Roberta put her in the hutch with some clean straw and gave her a great big carrot. What do you think Roberta did then? Yes, she shut the door *tightly!*

How do you think Ms. Puff knew that she could keep warm by crawling under the big paper hat? I wonder how she knew.

The Ladybug Helps Kendra

Some answers to all three of the children's big questions are found in this story. Every child from time to time feels alone, rejected, and unloved, as Kendra feels in this story. Kendra's good feelings about herself and other people were restored when mother helped her find a jar and when Jan and Carl showed interest in her "pet." Kendra learned more about what the world is like, too, as she discovered that the ladybug's feet tickled her and that the ladybug needed air when she put it in the jar.

Can you find a ladybug to bring to the class? Your children will have as much fun with it as Kendra did. Then, together, you can set it free.

Kendra wanted someone to play with her.

Her big brother, Carlo, wouldn't. He had gone to play ball with his big friends.

Her little sister, Jan, couldn't. She was napping.

"Will you play with me, Mommy?"

"I just *have* to finish this baking, Kendra," her mother told her. "Can you bring something to play with into the kitchen with me? We'll talk together while you play and I cook."

Kendra brought her hammer and a handful of nails and a little piece of wood. Kendra loved to pound nails.

But her mother would not let her pound nails. She said that the hammer and nails would make bad marks on the kitchen table or on the floor. Besides, the noise would waken Jan.

"Kendra, you can pound nails on the workbench in the basement," Mother suggested. Kendra didn't want to do that. "Or you can pound on the back porch." Kendra didn't want to do that either. "Or you can find something else to play with."

Kendra didn't want to play with anything else. She wanted to pound nails in the kitchen where her mother was. But when she did, her mother made her go out on the back porch.

There she sat. She felt very unhappy.

She sat there a long time. Nothing happened.

The shadows of the leaves danced like little fairies on the walk in front of her.

A big fat robin hopped through the grass quite close to her and pulled out a big, big worm.

Kendra felt a little soft tickle on her cheek. She reached up to rub the tickle off, and what do you think was there? A ladybug! It was a pretty, orange ladybug with black spots on her wings and a shiny black head.

Kendra watched it crawl up her finger. Then it crawled up her arm. Oh, how it tickled! It's little feet tickled and tickled, and Kendra laughed. "Ha, ha, ha, don't tickle me, ladybug. Don't tickle."

She picked the ladybug up in her hand again, very carefully so as not to hurt it, and she said to it, "Ladybug, ladybug, fly away home."

But the ladybug didn't fly away.

Then Kendra knew what she could do by herself that would be fun. She took the ladybug into the house to show her mother.

"Look, Mommy, a little ladybug came to play with me and it doesn't want to fly away. Could you get a little jar to keep it in?"

"Yes, I surely can do that," Mother said as she put down her spoon. She looked in her cupboard for just the right-sized jar. Then she showed Kendra how to punch holes in the paper cover of the jar so that the ladybug would have some air. She had Kendra bring in some leaves and showed her how to put them in the jar for the ladybug to crawl on.

Kendra played with her ladybug all afternoon.

When Jan woke up, Kendra told her all about the ladybug. Jan watched it and watched it for a long, long time.

When Carlo came home, Kendra told him all about the ladybug. Carlo said it was the biggest, brightest ladybug he had ever seen.

That night before dinner, Kendra went outside, uncovered her jar, and sang to the ladybug again: "Ladybug, ladybug, fly away home."

This time the ladybug flew away. Kendra took the jar to her mother.

"Thank you, Mother, for the jar," she said.

"You're welcome, Kendra. You aren't angry any more about the pounding?" Mother asked.

"No. The ladybug was more fun," Kendra answered.

"I'm glad, Kendra," said Mother. And she gave her a great big hug.

A Little Boy Wonders

Imagine what the world is like to a young child. It is all new and wonderful and full of things many folk do not understand. A child's response to the marvels of nature may be one of joy and wonder. We can help the child begin to develop a sense of awe and appreciation (which may later become reverence and praise) for God's creative activity in the world of nature by feeling and expressing wonder with the child rather than trying to provide detailed scientific explanations.

If possible, bring a small branch or twig with leaf buds just bursting open, a bird's nest, and a bright flower to show when telling this story. (There is undoubtedly a Boy or Girl Scout or someone else in the church who has or can find an abandoned bird's nest for you to show the children. One teacher kept a well-preserved nest packed in tissue paper in a small box. Several times during the year the nest would be put on the special table or on the wonder table for the children to examine.)

If you cannot bring in the real things, try to find magazine pictures to illustrate this story as you tell it. You might make a large picture from several smaller pictures pasted along a "path" you draw on a large sheet of heavy paper. Slit the picture along the center of the path. Attach a cutout of a little boy to a six- or eight-inch strip of heavy paper or cardboard. Insert the figure of the little boy through the slit and let him "walk" along the path (moved by means of the cardboard strip) as you tell the story.

It was spring. A little boy walked alone over the green hills near his home. He stopped and looked at them. Perhaps he asked, "Trees, where did you come from? And where did you get your new green leaves?"

The trees did rustle
And tried to tell,
But the people could not
Understand very well.

And the little boy wondered.

The little boy walked on. Suddenly he spied a bird's nest hidden in some bushes. He looked at it but did not touch it. He said, "How wonderful it is!" He turned to its maker perched up in a tree and asked, "Little bird, where did you learn to make this nest?"

The bright little fellow
Never did say,
It twittered and twittered
And then flew away.

And the little boy wondered.

The little boy walked on. He saw bright flowers covering the hillside. He sat on the ground to look into one of the little red cups. He cried, "How wonderful it is!" He asked, "Little flower, where did you come from? And where did you get your dress of red?"

The red flower nodded
But said not a word,
At least not any
That could be heard.

And the little boy wondered.

The little boy felt the wind blow through his hair. He heard the rustle of the leaves. Perhaps he asked, "O wind, where do you come from and where do you go?"

And the warm wind blew
And blew and blew,
But what it said
Nobody knew.

And the little boy wondered.

He wondered about these things all the way home. On the way he picked one of the bright red flowers. He said to his mother, "I wonder how the trees get their new leaves. I wonder how birds learn to make nests. I wonder where the winds come from and where they go. I wonder how this little flower got its red dress."

The mother looked with the little boy into the red flower cup and said softly, "I wonder!"

—*Esther Freivogel*

When Mother Goes Away

"God is love" (1 John 4:16b). God's "benevolence endures forever" (2 Corinthians 9:9). Faith and trust in God's love and steadfastness are beyond the preschooler's ability to understand. This is a here-and-now child busily learning about self, others, and the world. The child may come to know God and respond to God as the child grows older if present experiences help develop a sense of trust.

You know, and I know, that when a parent hires a baby-sitter and goes away for a few hours (sometimes for several days) the parent will come home again. The preschool child, however, may not know this. When the parent leaves, the child may be extremely upset. The child needs constant reassurances that the parent (or whomever the child depends upon) will come back.

Do you remember the conversation about baby-sitters in the letter "Listen: What Are They Really *Saying?" (page 119)? You may have children in your group who feel just as Chano did in his account. It would be good to have this story, "When Mother Goes Away," at your fingertips to tell the children whenever the occasion arises.*

Use any picture you can find that will fit this story. Give the children an opportunity to talk about any fears they may have about a parent going away and coming home again. You may lead into a good conversation about baby-sitters as friends and about what children can do when they are with sitters. After the story there may be happy speculation about the packages Ruth's mother brought home. Yet children should not be encouraged to expect gifts every time a parent goes away.

Ruth didn't like to have her mother go away. Ruth wanted to go too. She didn't like to stay at home alone with the sitter, Mrs. Johnson. She wanted to go with her mother.

But Mother said that she *had* to go away.

And she said that Ruth *had* to stay home.

And Mother said that she would come back.

Ruth cried. "I don't feel good in my stomach," she said. "I'm sick."

"I know how you feel," said Mother. "I have just the thing to help you." From her purse she took a little mirror. "Ruth, here is a special mirror. You may keep it near you; and whenever you miss me, look at the mirror to remind you of me."

Ruth looked in the mirror. She remembered how people said she looks like her mother.

Mrs. Johnson came. Ruth's mother went away.

Ruth didn't cry. She played.

She put her dolls and teddy bear to bed. Mrs. Johnson helped her with the fasteners on the nighties.

She read some books. Mrs. Johnson helped with the reading. She colored a picture. Mrs. Johnson wrote Ruth's name on it.

She and Mrs. Johnson had a snack of lemonade and cookies that Mother had left for them.

Then Ruth wondered when her mother would come back.

"Pretty soon now," said Mrs. Johnson.

Then Ruth remembered her mirror. She looked at herself and thought about Mother.

Then Ruth and Mrs. Johnson sat on the front step and waited for Mother.

They saw a little boy go up the street with a furry brown puppy in his arms. That wasn't Mother.

They saw a lady pushing a baby stroller. A little boy on a red and white tricycle followed her. That wasn't Mother.

They saw another lady with a blue coat. She was carrying many packages. That was . . .

"Mother!" called Ruth. "You came home! Mrs. Johnson, Mother came home!"

Mother put down her packages and gave Ruth a big hug. "Yes, I came home, just as I said I would.

I always come back to you, Ruth. You know that."

Ruth did know that, and she was glad.

Mrs. Johnson put on her hat and coat, ready to go home.

"Good-bye, Mrs. Johnson. Come again."

"Good-bye, Ruth. I had a happy time sitting with you," said Mrs. Johnson.

Then Ruth told her mother all that she had done with Mrs. Johnson while her mother was away. And Mother showed Ruth what was in the packages she had brought home.

Baby Bear's Adventure

Being lost is a terrifying experience and one that happens to almost every young child. Usually the child is lost for just a few minutes before mother or father or whomever the child is with finds the child. But it is comforting and helpful to know that if you get lost there are many grown-up friends who will help you find your home and family.

If you have or can find a picture of a friendly police officer helping a lost child, you could show it after the story and talk about friends who help us when we get lost.

Your conversation might include talking about the things Baby Bear knew about herself: her name, her family's name, her address. It is important for children to know these things so that friends can help them find their homes if they become lost.

One day the Bear family went for a walk in the woods. There were Father Bear, Mother Bear, Sister Suzy Bear, and Baby Bear.

Father and Mother Bear walked pretty fast. Suzy Bear skipped alongside them. She could keep up with them pretty well. But Baby Bear just couldn't walk fast. Besides, he liked to stop often and look at things.

Once he chased a pretty brown and yellow butterfly. It flew back and forth from bush to bush, and then suddenly it was gone. Baby Bear couldn't see it anywhere. Then he looked for Father and Mother Bear and Sister Suzy. He couldn't see them anywhere either. He called them, "Mother . . . Father . . . !" No answer. He called again—still no answer. Where could they be? They must have walked too fast and walked right away from him. Or maybe, just maybe, he had chased that butterfly so far that he had gotten off the path.

Baby Bear was lost. He didn't know where he was or which way to go.

Never mind. Baby Bear knew *who* he was—Barton Bear, that's who. And he knew he was three years old. He knew that he belonged to the Bear family. And he knew where he belonged. He belonged in the Bear family house, which was a cave in the woods, Number 123 by the thornapple tree.

But he did not know where he was or how to get home.

He walked a little this way and then a little that way. Then he met Mrs. Raccoon.

"Mrs. Raccoon, I'm lost. Can you help me to get home to my cave? It is Number 123 by the thornapple tree."

"My goodness, Barton Bear, there are many thornapple trees in the forest. How can we tell which cave is 123?"

"Oh, I know my own cave, Mrs. Raccoon. It has a low hook right inside the front door for me to hang my coat on when I come in."

Mrs. Raccoon took Barton Bear to the only cave she knew. Barton Bear looked in. There was no hook for a three-year-old bear's coat.

As they walked on, they met Brown Stag. He had traveled all over the forest and knew nearly every cave there was.

"Brown Stag, I'm lost," said Barton Bear. "Do you know where my cave is? It is Number 123 by the thornapple tree."

"My goodness, Barton Bear, there are many caves and many thornapple trees in the forest. How can we tell which cave is yours?"

"Oh, I know my own cave, Brown Stag. There's a little chair there just my size. I sit on it when I play pizza party with my teddy bear."

So Brown Stag took Baby Bear to the first cave he knew. Baby Bear looked in. There was no little chair there.

"What else is in your cave, Barton Bear, that we can look for?"

"Oh . . . my toys. I've got a teddy bear, some blocks, and crayons my gran'ma gave me."

So Brown Stag took Baby Bear to the second cave he knew. Baby Bear looked in. There were no toys there, none at all—no teddy bear, no blocks, no crayons.

Baby Bear didn't feel very good. He thought maybe he was going to cry. "Don't worry, Baby Bear," said Brown Stag, "we'll find your cave."

"I'm hungry, Brown Stag, and I'm very tired," Baby Bear said.

"I know one more cave by a thornapple tree, Baby Bear. Let's try that one."

That one was Baby Bear's own cave. That was where he belonged.

There was the hook for his coat.

There were his little chair and all his toys.

Best of all, there were Father Bear, Mother Bear, and Sister Suzy. They were glad Barton Bear was home again. Barton Bear was glad too. He felt best when he was home with his own family where he belonged.

And do you know, the very next time the Bear family went walking, they didn't go as fast as Father Bear or Mother Bear or even Sister Suzy Bear could walk. They went just as fast as Baby Barton Bear could walk because no one wanted him to become lost again.

People Are Friends

Many children at some time or other feel uneasy, perhaps a little afraid, of people whom they do not know.

Trying to talk a child out of this feeling by explaining who another person is in terms of the good things this person does—the doctor makes you well and the sitter takes good care of you—does not often work. The child grows to appreciate and trust other people as the child builds a trusting relationship with them, regardless of who they are and what they do.

The Little Girl liked the little boy. Then she liked his daddy with the big glasses and his mommy who smelled like flowers. In time, she came to see that other people were friends. She did different things with each one, but she enjoyed them all.

Telling this story will not turn any child into an outgoing, friendly person overnight. No story alone can do that. But it may provide some assurance.

Once there was a Little Girl who did not know about other people. Other people did not know about her either.

She did not know about the big man who came to see her daddy. He looked as high as the door. When he laughed, the laugh went all around the room with a ho, ho, ho.

The Little Girl sat far away in her little chair and looked at him.

The Little Girl did not know about Mrs. Prentiss who lived next door. Her face was wrinkled and she always said, "How are you today, Little Girl?"

The Little Girl did not answer. She sat in her sandbox and felt the sand.

The Little Girl did not know about the sitter who came to stay with her and her big brother when her mother and father went away. The sitter brought a book about kittens to read.

The Little Girl held her blanket and sat beside her brother and listened.

The Little Girl did not know about the little boy who came to visit her.

The little boy had a daddy with big glasses and a mommy who smelled like flowers. The daddy smiled at her. The mommy said, "How big you have grown!"

The little boy said, "Let's play." The little boy was fun to play with. They played firefighter for a long time. Then the little boy had to go home.

The Little Girl said, "Good-bye." And then she said, "Come again."

The little boy said, "I will."

The daddy with the big glasses said, "We had fun at your house."

The mommy who smelled like flowers said, "You are our friend and we like you."

Now the Little Girl knows more about some people. She knows that the little boy and his mommy and his daddy are her friends. The little boy and the Little Girl play together often.

She knows that the sitter is her friend. She reads stories to the Little Girl every time she comes.

She knows that Mrs. Prentiss likes to talk to little girls. And the Little Girl likes to talk to her.

She knows that the big man with the big laugh is her daddy's friend. She sits with him as he tells her a funny story, and she laughs a big laugh right along with him.

Mr. Red Ears

Death is a puzzling and sometimes emotionally distressing experience to a young child, as indeed it is to all of us. The child cannot understand what has happened and will ask many questions, perhaps over a period of months, in an attempt to discover some meaning behind the experience.

The meaning that death has for you very likely will be the meaning death has for the child. The child will grasp this meaning whether you say anything or not.

We cannot declare the immortality of turtles or of any pets. But as Christians we believe that death is the door to another life. It is appropriate that joy and a note of celebration should be part of the ritual of burial.

Amy, as she buried Mr. Red Ears, played with her pretty stone markers and sang and sang. This is as it should be. Life and death are related and go on at the same time.

The death of a person close to the child calls for wise and sensitive handling. Consult your minister for some reading help as well as good counsel.

Amy had a little turtle. The turtle was her pet. She called him Mr. Red Ears.

Mr. Red Ears was green all over. On each side of his head where his ears should be was a red spot. Because he had these red spots, his name was Mr. Red Ears.

Amy also called her turtle Funny Fellow. He was a funny fellow because he carried his house on his back. His green shell was his house. When Mr. Red Ears went swimming, so did his house.

When Mr. Red Ears climbed on the stones, so did his house. When Mr. Red Ears sat in the warm sun, so did his house.

When Mr. Red Ears became afraid, he pulled himself inside his house all still and tight. He almost looked like a small green stone. When he did this, Amy laughed.

"Come out, Funny Fellow, come out. I'm going to feed you and give you some clean water." Then Amy put Mr. Red Ears into his feeding dish with some bits of red meat. Soon out came his head and his legs and his little pointed tail. He looked around with his teeny-tiny black eyes, saw the meat, and gulped it down.

After he had eaten, Amy put him back into the water. Funny Fellow Red Ears crawled right out of the water up onto the stones, house and all. He sat there in the sun and went to sleep.

Amy made up a little song about him. "Funny fellow, Red Ears, funny fellow, Red Ears, swim, climb; swim, climb, go to sleep."

One day when Amy picked up Mr. Red Ears, he didn't pull in his head or his legs or his little pointed tail. His teeny-tiny black eyes were closed tight.

"Mommy, Mommy!" called Amy, "Funny Fellow is still asleep. He won't wake up even when I touch him."

Mother came and looked at Amy's turtle.

"Honey, your turtle is not asleep. He is dead."

"What's dead?"

"Well . . . dead is something like being asleep," her mother said. "It is a change. Your turtle is different now. He will not eat any more or climb on the stones or sit in the sun—not any more."

"What made him dead, Mommy?"

"I don't know, dear. Maybe he couldn't stay warm enough after the sun went down. Maybe he was sick and we didn't know it."

"Where will we keep him now, Mommy?"

"We will bury him, Amy. I will show you how."

So Amy and her mother dug a hole in the soft earth at the edge of the garden. Amy put Mr. Funny Fellow Red Ears into the hole and carefully covered him. Then she took some pretty stones and put them around the edge of the hole.

Amy sang, "Funny fellow, Red Ears, funny fellow, Red Ears, swim, climb; swim, climb, go to sleep."

FINGER PLAYS

Little Chickadees

Five little chickadees, *(Hands up, fingers and thumb showing)*
Peeping at the door;
One flew away, *(Make flying motion with arm)*
And then there were four. *(Show four fingers)*
Chorus: Chickadee, chickadee, happy all day, *(One finger)*
Chickadee, chickadee, fly away. *(Flying motion)*
Four little chickadees, *(Four fingers)*
Sitting on a tree;
One flew away, *(Flying motion)*
And then there were three. *(Three fingers)*
Three little chickadees, *(Three fingers)*
Looking at you;
One flew away, *(Flying motion)*
And then there were two. *(Two fingers)*
Two little chickadees, *(Two fingers)*
Sitting in the sun;
One flew away, *(Flying motion)*
And then there was one. *(One finger)*
One little chickadee, *(One finger)*
Sitting all alone;
He flew away, *(Flying motion)*
And then there were none. *(Hands behind back)*

From *Songs and Games for Little Ones*, by Harriet S. Jenks. Boston: Oliver Ditson, 1915, adapted.

Wee White Rabbit

Once there was a wee white rabbit *(Two fingers up, right hand)*
And a green little cabbage head. *(Clenched left fist)*
"I think I'll have some breakfast," *(Bring right hand to left)*
The little rabbit said.
So he nibbled and he nibbled
And he cocked his ears to say, *(Right hand cocked)*

"I think it's time for me to run away." *(Hands behind back)*

Author Unknown

Two Funny People

(Two doubled fists crossed at wrists; thumbs represent the people)
There's a funny person, in a funny little house,
And right across the way,
There's another funny person in another little house,
And they play hide and seek all day.

One funny person through her window peeps,
Sees no one looking, then softly creeps
Out of her door, she comes so slow,
Looks up and down, high and low,
Then back into her house she goes.

Then the other person through her window peeps,
Sees no one looking, then softly creeps
Out of her door, she comes so slow,
Looks up and down, high and low,
Then back into her house she goes.

Sometimes these two forget to peep,
And out of their doors they softly creep,
Look up and down, and high and low,
See each other, and laugh—ho, ho, ho!
Then back into their houses they go.

Author Unknown

POEMS

Rain

The rain is raining all around,
It falls on field and tree,
It rains on the umbrellas here,
And on the ships at sea.

From *A Child's Garden of Verses*, by Robert Louis Stevenson. New York: Charles Scribner's Sons, 1910.

Who Has Seen the Wind?

Who has seen the wind?
Neither I nor you;
But when the leaves hang trembling,
The wind is passing through.
Who has seen the wind?
Neither I nor you;
But when the trees bow down their heads,
The wind is passing by.

From *Sing-Song*, by Christina G. Rossetti. New York: Macmillan, 1915.

PRAYERS

These prayers are samples for you to use in creating your own prayers. The best prayers for preschoolers are just two or three short sentences that express some concrete experience the children have had. Read the letter "What Kind of Prayer for Preschoolers?" (page 179) for more help in making prayer a meaningful part of your work with the children.

Dear God, we had a lot of fun this morning playing with the snow. Thank you, God, for snow. Amen.

We are glad, dear God, that Ms. Puff knew how to keep warm on a cold night. Your plan for animals to know what they should do is very wonderful. Amen.

Dear God, we liked the story of Jesus. He was friendly to little children. Thank you, God, for Jesus. Amen.

Dear God, we wonder how the birds make their nests. We love to hear them sing. We are glad we can give them food to eat. Amen.

SONGS

From *Songs for the Nursery School*, Copyright 1937 by The Willis Music Company. Used by permission.

It's raining, it's raining, It's raining all around!
It's splashing in puddles, With circles going 'round.

It's blowing, it's blowing, It's blowing all around!
Oo-oo, oo-oo, It's blowing all around.

From *Nursery Songs and Rhythms*, compiled by Margaret L. Crain. Philadelphia: Judson Press, 1953.

From *Songs for the Nursery School*, Copyright 1937 by The Willis Music Company. Used by permission.

All the Birds are Singing Again

Sing joyfully, not too slowly

Flow'rs are bloom-ing, Flow'rs are bloom-ing, Spring-time now is here.

Flow'rs are bloom-ing, Flow'rs are bloom-ing, Spring-time now is here.

Adapted from *Nursery Songs and Rhythms*, by Margaret L. Crain. Philadelphia: Judson Press, 1953.

Birds are singing, Birds are singing,
Springtime now is here.
Birds are singing, Birds are singing,
Springtime now is here.

Bells are ringing, Bells are ringing,
Hear the Easter bells.
Bells are ringing, Bells are ringing,
Easter day is here.

From *Songs for the Nursery School*, Copyright 1937 by The Willis Music Company. Used by permission.

Sing this song with substitutions such as plane, car, subway, truck.

Photo © Kathryn Abbe

Part III

Guiding the Children

Growing "in wisdom and in years, and in divine and human favor."
—Luke 2:52

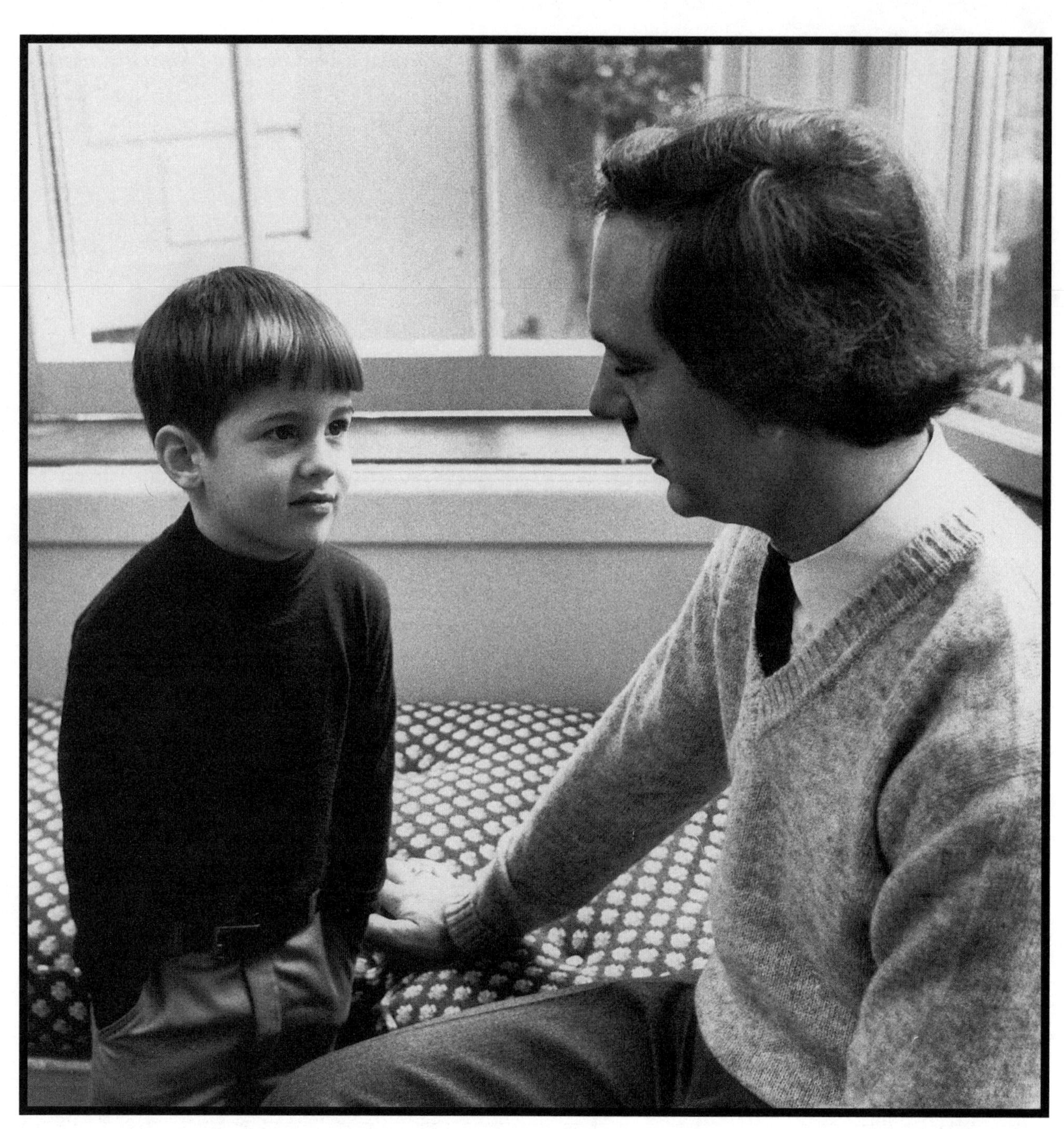

Photo © Kathryn Abbe

Letter 17 Lynn's Father Asks: "Is This *Christian* Education?"

I shall never forget Lynn's father. He thought clearly, spoke precisely, and reasoned closely. He had had no experience with the person-to-person relationship that we have been talking about as the basis of church school teaching. It is not easy to see this relationship at work between teacher and child in a casual five-minute observation as the children are arriving. Even after an entire morning's observation, he said to me, "I don't know what the kids learned, but you are very good with them and to them. This is an interesting place you have fixed up for them; I'm not surprised that Lynn can't wait to come. But what I want to know is, when do they learn about Jesus and the Bible?"

Lynn's father was sincere in what he said. He could not believe that fifteen preschoolers could get along together so harmoniously when his one at home could get her two brothers and her mother into a scrap about rights and property almost any time she took the notion. He attributed the harmony to the teachers' skills. He could see that the experience the children were having was good. He could not see that it was religious or Christian. It was good psychology.

CHRISTIANITY IN SECULAR PRESCHOOLS

Another parent, having come to nearly the same conclusions about our work with the young children, asked, "Doesn't a good secular preschool or day-care center do the same thing that you are doing?" This question I always answer slowly, for I always have to think it through again for myself.

A good secular preschool or day-care center could be doing this kind of teaching. In fact, I think there are many schools in our country where the relationship between teacher and child and the understanding the teacher has of the needs and problems and the capacities and joys of each of the children are about as excellent as our human abilities will permit.

I have seen public school teachers treat the unlovable with great love and accept the bully and the lonely child with persistent respect and understanding. In such experiences the power of love to lessen a child's feelings of rejection, to relieve hate and urges to destroy, to remove fears of other people and feelings of inadequacy—in short, to redeem or save the child—is the power of God working through these teachers, whether they call it that or not. Mostly they do not call it that. The principle of the separation of church and state, which is one of the cornerstones of our democracy, prohibits our teachers from mentioning God, except in casual and incidental ways. Only the parochial schools and church-sponsored schools are under no such constraint.

Some of these public school teachers feel that teaching is their Christian vocation. They strive continually to make their lives a channel of God's love toward the children they teach. Their teaching is a commitment of their lives. These are the patient, sensitive, understanding, praying teachers. Other teachers may not see their lives or their job in terms of God's will, but they are no less dedicated to children.

THE DIFFERENCE IS THE GOAL

Yes, the teachers of our secular preschools can live this way with children. Thank goodness, God's love cannot be confined to a particular place or a particular people.

The difference between the preschool experiences in the church and those of a public preschool may not be a difference of method, but it is certainly a difference of goal, of end in view. What we are doing in the church preschool is helping to establish the foundations for the child's relationship to the church, the body of Christ, the people of God. We want the children to experience, at their own level, the Christian life. We love children and trust that they will learn to love. We present ourselves to them as trustworthy and dependable and help them learn to trust and to grow in faith. We accept their angry feelings, understand their fears, forgive them their errors, believing that they can learn to handle their anger, their fears, and their guilt. We have been helped to experience and know God's love for us. And we want to share our understanding with the young children. We want them to experience the gospel, the good news. The secular school has no such motivation.

At the preschool level we do not do a lot of talking about the gospel because the young child has a limited understanding and an even more limited vocabulary. We do not say a lot about God, Jesus, the Bible, and prayer. However, what the children are learning through their experiences is Christian love—the Word. This is basic to understanding every aspect of the Christian faith—the words. Later, when the child can use words and ideas easily, conversation about and study of the facts of our Christian faith begin.

Lynn's father did not disagree with this goal for the church preschool after I had explained it. Very likely the parents of your children will not either. Lynn's father wanted his daughter to grow up to be good and upright and honest, and he thought that exposing her to church school would help. He had felt that the church school should be teaching her some ideas about God and Jesus, the Bible and prayer that he felt inadequate to teach her. What he saw was space and equipment for children's play and children playing. What they were learning, and how, completely escaped him because they were not learning in the same way he did when he went to church school.

MATERIALS ABOUT RELIGION OR EXPERIENCES OF RELIGION?

There is a great deal of vague thinking in the minds of Christians, including parents and teachers, about how growth toward Christian maturity begins. Too often they mistakenly rely on the transmission of ideas.

When our son Jon was four years old, he attended a weekday preschool that used the excellent facilities of a church but was not part of the church's Christian education program. It was a fine school with an especially good working staff.

A few months later we joined this church, and Jon went to church school there for the first time since we had moved to the community. His group met in the same room that the weekday school used. He was happy about that and went immediately to the bookshelf for his favorite storybook, *Curious George*, that he looked at every day at school. It was not there. Neither was the *Big Book of Real Fire Trucks* nor *The Sailor Dog*. He looked through the half-dozen books that were there and decided against all of them. Then he walked to the table where the puzzles were and looked for the tractor puzzle. He found in its place a puzzle of two children in front of a church, another of Jesus with some children, and another of a big church. At the creative activity table the boys and girls were pasting small pictures of Jesus with the children on colored construction paper and placing a Bible verse underneath. He wanted to play with dough clay, but there wasn't any.

When he came home he told me about these disappointments and said he guessed he would not go to that school on Sundays. It wasn't much fun. I persuaded him to try it again and went in with him the next Sunday to see if his report was accurate. It was.

Curious George and *The Sailor Dog* were nowhere to be seen. In their place were several small books of prayers and Bible stories and one about stars. As for the puzzles, the available ones all had religious pictures and were highly uninteresting. Even the happy, bright, summertime pictures of children playing, families picnicking, the balloon man, and the merry-go-round that had been on the walls had been replaced by religious pictures. These new pictures held little appeal for any of the children because they were not related in any way to their experiences.

I think many teachers feel that there is so much to learn about Jesus, God, the Bible, and the history of our faith, and that one hour a week is so short a time, that they must use both the time and the environment to impress their young pupils' minds with the important facts, the high spots. Sad to say, the consequences of such devotion to the facts are often a hodgepodge of facts, half understood because they have little meaning to the child.

Do not misunderstand me. There was nothing wrong with the books, puzzles, and pictures the teacher had chosen, except that they were not very interesting or fun. But neither was there anything wrong with those that Jon so enjoyed. The mistake the teacher made was in deciding to make the environment seem religious. The teacher assumed that something better was happening to the children if they put together a puzzle of Jesus (that they likely would not recognize) than if they worked on a tractor puzzle that fascinated them because they once had seen one work.

Suppose that Jon had chosen to work at the puzzle of Jesus and the children and that he had asked who that man was. And suppose the teacher had told him the story of the picture. Would even that have been a help to the child in his growth toward Christian maturity? We cannot know for sure. The story would have given Jon a name to attach to the picture. What other ideas he might have gotten no one knows. This we do know, however. It is *the way* you help Jon work his puzzle, the way you help Carmen and Carlos in their struggle for the same book, rather than the subject matter of the puzzle or the book, that will spell the difference in the children's feeling about the church and the difference in their behavior. *What any child learns in the church preschool depends more upon the kind of experiences the child has than the kind of materials employed in teaching.*

WHEN PARENTS ASK YOU THESE QUESTIONS

"What is Christian about this preschool room? What are the children learning by playing all the time? When will they learn about Jesus and the Bible?"

Do not try to answer in the five minutes after church. That is not enough time for either of you. Say instead, "I would like to talk with you about that, but could we find a better time?" Make an appointment to visit their home, perhaps some evening when the children are asleep. The parents might invite some other parents; then you, with them, could plan a parents' meeting to explore the subject. You may feel as though you could not possibly do this; you don't know enough. Take heart. If you have worked with this material and tried to follow these practices with children up to now, the chances are good that you will be able to be of real help to the parents. Lynn's father has just faced the question you have been answering for several months as you have lived with your group of young children.

Photo © Kathryn Abbe

Letter 18 The Use of the Bible with Preschool Children

You will want to know how to use the Bible with your group of preschoolers. Parents will want to know, too, how you are using it, and some may want you to suggest how they should use it at home.

Should you have a Bible in the space where you are working with the children? If you do have one, where do you keep it and what should you do with it? Are there some Bible stories suitable for young children? What of Bible verses, such as "Be kind to one another"?

A BIBLE IN THE PRESCHOOL

Yes, you should have a Bible in the preschool room. An attractive one in good condition is my preference, although a well-worn one, still carefully treated, could be a conversation piece with the children. And that is just what the Bible is in preschool education, a book that can be a topic of conversation. During one session, in your talking time on the rug, say to the children who come, "Girls and boys, I want to show you a very special book that we have in our church." Pick up the Bible and hold it. "Who knows the name of this book?" Some will know it is the Bible. Some will tell you they have one at home.

As in most conversations with children, they may miss entirely the facts you tell them about the Bible, such as, "It has stories in it and other reading, too, which you will read when you are older." They will not miss, however, your attitude toward it, how you hold it and put it down, and where you keep it. If you brought and shared your own Bible, it would have personal meaning which you could not help but convey to the children.

If you do not have too many children, they could take turns holding the Bible, feeling how heavy it is, looking at the thin paper pages that are not one bit like those in their own books.

If your Bible has pictures, examine them carefully before the children do. I remember, as a child, a Bible that worried me greatly. It had a picture of the disciples in a small boat in the midst of a fierce storm and another of the last moments of the Crucifixion, when the heavens were rent by a thunderbolt and a black cloud covered the sun. There are many Bibles with pictures that would be distressing to a young child. If you are not sure about the pictures, choose a Bible without pictures. Do not use any faded, dusty Bible that you take off the stack in the corner cupboard. You will not handle it as something to be cherished, and the children will not see it as a very special book at all.

WHERE WILL YOU KEEP THE BIBLE?

One good place is on the special table. Here the children will see it each session, and a child might pick it up occasionally, look at it, and put it down again.

I am here reminded of a delightful true story a friend told me about a preschool child's use of the Bible in her church. A member of the Christian education committee visited the preschool one Sunday morning. One of the little girls decided to show the woman around and did a very good job of being hostess. They ended up at the book table, and the little girl offered to read a story. The woman, of course, said she would be delighted. The little girl passed up the children's picture books, went to the special table, and picked up the Bible. She proceeded to "read" a wonderful story of cowboys and Indians to her astonished listener!

Doesn't that tickle you? That little girl knew the Bible was an important book with important stories, and luckily, she happened to know an important story. I am not poking fun or being irreverent. I think the teacher had done a good job in conveying an appreciative attitude toward the Bible.

WHICH BIBLE STORIES?

Are there Bible stories suitable for preschool children? Not very many. In fact, I have not been able to find more than two, the story of Jesus' birth and the story of Jesus and the children. Most of the Bible stories are beyond the experience and understanding of young children. And when we try to simplify them we usually do violence to the real meaning of the story.

VIOLATION OF MEANING

Take the story of the baby Moses for example. There are many problems in making this story suitable for preschoolers. One is the language. "Bulrushes," "wicked Pharaoh," and "handmaidens" all have to be explained.

A more difficult problem has to do with the ideas of the story. What is wrong with boy babies that the bad king sent soldiers to kill them? Are there bad kings now? The fear and concern that the children will feel for the little baby Moses and for themselves will be real. Saying that it happened long ago will not relieve their distress. They have no way of understanding that long ago was not sometime before breakfast. This story as it is told in the Bible will make some young children fearful and anxious.

If you leave out the bad king part, then you are faced with explaining why the mother put the baby in a little basket in the high grasses with the sister watching. The mothers of your children do not do that.

But even if you can fix the story so that it is plausible and not frightening, there is yet another difficulty. The story, as amended, is no longer true to what the story of Moses actually means, both to the Christians and the Jews of today or to the Jews who told and retold the story hundreds of years ago. The story of Moses is one of the many stories illustrating the same truth; namely, that God was caring for the people even when they had forgotten God and that God had chosen them for a special task and purpose. The Jewish people wrote the stories of Moses long after the events had happened, when they had begun to understand their history and their destiny as a "chosen people."

This meaning of the story of Moses cannot be understood by preschoolers. If we use the story just as a story, we have taken the fun and discovery out of it for fifth-or sixth-graders, who can understand it in its full meaning. They say, "Who? Moses! Oh, we know that already. He was that kid saved by the princess." But Moses was a strong and courageous man of God whom many of us have never known because we never got beyond the baby hidden among the bulrushes.

BASIS FOR JUDGING STORIES

How can you decide whether a particular Bible story is suitable for the young children in your group? Use these questions as a standard for judgment:

1. Is the story within the experience and understanding of preschoolers? (One big difficulty with Bible stories is that their setting is always long ago and far away. Young children are creatures of the here and now. Places they do not know they can hardly imagine, and time before yesterday or beyond this afternoon has no importance.)
2. Will it confuse or frighten the children?
3. Will the real meaning of the story as it is in the Bible be understood by the children? (You may want to ask the director of Christian education or the

minister for help in establishing a Bible study group for church school teachers.)

TESTING THE CHRISTMAS STORY

Now let's look at the story of Jesus' birth, the Christmas story, in terms of these questions.

Is the story a good one for young children? True, the story is long ago and far away, but it is also here and now to young children because they have had some experience with mothers and babies. The story of a mother caring for her baby is not limited to time or place or nationality.

Some parts of the Christmas story are not within the experience and understanding of young children—angels, Magi, and kings. These parts can be omitted, however, without changing the meaning of the story.

DISTORTING THE STORY

I have no quarrel with angels. I think they are quite nice to have about, but some children might be frightened by the idea of winged, white-robed people flying in the sky. Since I cannot explain the angel part of the story to young children so that it is true to its meaning, I omit that part entirely. Leaving out the angels does not distort the meaning in the same way as omitting Pharaoh changes the Moses story.

The episodes of the shepherds and the Magi put the story into the category of long ago and far away, simply because most children in our country today have had little or no contact with shepherds or Magi. These episodes also make the story more complicated and are not essential to the understanding of the central meaning.

Will the real meaning of the story as it is in the Bible be understood by the children? The story of Jesus' birth is the story of God's love being made known among us—a love greater than anyone had ever known. Looking back at it, the writers of the story felt that surely the whole universe might have sung with joy. Young children cannot grasp these ideas, but they can understand the love of a father and a mother for a baby. The part that they can understand is part of the whole meaning and not a distortion of it or a different emphasis.

JESUS AND THE CHILDREN

Much the same kind of reasoning lies behind my choice of Jesus and the children as a good Bible story for preschoolers. Children know that they like to be around some grown-ups, and they are afraid of others. They can feel the joy of the children whom Jesus welcomed after the disciples had tried to shoo them off. In the sense that they feel with the experience, the story is "here and now" for them.

I think at least part of the meaning of this story is that children are acceptable, of great worth to God, and should also be so to grown-ups. That idea may not be so startling today in our country as it was in Palestine in Jesus' day. Indeed, if it had not been revolutionary and upsetting, it would never have been recorded. Someone has said that Jesus did more for women and children than any other person who ever lived—but I do not mean for you to tell the children this.

Young children can understand some of the meaning of this story without closing the door to further insights at some later time. Such was not the case with Moses, you remember. The meaning that the children may have gotten from the Moses story was entirely different from the meaning of the story in its totality.

OTHER USES OF BIBLE STORIES

There are some Bible stories which reveal a meaning that can be understood by preschoolers, even though the stories themselves are difficult. These stories cannot be used as they are, and any attempt to simplify them for young children does violence to their true meaning. Yet there are ways in which the meanings of these stories can be made available to curious, wondering children.

Take the story of creation. As this story appears in Genesis it is beyond the experience and understanding of preschoolers. But I think the meaning of the story is not.

I think the story of creation says that the universe is not in our hands. There is a power beyond and within the cosmos, the magnificence and greatness of which we only glimpse, even in this space age. People have never fully understood the universe; we have always stood in awe of it and the power that created it. The Christian says this power is God who is the creator.

If you can accept this meaning of the story of the creation, I am sure you can see that you are teaching children its meaning with the experiences you can plan with plants, animals, the seasons.

If the children plant seeds and water them and put them in the sun and finally see them sprout, you marvel with the children. "I don't know what made that little seed grow into a bean plant. We gave it water and put it in the sun, and it just grew. God planned for things to grow."

In all your conversations about life and growth and creation, avoid saying that God made babies or made the plants grow or made the moon and the stars. Young children are literalists; they have limited experience with the word "made." They know that you make a cake or pudding by putting things together and stirring them up. Nothing in our universe was *made* quite that way. It is better to say, "I don't know how the moon got up there, Jennifer. I believe that God *planned* for the moon to be there." Such a statement is true to the facts as you know them and will not have to be changed if Jennifer learns many more facts about the moon, space, and planets than you will ever know. In our age this is very likely!

SHALL WE LEARN BIBLE VERSES?

To answer this question, we need to have an understanding of what the Bible is. That is, what use is it, what value is it to us, why do we Christians treasure it?

The Bible is the record of the revelation of God to people, of people's response to God as seen in their relationship to God and to one another. It is a record that developed and changed with the history of a small group of people, the Jews. It tells of their growing awareness of what God requires of us: responsibility for one another; and an increasing understanding of the meaning of justice and righteousness. Throughout, the Bible tells of God's continuing love and forgiveness, in spite of our sin and forgetfulness.

The Bible is a book written by adults for other adults. Many of us adults do not understand it. Many of us have never read or studied it or thought about it as a whole. We know little bits and pieces.

But the Bible is more than a collection of little bits and pieces; it is a powerful, gripping drama of God's struggle with us and of our struggle with God. Learning by heart little snippets taken from here and there will never really teach a child what is in the Bible. In fact, the process of memorizing may set children firmly against ever wanting to know any more about it.

For children to memorize verses of the Bible so that they will begin to "know" the Bible is something like memorizing a few outstanding directions from a new cookbook in order to know the cookbook. Our short time with children should have more meaning and be more satisfying to all children than rote memorization. Since some cannot memorize, they fail.

One reason I have heard for teaching children Bible verses or passages is so they will learn how to live. "Love one another" (Rom. 13:8a) and "Be kind to one another" (Eph. 4:32a) fall in this category. By now the answer to this point of view must come to your mind as quickly as it comes to mine. Children learn how to live together in love and understanding by experiencing love and understanding rather than by being admonished to love and understand.

If anyone should ask you, "Are you teaching the children the Bible?" answer surely, "Yes." We cannot teach young children many of the *facts* of the Bible, but we are doing a more important, more basic job than that. We are teaching them the *truths* of the Bible by living these truths with them. They are learning love and kindness and forgiveness by experiencing them with a Christian teacher in a Christian church. This kind of relationship between teacher and child is at the core of the biblical faith. This is the best beginning for learning about the Bible and for growing toward Christian maturity.

Letter 19 What Kind of Prayer for Preschoolers?

Did you wonder about the way prayer was introduced in the sample Sunday sessions ("The First Sunday," page 23, and "The Second Sunday," page 31)? Should we instruct children to use a form, a posture, a practice that most likely is not their own doing or self-expression?

I have wondered about this too. I have talked with many experts who do not altogether agree. What is the best way to teach children how to pray? I am not sure anyone knows. Probably there are many good ways.

Prayer is a communion with God. According to this definition, it is doubtful if many really pray in those moments of the preschool session that we label prayer. We do not know whether children have enough awareness of God to commune with God in spoken prayer. You are trying to put into words what you think the meaning of the children's experiences has been, to give voice to the community experience. While the words may not be your own, your thoughts and feelings as a part of the community should be included.

Although the preschool group's moment of prayer may not result in real communication with God, it does do something else. It acquaints children with the practice of Christians. It introduces them to a practice of the Christian community. The church and their homes should help them invest the form they learn with particular meaning. Not this year, perhaps, nor for a few years more will the children really pray. No one knows for sure when or how it will come about. However showing them a way to pray, helping them to create and recognize the conditions of prayer, are a beginning we should make.

We guide children in good habits of hygiene and in various social proprieties, too, years before they can understand the reasons or meaning behind the form. It is good to cover your mouth when you sneeze. Although preschool children may not understand the reason for this practice, many of them will do it. Children love to copy adults; to be able to do what adults do is a sign to the children that they are growing up. For that reason, the children I have known have been eager to "learn to pray the way adults pray in the church."

However, no child can learn the fullness of the Christian experience of prayer. If the young child prays at home and participates in family prayer, when older that child probably will adopt prayer as a practice of daily life. If, however, through the years the child does not come to find any personal meaning in praying, prayer may be regarded as something done only in church or at a banquet.

MEMORIZED PRAYERS

The daily practice of prayer is more likely to be adopted by the child as a part of life if the experience of prayer has been meaningful. For that reason I would not set about to teach a child to memorize a prayer; but neither would I hesitate to use a prayer

Photo by Rohn Engh

repeatedly. Memorized prayers often carry meaning when they are first learned; but their meaning may be lost if they become empty forms of repetition. We need to recognize that prayer is an act of Christian faith; we cannot say when or how it has meaning for an individual or exactly what that meaning is.

CREATIVE PRAYER

Instead of using a memorized prayer, create the prayer with the children right during group time and say it. On your best days, when the children have had a good morning and the story or conversation time has been alive and interesting to them, they may have many ideas of what they are glad for. Accept them all, even if you think a child may be pulling your leg or angling for a laugh from the other children.

Child: "How about snakes? Ish!"

Teacher: "You don't like snakes?"

Child: "Ish! No."

Others: "No." "Neither do I."

Teacher: "Who knows what snakes do?"

(No one.)

Teacher: "Let me tell you a story about snakes. When I was a little girl I lived with my mother and father on a farm. We had a big garden. I had to do my share of work in the garden, and I always used to hope that I would not disturb a sleeping snake with my hoe.

"Then one day my father said to me, 'Don't worry about the snakes. They are helping us to take care of the garden, for they eat many of the bugs that would eat our plants.'

"Did you know that garden snakes are very helpful to the farmers?"

Children: "No-o-o-o-o-o."

Teacher: "I didn't know that either. I think that it is a pretty good thing to know about snakes, don't you? You may close your eyes and bow your heads and fold your hands the way I do, and I will say our prayer: 'Thank you, God, for robins that sing, for our rabbit with the red eyes, and for the snakes that live in the gardens and eat bugs. Amen.' "

On other days the children may not have any ideas. In fact, the conversation or story time may have been so animated that the children cannot shift their thinking to a prayer. When you try it, you lose the group. They talk to one another, one pulls out a book that has been used as a "cushion" and starts "reading" it, another stands up and announces he is too hot and takes off his new, itchy shirt.

At this point I would pass the crackers and have one myself. If the children would like to say their prayer for the "good cracker when we are tired and hungry," that would be appropriate. If not, forget the prayer this week.

I do not mean to imply that this prayer time will ever attract total participation. It may, but I would not count on it. Just as coming to the rug for singing and story and talking time should be an activity offered to children but not expected of them, so it should be with prayer time. At the beginning of the year, more than likely only a few children will participate in prayer. By April or May, when many of them are turning four or five, you may have an occasion when nearly all the children enter into prayer time. Do not worry about those who do not. There is still time for them—many years of time.

PRAYERS OF AWE AND WONDER

There is another kind of prayer that has real meaning for a preschool child. This is the child's response of awe or wonder or delight to some experience.

I once taught in a church preschool in the summer. It was very informal. The children often spent the entire hour outside, and they came to church in their play clothes. One Sunday morning Ariel, who was teaching with me, and I took our eight children to a meadow right next to the church. There we had "nature study" at the children's level. The meadow was full of dandelions. We found some dandelion buds, some rich yellow flowers, and some hoary-headed ones which the children blew on as hard as they could blow. We caught some of the seeds and examined their little soft white wings. We watched the sticky dandelion milk come out of the broken stems. Ariel made dandelion chains, and the children picked bouquets to take to their parents. It was loads of fun for all of us. I, for one, am grateful for the lowly and despised dandelion. Here is a flower that children can pick by the handful and no one cares, or they can trample them down and still no one cares.

As we were walking back to church, Jimmy was holding and swinging my hand. Then he stopped and said with a deep sigh, "Wasn't it fun in the dandelion field today?"

"Yes, Jimmy," I said. "We all had lots of fun. Thank you, God, for fun in our great, big, wonderful field of dandelions."

We went on into the church.

Moments of awe and wonder and delight do not happen every session, and they usually do not occur to a group of children at the same time. Often the feeling is experienced by one child alone. Have you ever watched the facial expression of a child who is listening to a large seashell for the first time?

"What makes the noise, I wonder?" Cindy queries, thoughtfully.

"I wonder too, Cindy. Once an animal like a snail lived in that shell in the ocean. Now the air moving in the empty shell makes a sound that's fun to listen to."

When you catch those fleeting expressions of delight or wonder with the world, enter into them with the child. Enjoy or wonder too. It is not necessary or even desirable to utter a short prayer of thanks to God on each occasion. Many times this could be a false note. Sometimes you may respond with "God has planned a world full of surprises. I find new ones every day." Sometimes all you will say is simply, "I wonder too." You have to keep remembering how the world looks and feels to young children, lest you miss these moments.

Worship is called celebration. Some of the parts of worship are adoration and praise of God, communion with God, dedication to God. Awe and wonder are the feelings that underlie adoration and praise. An adult may say:

When I look at your heavens, the work of your fingers,
the moon and the stars that you have established;
what are human beings that you are mindful of them?
—Psalm 8:3, 4a

The three year old may be expressing some of the same feeling:

Look! Mommy, the moon!
The moon, up in the trees!
The moon! Look, Daddy!

OTHER PRAYERS

Expressing thanks is one way to commune with God. Our thank-you prayers lay the foundation for that kind of prayer.

Prayers of petition, asking for help to be kind and good, require some ability to stand off and look at one's behavior. Likewise, prayers of intercession, such as a prayer for a sick member of the group, cannot really be understood if the sick child worsens. These prayers should therefore be left for later years.

I am sure you know now, without my discussing it in detail, why the Prayer of Jesus is definitely not for young children. To preschoolers it is incomprehensible. The experience we want most to avoid with all praying is using words that convey either no meaning or the wrong meaning.

This whole matter of prayer is not as complex as it may at first seem. Tap every resource you know, and do not forget to set aside time for your own study and thoughts and prayers. The teacher who prays earnestly may have an enthusiasm and a dedication that could inspire a whole church school.

Letter 20 Art Is Not for Art's Sake in the Preschool

Preschool and kindergarten rooms used to include as their main furnishings enough tables and chairs to seat every child at the same time. Those were days—and they are not long past—when a good church school session for children was thought of in terms of singing the old songs, telling a Bible story or two, taking up the collection, saying a prayer, dropping in the birthday pennies, and then spending the remaining minutes in some kind of handwork that the children could take home. It was reported that "the children loved it," and that response we accepted as proof enough that what we did with them was good.

Now we know better. We know that children are pliant, usually agreeable creatures, especially in unfamiliar surroundings, and they will go along with many activities that adults engineer, whether it means much to them or not. Children discover early that if they want to do things with grown-ups, and nearly all children do, they must let the grown-ups have their way about what to do and how to do it. This explains, at least partially, why "the children loved it."

We know, too, that children become creative, adequate, self-confident, independent persons as they grow up with adults who intentionally help them grow this way. Sitting children in chairs is one of the least effective ways of aiding this kind of growth. Children need opportunities to explore the world of people and ideas and things in the manner and at the time that seems right for them. The younger the child, the more true this is. A three year old, for example, has little time sense beyond now and little sense of social responsibility or of belonging to a group. It is literally impossible for some children to sit still and listen to the story "like good children" until later when they can play where and with whatever they choose. Children do not know what you mean by "later." Likewise this lack of a sense of social responsibility makes the appeal to "sit still so the other children can hear the story even if you don't want to" meaningless. A child's need *not* to listen to the story, but rather to be exploring the world, is *now*, and it is demanding.

So we have done away with most of the tables and chairs. In their place we have endeavored to set up a children's world of materials and things that they can work with, talk to and talk about, manipulate, control, rearrange, and reconstruct. As we have said before, our theory is that the experiences of the children with the kinds of equipment and materials described in the earlier letters ("Company's Coming" and "Doing Big Things in Little Space") and with understanding Christian teachers provide sounder first steps toward Christian maturity than the old handwork at tables-and-chairs Sunday school did.

WHEN TO USE TABLES AND CHAIRS

If you have enough space, provide tables and chairs to seat a third of the group for whatever creative art activity you decide to make available each session. It

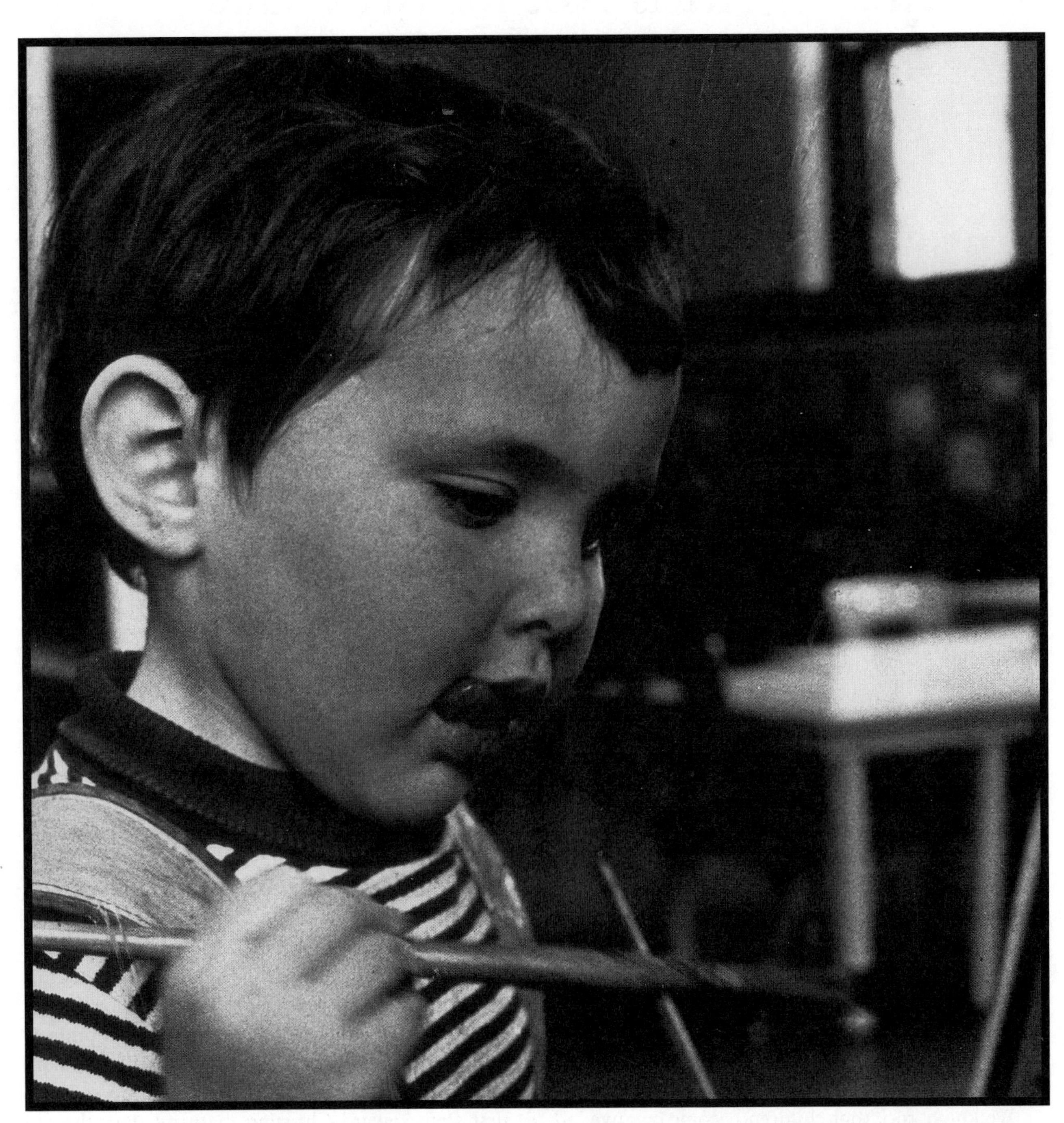

Photo by Sunrise/Trinity Photos

may be cutting and pasting, coloring with crayons, modeling with clay or dough clay or other pliable material, finger painting, or brush painting. This last activity is done better at easels (see page 222). If you can arrange to have two small tables that will seat four children each, instead of one long table, you will find that you can work with the children with less strain and stretching and walking around them and that you can carry on two creative activities during the same session: for example, modeling *or* finger painting at one table, or crayoning *or* pasting at the other. The children using finger paint will need considerable help to learn how to handle the material. The children at the other table will need little help.

RULES FOR ART ACTIVITIES

There are only a few rules for working with children in any art medium.

1. Accept with interest and with some comment of approval whatever a child has done.
2. Do not ask, "What is it?"
3. Do not make anything for the child: neither a snowperson out of clay, nor a picture of a house with crayons, nor a tree with the paint. Do not do anything with the child's materials. This does not mean that you should never help a child do something when you are asked for help. A child has often asked me to roll a clay ball between my palms. So I do. You demonstrate with your own materials, and then let the child try with their own.

RULE ONE

Let us consider some of the reasons for these rules. Why do you accept whatever a child has done as having worth? Because it does have worth, although by our adult standards of judgment, we may fail to see it. We call these activities art activities, but we are not concerned with talent.

The reason we have these activities is to provide another means by which the child can discover answers to the big questions about self and other people and the world. For some children, finger painting is an exciting, happy thing to do, a rhythmic activity through which they can express how they feel. They may sing and talk as they move hands, arms, and even their bodies in response to the wet, bright-colored "squishiness." For others it is a silent, engrossing, thoughtful occupation that lifts them completely out of the busy activity all about them. For still others, it is almost a purely physical experiment, feeling the paint with one finger, then with five, then with both hands, palms and backs, moving it, squishing it, slapping it; adding more water and then more paint to make a smooth, slippery, wet panorama of changing lines and curves and swooshes and stops. For most children it can be releasing, relaxing, absorbing fun.

Since finger painting—to stay with this example—can mean all these experiences for children, it is clear that there is no single standard of judgment for the finished product. In the preschool there are no good and no poor pictures. Instead, there is an attempt to understand the meaning the child found in the activity.

JOHN: "I'm all finished finger painting, Teacher."
TEACHER: "All right, John, I will help you with your hands and the apron. We will hang your picture here to dry. You had fun finger painting today, didn't you?"

John may respond to that, and he may not. It does not matter. He feels good about what he has done. Naisha may have used her hands with more skill than John. Spike may have painted with much more freedom and creative expression. Yolanda may have dared put only one finger in the paint. No child's effort should ever be compared to those of any other child or judged by any general standard supposedly true for preschool children. Whatever a child does is right for that child. Only as every child feels your acceptance of what they have done—and therefore, in their minds, your acceptance of them—will they be free to experiment and explore again another day.

RULE TWO

Why do you not ask, "What is it?" Because in most cases it is not a representation of anything. Preschool children do not usually first think of something to draw or paint or mold and then set about doing it. They experiment with the material, its color, feel, and form; when they are finished they look at it. It may suggest something to them or it may not. If it does, the child will usually tell you.

Treva was standing at the easel painting thoughtfully. Several painting partners came and went on the other side of the double easel, yet Treva continued, engrossed, oblivious to noise, laughter, truck and doll-buggy traffic. Finally, she was finished. She put the brush in the jar of paint and stepped back to look at her picture. Suddenly she began to laugh. She laughed so infectiously and with such merriment that several children gathered around to ask her what was funny. The teacher did too. "It's an elephant . . . a big elephant . . . ha, ha, ha; and he sat on a piano stool and it broke," and off she went again. The children enjoyed the joke and laughed with her. The teacher did too, but as she draped the painting over the rack to dry, she found herself wondering which color was the elephant and where the piano stool was.

If your abstractionist does not volunteer any interpretation, you might occasionally say, especially if the child seemed particularly thoughtful and intense in the creation of the work, "Would you like to tell me about your picture?" The child may be able to respond very easily, and will probably appreciate your writing the words on the picture to show to parents. If the child has to hunt around for something to tell you, simply say, "I like the colors you used, Pedro" or "That is an interesting design, Sasha." This relieves the child from feeling pressed to provide an interpretation.

Occasionally there will be a child—often one who is not free to work with art materials—who will be derogatory of other children's work. "That's not anything; that's just scribble-scrabble."

Usually young children cannot emotionally handle deflating opinions about themselves or their art work by other children. The teacher can and should. However, the teacher must not take sides, but rather must help both children at once.

"Ina is having fun with the crayons on that big sheet of paper, Harry. It doesn't matter what she makes or what she calls it. All that matters is that she is having fun doing it. Did you ever watch what colors you could make by putting one color on top of another? Would you like a sheet of paper of your own to work with?" If Harry declines, perhaps he will be interested in whatever other art activity you have available for the day. Whatever material you offer him, focus his attention on the fun he will have playing with it—the feel, the color, and the patterns that form. Say no more about what he or anyone makes with the materials.

RULE THREE

Why do you not make anything for a child, not even when you are asked, "Draw me a house"? There are several reasons. If you make something, anything that you name or that the child can recognize, you imply a standard for the use of the material that few children can attain. For that reason they may feel unsure about handling the material.

Children may come to feel that the purpose of all art material is to make something. If they feel they cannot make anything, they miss the fun of exploring and experimenting with the material. Perhaps you can encourage a child by saying, "You can make the kind of house you are thinking of better than I can. You do it, and then it will be yours. Have fun making it."

In everything we do, our feelings about our worth and competence are at stake. If we have repeated experiences of feeling incompetent and not up to standard, we grow up to dislike ourselves and to dislike and fear other people. We cannot then extend love or trust or forgiveness; we cannot freely relate to anyone. We are not on the way toward Christian maturity. Art activities in the preschool can help build feelings of confidence and self-esteem *when the activities belong to the children.*

Letter 21

Discipline, Hurtful or Helpful?

I was working with a group of teachers from some of our churches not long ago. The discussion came around to discipline, as it nearly always does. One experienced teacher spoke of discipline in terms of "short-circuiting live wires." It was a highly entertaining and helpful way of thinking about methods to help children learn and grow.

Do you have a few "live wires" in your room? Do they perplex you, disturb the other children, and in general create pandemonium? Sooner or later, everyone has a child like this. Many times we do not know what to do. We must confess we are half glad on the days when such a child does not come. And on the days that child is there, we could do with a little short-circuiting know-how.

By now you know that I have no specific directions for handling your various "live wires." It would be most convenient if I could enclose a little booklet with a thumb index indicating such kinds of behavior as hitting, knocking over blocks, upsetting all the newly planted seeds, pocketing the offering, squirting the bathroom—finger-under-faucet method. But I cannot do that.

Each child is different. That fact both delights and bewilders us. The reason why Masaki knocked over Samantha's block building is not the same reason why Samantha herself knocked it flat ten minutes later. Hence, no instruction booklet.

Nevertheless, some understanding is in order and should be helpful. All behavior is caused. This means simply that there is a reason for the way a child acts. As adults we feel quite certain that we have good reasons for what we say and do. We often act, however, as though we do not believe this about children.

At one time people believed that children were born bad. From birth they had some undesirable traits, some ornery streaks that were part of their makeup. The job of the parent and the teacher was to eliminate these traits in any way they could. Not many people believe this about children any more, thank goodness. The current thinking about children and their behavior is that there is a reason for the way a child acts.

WHAT ARE SOME OF THE REASONS FOR MISBEHAVIOR?

1. The child does not understand the limits or the rules, or the reasons for them. For example, a child who does not know that clay is to remain on the table may carry clay to the housekeeping corner or load it in a dump truck.

2. The child does not know a better way to do or to get what is wanted. For example, grabbing, hitting, pushing are often the only ways some children know to get a turn with a toy.

3. The child is bored. Nothing seems interesting. For example, you may have a child who has had much preschool or day-care experience. This child finds the church school program uninteresting because it offers little that is fun, different, or new.

Photo © Kathryn Abbe

4. The child is not at ease, but rather hurt or unhappy. Something is wrong, and the child feels unloved or unworthy. Bad feelings beget bad behavior. Possibly the child is coming down with the current "flu bug" or may be overstimulated or overtired from a late night of television.

THERE ARE MANY POOR METHODS OF DISCIPLINE

They are common methods that many of us use and that were probably used with us when we were growing up. Their effect is more hurtful than helpful because they increase a child's bad feelings and do not suggest a way or offer any help for changing behavior.

What are some of these common methods of discipline that are more hurtful than helpful?

1. Saying or doing anything to a child that shames the child: for example, "Big children don't cry." Such words could lessen a child's feeling of worth in his or her own eyes, and, if overheard by the other children, in their eyes as well. Of course, as adults we know that almost everyone cries.
2. Making a child feel guilty: for example, "You are bad to say such a thing." The child already feels bad. This makes the child feel worse.
3. Threatening a child or making that child fearful: for example, "The children will not like you if you do that." It is hard for anyone who is afraid to find the right way to do something.
4. Inconsistent or unfair consequences: for example, denying a child a cookie or hearing a story at rest time for something that happened yesterday; or punishing the group because of the actions of a few. Unfair punishment produces smoldering anger rather than helping children learn and understand why there are limits and what the consequences of going beyond those limits are.

GOOD DISCIPLINE

What, then, should you do? What is good discipline?

Good discipline is helpful, not hurtful. It is loving and diminishes a child's bad feelings. Read again the letter "Dealing with Fears and Feelings" (page 123). Good discipline helps a child feel more like a member of the group rather than adding to a sense of isolation and rejection. It teaches the child how to use things and how not to use people. It is education, not just training. It helps a child develop an understanding that puts an inner discipline to work. It helps the child develop self-confidence.

Young children know little of the rules that govern human behavior. They have no clear sense of mine or yours, of right and wrong, of sharing and taking turns, of being responsible members of a group. They need to learn these things. They want to know.

Our job is to help children find their way through the maze of regulations, of dos and don'ts. We must teach in such a way that the relationships between us and the children are not weakened or broken. Indeed, they should be strengthened.

Observe carefully the "live wires" who perplex you. Get to know them as well as you can. Try to imagine how life looks and feels to them. What are the reasons for their behavior? When you have done this, there are two thoughts and two big questions that may help you decide what you should do and how you should do it.

The first thought is: Consider the child's intentions as well as their actions. One of the children remembers to feed the fish and then overfeeds them. Then fish die, but the child did not intend to kill them.

The second thought is: Remember that a child needs love most when that child is most unlovable. Misbehavior is often a red flag of distress, a cry acted out to tell you that all is not well and that help is needed. Sometimes in dealing with the misbehavior—the symptom—we neglect entirely the deep need. Worse, we often increase the child's basic distress or bad feelings instead of offering love and help. For example, a child creates one disturbance after another all morning. Finally the teacher resorts to making that child sit on a chair. If a person (you or I included) is feeling angry or hostile, forcing that person to sit on a chair may only increase their hostility. The teacher may be adding to it by not understanding the child's need and unhappiness. If a child is feeling bored, sitting on a chair only adds to the boredom.

The first question is: Will the discipline help the child to handle this situation or a similar one with more skill, more satisfaction, and more acceptability the next time? In other words, will the child learn something about right and wrong, mine or yours, the laws that govern the relationships between people, and cause and effect, or will the child learn merely what makes the teacher angry and what the teacher does when angry? To put it another way, will the discipline be helpful rather than hurtful?

Question two is: Will this experience of discipline strengthen the relationships between the children and their teacher—me? Will it increase their self-confidence and trust in me? Will it begin to help them act out of an inner concern for people rather than out of fear?

You see, we do not really want to "short-circuit" our "live wires." We want to help them direct their energy into creative, satisfying relationships.

Letter 22 Summertime

The word "summertime" to me is a word to be sung, not said. It has three musical notes, followed by "when the livin' is easy." And that is just what summer in the preschool should be—livin' easy.

Because summertime is vacation time for most people, if you have a summer program, the attendance of the children will be irregular. You may have more visitors than you have during the winter. Or you may have all the preschool children together—twos, threes, fours, and fives—under your wings, or should I say feet?

For these reasons, the program should be very flexible. For one session you might take a walk to a special place, such as the firehouse. For the next, a visitor might come. Who in the community plays an instrument or sings and plays folk music? Children love to know people who do interesting things. During one session you might play in the churchyard or in a nearby park.

OUTDOOR EQUIPMENT

Spending your session outside with the children can be a fine church school experience if you can plan to do it safely. You will need a space away from traffic and away from the open church windows, as well, but not too far from water and the restrooms. This area should be grassy, not asphalt, if possible, and with some shade. If you plan to spend an hour or more outside each session, you will need some equipment: a sandbox (with seats) no smaller than ten feet square and pails, shovels, colanders, funnels, cups, plastic bowls, small trucks and cars, and a few boards for sandbox play; a dishpan for sailing boats; and pans and straws for blowing bubbles. Bring some plastic containers or boxes for holding little discoveries, such as bugs, leaves, worms, or pretty stones. Take some books to look at in the shade. Be sure that there are at least three teachers so that one may be spared to bring a child back to the church, if necessary, while two remain with the rest of the children.

SUMMER GROUPINGS

Some churches carry on the church school program with the same classes and the same teachers for twelve months of the year. Other churches have a closely graded church school for nine months and a group-graded program in the summer; this means separate preschool and kindergarten programs in the winter, all preschool children together in the summer. Some churches have a school-year staff of teachers and a summer staff of teachers. Some have volunteers who rotate throughout the summer, which means different teachers every session. This latter is a baby-sitting service, not an educational program. Some promote in June, others in September. Some church preschools have new threes in the summer; some have old threes who are all nearly four.

Photo © Kathryn Abbe

You will have to work out your program according to the circumstances of you situation. If you are a year-round teacher, your year's work may be coming to a happy climax at the end of the summer. Or you may be starting in July with a new group of preschoolers. If this is the case, it will be helpful to read again some of the letters at the beginning of this book about a child's first venture to church school.

If you are a summer teacher with a group of children from three to six years of age, make the most of it. Think of yourself and the group as a big family where the big children help the little children, the older ones help the young ones, and all persons live their lives according to family needs and their own interests and abilities. Try hard not to bore kindergartners, but do not get projects underway that frustrate the threes. A well-equipped room appeals to most preschool children. All children can work and play in it according to their abilities and inclinations. The five year olds may need some extra activities and more ideas from the teacher of things to do, such as collecting and arranging and identifying summer wonders of the out-of-doors or making leaf scrapbooks. They will enjoy more complicated books and stories, songs, puzzles, and art activities.

KEEP PURPOSE AND STANDARDS HIGH

The summer program, like the school-year program, should offer each child an experience of love and acceptance in the church. Each child should feel secure and at home there. With a frequent change of summer teachers this is not likely to happen. I suspect one reason why summer attendance falls off is that the church school becomes an unpredictable experience to children, and they do not want to come.

We should not forget our standards in the summer. There should be one teacher to six children and at least two teachers with every group. There should be thirty-five square feet of play space per child indoors, seventy-five square feet outdoors. Play equipment should be designed for learning, creating, experimenting, manipulating, and expressing ideas and feelings. Finally, there should be teachers who respect and delight in children, who are growing and learning themselves, and who know that Christianity is learned through a loving relationship that begins with parent-child, then teacher-child, and is based upon God-child.

Photo from Sunrise/Trinity Photos

Letter 23 They Are All Growing Older

Toward the end of the church school year you may suddenly realize how different your sessions are compared with those in the beginning. Even if you are not aware of any differences, there will be some. Your children will be almost one year older. Since September they will have changed in many ways.

BECOMING A GROUP

Once you start to look back and think back to the beginning of your church school year, you will see other evidence of the children's growth. I think the biggest and the most thrilling change comes when fifteen separate and unrelated children and three teachers become a *group* of fifteen children and three teachers. It is like having eighteen newly shelled fresh green peas in a pan. They are held together only by being inside the walls of the pan. But cook them in a good buttery sauce and they are different. They are still peas, but they are held together in a new way that makes each pea a little different.

The experiences you and the other teachers and your children have together in the preschool this year will become a kind of sauce that holds you together. Both you and the children will come to feel that in a very real way you belong together, that you are somehow related to one another. You will be held together by more than the four walls. When the year is over, you will still be you, yet each of you will be a different you. Why? Because you will have shared yourselves, revealed yourselves, given yourselves away to some other selves; in the process something of great significance happens to each of you.

I believe that this something is growth in the power to love, to accept, to trust, to forgive. It is growth in the feeling of belonging to the people of God, the church, and in the feeling of worth as children of God. You and the children will have become a small and still imperfect "community of those who care." Not every child or every teacher will grow alike in these respects, just as people do not grow at the same pace in other respects, such as language, social awareness, or physical development. Nevertheless, given favorable conditions, we do grow.

CONDITIONS FOR GROWTH

I have already written to you at length about what these favorable conditions are. You know about loving the unlovable; accepting the quiet ones, the rambunctious ones, the lonely ones; understanding what seems to be foolish fears and hostile feelings; forgiving, "for they do not know what they are doing" (Luke 23:34). A great deal depends on you, dear teacher. If you can even partially achieve this kind of relationship with the children, you will have served God and the church well.

One day, when you least expect it, you will hear one of the children accept another one's bad feelings and extend help and affection.

Douglas, who was new to the preschool, came every morning with a big chip on his shoulder. Getting started each day was a difficult thing for him, the children, and the teachers.

On the fifth day, Douglas arrived, walked right up to Tonweya, doubled up his fists, and said, "What are you doing here? Wanna fight?"

Tonweya stood and looked straight at him. "No, I don't wanna fight. I want to play cave under the climbing gym. Come and play with me." Douglas was taken off guard. He slowly relaxed his fists and followed Tonweya to the cave.

Are you thinking that this couldn't really happen? Well, it did happen, just like that, in a church weekday preschool that I know. It would not happen so quickly in a Sunday-only program, but it could happen, if the conditions were right.

You and I have spent many hours and have used a good number of words thinking about these conditions. We have worked through the need for a light, clean room; for useful, sturdy equipment; for enough time to play, to experiment, to think, to listen, and to talk; and, most important, the need for loving, understanding, Christian teachers.

THE CLIMATE OF BELONGING

These conditions, all working together, create another condition. You cannot see it or touch it or order it from the equipment catalogs, but it is real. If your preschool has it, all of you will know it. It is a feeling that pervades the atmosphere. This feeling grows in the preschool at the same time that you and the children are growing. It is a secure feeling, a "we do things this way" feeling. It includes such concrete experiences as sharing the crayons, taking turns, sitting flat on the rug so that all can see, playing quietly while other children are listening to a story, and taking part in the group time. It is a happy feeling; it is also a feeling of concern and responsibility, each for the other. It includes the habits, the attitudes, the recollected joys, such as planting our bulbs or cutting our Halloween pumpkins, and the anticipated pleasures that the children and you have.

It is this quality of living in the preschool that is the cement or sauce for the feeling of belonging. It was this climate, this intangible feeling about how we live and play together, that Tonweya knew so well and that she expressed toward Douglas.

THE CHRISTIAN COMMUNITY

If you and the other teachers work as conscientiously as you know how this year, by spring you and the children will surely become "members one of another" (Rom. 12:5). Together you will have built a climate in the preschool, a climate of love, acceptance, understanding, and forgiveness. The children would not be able to do it without you. You would not be able to do it without the help of friends, parents, other teachers, your minister, books, prayer, and study. I think it is this climate that ministers have in mind when they talk about the power of the Holy Spirit. "For where two or three are gathered in my name, I am there among them" (Matt. 18:20).

Call it sauce, a climate of shared concern, or the working of the Holy Spirit—it makes no difference. It is enough to witness to the fact that together you are growing "in wisdom and in years, and in divine and human favor" (Luke 2:52). Together you will experience a taste of creative, abundant, life, expressed to one another, shared with one another.

"So then you are no longer strangers and aliens, but you are citizens with the saints and also members of the household of God, built upon the foundation of the apostles and prophets, with Christ Jesus himself as the cornerstone. In him the whole structure is joined together and grows into a holy temple in the Lord; in whom you also are built together spiritually into a dwelling place for God" (Eph. 2:19–22). This is the life to which we have been called, the Christian life.

Having been so fortunate as to experience much of the Christian community myself, both with children and with adults, I know why the early Christian cried, "Good News!" and talked of shouting it from the housetops. They felt like that. I do too.

Times have changed. I have no clarion voice, no lofty housetop. But the printed page may do as well for this day in this age. I hope so. And now, God bless you. I hope I shall meet you face-to-face one day.

Resource Section III *Contents*

TEACHING PLANS 198
Theme: Growing 199
A Sample Teaching Plan for *Growing* 201
Theme: Summertime 202
A Sample Teaching Plan for *Summertime* 205

BOOKS 207
- Vacation Reading 207
- Care of Books 207

PICTURES 207
- Teaching Pictures 207
- Additional Pictures 207

ACTIVITIES 207
Activities Related to Growing 207
- A Group Picture 207
- See How I Am Growing 208
- Visitors Come to the Preschool 208
- Guess Who 208
- Match Colors 208

Summertime Activities 208
- Parades 208
- Rhythm Band 208
- Treasure Walks 208
- Making Bouquets 208
- Making a Garden 208
- From Bud to Seed 209
- Outdoor Play 209
- Outdoor Water Play 209
- Shadow Play 209
- Show and Tell 209
- Visit the Sanctuary 209

STORIES 209
- *Beverly Beaver Grows Big Enough* 209
- *Peter's Wonderful Day* 210
- *The Five Toots* 211
- *Anna's Mistake* 212
- *The Little Boy Who Didn't Know Who He Was* 213
- *Big Tree* 214
- *Summer Fun* 215

FINGER PLAYS 216
- *Eentsy Weentsy Spider* 216

POEMS 216
- *At the Seaside* 216
- *Thank You, God* 216

PRAYERS 217

SONGS 218
- *Looby Loo* 218
- *Ring Around a Rosy* 219
- *Pop Goes the Weasel* 220

TEACHING PLANS

Two major themes are suggested for the months of May through August with several subthemes and alternative ideas for different groups and situations. It is most important to be familiar with the letters "They Are All Growing Older" (page 195) and "Summertime" (page 191) as background for developing the following two themes.

THEMES

Suggested themes for summer are:
Growing ("Big Tree," page 214)
Summertime ("Summer Fun," page 215)

For many groups, May and June mark the end of the church school year. Your children are almost all a year older or will have their next birthday during the summer. You and the children may have grown from a number of vaguely related individuals into a group of persons who have played, worked, and learned together. It is fitting to place an emphasis upon the growth of each individual and the total group as you come to the end of your year together.

Some groups will be continuing throughout the summer, moving to another class the last of August or the first of September. The suggested resources for use during the theme on growth may be used over and over again during the summer, as they relate to particular themes such as family fun in summer, God's world in summer, friends, or pets and animals.

NEW GROUPS

Many of you whose children come to you in June will be getting acquainted with a new group of young children during the summer months. You will want to go back to the beginning of this book; review the letters "Meeting Charles," "Company's Coming!" and others in the first section. You, too, have learned much during this year. The ideas in these letters had one meaning to you when you first read them. Now, having experienced another year of teaching, you will be able to evaluate your own work as you read the letters and get fresh ideas of ways to work with preschoolers. You will want to use the themes and many of the materials suggested in Resource Section I, supplemented by stories, songs, finger plays, and activities found in that resource section.

CHURCH SCHOOL DAY

Many churches have dropped the observance of Children's Day, as such, in favor of a more inclusive celebration involving the entire church school—children, young people, and adults. In some churches, Church School Day has a three-fold emphasis: a program summarizing and highlighting the year's study, promotion, and teacher recognition.

Whatever this day is called in your church and however it is celebrated, preschool children should stay in their own group, following their regular schedule for some or most of the time. But this may be one of the days you will take the group to the worship service for a few minutes. The children probably would be particularly interested in listening to a children's choir sing, a class reading of scripture, or any older groups of church school children who are participating in the service of worship on this day.

PROMOTION

If promotion is part of the program for this special day, there are at least two things you can do to help children understand and anticipate promotion. First, invite the teachers of the next older group to come to visit the preschool for a few minutes. Ask them to tell the children a little about the class they will soon join and to say how glad they will be to have this group of boys and girls join them. Second, one teacher might take three or four children at a time to visit their new class. Explain that this is the place or room where they will go the next time they come to church school.

Promotion certificates (if your church uses them and does not give them during a service of worship) may be given to the children during a special group time at the close of the session.

Another plan to celebrate promotion would be to arrange a time for parents and children to get together (also brothers and sisters). Play a game together. See pages 218–20 for song games. Have simple refreshments such as fruit or cookies and lemonade. Gather in a group and let the children join you in singing one or two of the songs they have most enjoyed during the year. You might do a finger play or two and read a poem or tell a story such as "A Little Boy Wonders" (page 156). Talk a little about the fun you have had together in the preschool and the ways everyone has grown. Give the children their promotion certificates. Then everyone goes to the new space or room. If possible, have the new teachers meet the parents and welcome the children to the group.

Theme: Growing

"Will I ever grow big enough to . . . ?" is the never-ending question of young children, expressed by Beverly Beaver in the story "Beverly Beaver Grows Big Enough" (page 209). No one can see their legs growing or their mind growing or their ability to live as a Christian person with other persons growing. Yet when preschoolers compare themselves as they are in the spring of the year with the children they were the previous summer or fall, they discover that they really have been growing. They are now taller and heavier; they can hop and jump better; they can cut or paint with more ease and control; they can sit longer or listen to a story; they can express themselves better with their larger vocabularies; they have grown in their ability to work and play with other children; they know many things they did not know when they started preschool.

Purpose: As you select resources and plan experiences related to the theme of growing, these general purposes should be your guide:

1. *To help the children find that they have grown in many ways*—that they have found many satisfying answers to "Who am I?"

2. *To help children recognize their growth in their relationships with other people*—answers to their question "Who are you?"

3. *To help the children become aware of their growth in understanding the world in which they live*—answers to their question "What is the world like?"

Of course, you will be working at all three of these purposes in almost every activity or experience you plan. They are really inseparable. In one session you may be primarily concerned with emphasizing physical growth and plan to tell the story "Beverly Beaver Grows Big Enough." The children will tell you of all the things they have grown big enough to do during the year. "Who am I? I'm a person who grows, who is big enough to . . . " But, like Beverly Beaver, your children are not just growing physically, they are also learning about other people. "I'm big enough to play games or climb trees with other boys and girls. We have fun playing together." They are learning about the world—how to make chocolate pudding or what people do at work or how to help seeds and plants to grow.

In one session during this theme you might celebrate the fact that the children are all growing older. A year of preschool marks a whole year of growth and achievement. The stories of "Big Tree" (page 214) and "Peter's Wonderful Day" (page 210) may give rise to a lively conversation about birthdays, growth, seasons, friends, and other subjects. You might have the group play "Guess Who" or "Match Colors" (page 208) to emphasize how they have grown in their ability to know their church school friends by name and to recognize colors.

Still other sessions could be planned around the difficulties that are part of growing. Accepting adult rules is part of growing. Children want to eat candy, and they do not want to go to bed; but they have to go to bed and they should not eat much candy. It helps children to discover that other people have the same problems and that it is quite all right to make fun of the whole thing, as in the story of "The Five Toots" (page 211). Making mistakes is another way through which children learn and grow. The children will readily identify themselves and their problems with Anna in "Anna's Mistake" (page 212). Self-acceptance is still another important aspect of growth, which is dealt with in the story "The Little Boy Who Didn't Know Who He Was" (page 213).

THE ROOM

The interest centers will remain the same as in previous units unless you are able to add an occasional new piece of equipment for the housekeeping or block center or a new puzzle for quiet play. Remove anything that is broken or dirty.

Major changes will be in the use of new pictures and books. Try to find pictures of a child being weighed or measured by a doctor or a parent, mother animals with babies, birds feeding their young, children with sleeves or skirts or pants that are too short, the seasons, and growing plants, trees or fields.

Books from the Bibliography (page 235) to add to your book corner may include:

See How You Grow
Whistle for Willie
What I Like
The New Baby

ACTIVITIES

One way children learn about growth is by observing mother animals with their babies. If you have not yet tried having a mother animal and her babies come to visit, you might do so during this unit. (See "Animal Babies," page 149.) If the animals cannot come to the preschool, perhaps you could take the children on a "Visiting Walk" (page 148) to see the mother and her babies.

Better yet, children learn about growth by seeing a human baby and thinking about how they themselves have grown since they were tiny babies. Adapt your activities to the particular needs and interests of the children in your group. Suggested activities related to growing are:

A Group Picture, page 207
See How I Am Growing, page 208
Visitors Come to the Preschool, page 208
Guess Who, page 208
Match Colors, page 208

ART ACTIVITIES

Use any of the art activities suggested on pages 221–24. Provide plenty of materials and encourage children to try different kinds of art work. If a child has done a lot of crayoning but little painting or working with clay, it may be that the child is afraid of getting dirty. Provide good smocks or coveralls that really protect clothes. You might also ask the parent to dress the child in play clothes.

SPECIAL EQUIPMENT

A yardstick or measuring tape
A bathroom scale
Paper for "A Group Picture" (page 207)
(If you can bring a yardstick and scale, the children's height and weight may be recorded on either the "group picture" or the "See How I Am Growing" outlines.)

GROUP TIME

Group time should be a time of lively conversation during this unit. The suggested stories usually produce an immediate response from most preschoolers because the subject of growing up is very important to them. Take plenty of time so that everyone may participate. If some of the children lose interest, they may quietly leave the group and return to their play in the interest centers. Encourage children to change their positions frequently so that they do not become tired.

The following resources might be used during group times:

Finger plays

Eentsy Weentsy Spider, page 216

Stories

Peter's Wonderful Day, page 210
Beverly Beaver Grows Big Enough, page 209
The Little Boy Who Didn't Know Who He Was, page 213
The Five Toots, page 211
Big Tree, page 214

Songs

Growing Up, page 96
This Is the Way, page 95
God, We Thank You, page 94

(Make up verses about planting and watering seeds and plants.)

Prayers

Sample prayers are found on page 217. As in previous units, the best prayers are those that express the immediate concerns and feelings of gladness, thankfulness, or wonder of the children. At the point in the conversation when you feel the children are really experiencing a feeling of gladness or thankfulness or wonder for new abilities or for the fact that they are growing, pause and say a thank-you prayer to God who "planned" for everyone to grow. The children may volunteer to pray. This is another sign of growth. Accept prayer suggestions with little comment.

Growing is such an important subject that you may want to plan six or more sessions to think about the different ways in which the children are growing. Use resources from throughout the book and your own ideas. You might tell the story "Karen Goes to Preschool" (page 80) one session to recall how much each one has grown since the first day they came to the group. Perhaps the children can join you in finger plays that they could not do earlier in the year.

A Sample Teaching Plan for *Growing*

Think about each child in your group. Do you remember how each one looked, how each responded, what interested each child when that child first came to the preschool? Day by day you saw only a little growth, but now in the long perspective you can see how much each one has changed. If you have kept diary notes on each child or had photographs taken during the year, you have an even more accurate picture of the development that has taken place.

Your purposes for one or more sessions might be *to help the children become aware of their own growth by discovering how tall they have grown and to learn that growing is a wonderful part of living—God has made a wonderful world in which all living things grow.*

PREPARATION

The Room

- Around the room place pictures of children in clothes that have become too small, parent animals or birds with their babies, and perhaps a picture of a flower garden with some plants just coming up and others in bloom.
- Have books about growing, such as *See How You Grow* (see page 237), on the book table.

Special Equipment

- If possible, bring a scale and yardstick or tape measure for weighing and measuring the children.
- Bring the outlines you made of the children at the beginning of the church school year for the activity "See How I Am Growing" (page 208).
- You may need some extra helpers for this session because most of the children will want to have their outlines drawn as soon as they see the outlines made last fall.
- Mark weight and height beside each new outline.

SESSION TIME

Greet Children

As you greet the children tell them about the special activity you have planned. Some of the children will want to find their "pictures" right away and have a teacher or parent helper start drawing their "growing pictures." Others will want to go to the interest centers as usual. Betsy may have been planning all the way to church school to head directly for the block corner to have a turn at building a castle before Ping or Letticia monopolizes the area. Betsy is not going to be lured away from her plan by a suggestion that she have her picture drawn so you will have to draw her some other time. *Do not forget!*

Free Play

The activity planned for this morning will occupy most of the children during free play time, although each child will have some time to work in the interest centers.

Group Time

The children may be full of chatter about their pictures and ways they have grown. Talk with the children about growing.

> How, when, and why do they grow?
> Do all things grow? Which things do not?
> Can they see things grow? Why not?

Story

You may not have time or want to interrupt the conversation to tell a story. Or you may want to tell "Beverly Beaver Grows Big Enough" or one of the other growing stories to stimulate further conversation.

Prayer

Say a thank-you prayer for strong, growing bodies if this is appropriate.

Song

"This Is the Way," (page 95)

> This is the way we grow up tall,
> Grow up tall, grow up tall.
> This is the way we grow up tall,
> Stretching to the sky.
> *(Suit the actions to the words.)*

Free Play, Going Home Time, Cleanup, Pick up, Saying Good-bye

There may not be much picking up to do if most of the time was spent on the special activity. You might spend a few minutes doing rhythms if you can play a medley that would suggest such things as "elephant steps, baby steps, rabbit hops, or fairy dancing." Do not tell the children what to do; let them respond to the music in any way they wish.

Rhythm records or tapes are available in most audio shops. If you have a record or cassette player to use in the preschool, invest in one or two good recordings for this activity.

Give the children their outline pictures to take home today.

AFTER THE SESSION

Were you as thrilled as the children about the ways in which they have grown this year? If any child did not participate in the conversation or the activities, what can you do to help that child feel more a part of the group? Are there special responsibilities you can give children who seem to need a sense of belonging, of being wanted and needed?

Theme: Summertime

How you plan your summer sessions depends entirely upon your local situation. If you have the children with whom you have been living and working for ten months, there is no limit to the interesting experiences you can have. Some sessions may be spent outdoors. Conversations and activities related to summer fun with families and friends may be the emphasis for many sessions. The joys and problems of growing older may be the major concern of other sessions.

If you have a new group of young threes, you will plan an entirely different development of the themes of family fun and the world in summertime, along with special emphasis upon the theme "The Child Goes to Church" (page 57).

You may have a combined group with three, four, and five year olds. Read the letter "Summertime" (page 191) for suggestions about ways these children can live and work happily together in the church school.

FAMILY FUN

Summer may be the most relaxed period of the church school year. Many children may be absent one or more sessions if their families take a vacation or special weekend trips. Anticipate these trips with the children, and include a "show and tell" period in your group time for children to tell the whole group about trips to the zoo, visits to grandparents, picnics, and other times of family fun. They may have brought back treasures or souvenirs to show to the group.

Use any of the stories in this book that tell about these experiences. Select songs, poems, and finger plays that relate to family fun—or any of the resources the children have enjoyed and asked for. I have seen preschoolers playing "Baby Jesus in the manger" in July and singing "Jingle Bells" in 100 degree temperatures.

SUMMERTIME FUN

The wonders of the out-of-doors are a never-ceasing source of interest to children. Take advantage of summer to include outdoor play whenever possible. Several of the activities suggested in this resource section make use of the out-of-doors. Of course, if the temperature is high and there is no shady lawn or park available, plan quiet play indoors with a cool drink of water or fruit juice as a midmorning treat.

If the children in your group have opportunities to go swimming—in their own backyard wading pools or lakes or ocean surf, as the case may be—include this experience in your conversations. Read or say the poem "At the Seaside" (page 216) if it is appropriate. Provide opportunities for water play (see page 147).

Sometimes summer is not so much fun. Days are long and hot, children get tired, and parents get frazzled nerves. Tell the story "The Ladybug Helps Kendra" (page 155) and talk about times when the children have felt alone, rejected, or unloved. They may remember times their parents helped them find something that was fun to do and realize that their parents did not intend to make them feel lonesome or unloved.

SPECIAL DAYS

Memorial Day and the Fourth of July may mean a great deal to preschoolers, in terms of family trips, picnics, or Fourth of July fireworks. Although they will not understand the historical significance of the event, these might be occasions for staging parades indoors or out (see page 208). But you need not wait for a special day to have a parade. Parades are good fun any time. You might call it a circus parade or the "hottest day in the year" parade. If you have a mixed age group, some of the older children could fold paper hats for everyone. Color and trimmings could be added by younger children. Perhaps you could have a pet parade or a "my favorite toy" parade. By all means, have some music for the marching, some with words the children can sing.

OTHER THEMES

None of the themes used earlier in the year has been exhausted. Friends and pets can come to visit, and whole sessions can be planned around these events. If you have a group of mostly four year olds or a mixed age group, you could plan a trip to a fire station, a forest ranger station, a farm, or other point of interest in your locality. You may spend just one Sunday on one of these special themes or you may develop two or three sessions around one of them.

PURPOSE

Your specific purposes during the summer months will depend upon your group and your situation. But whatever you do, you will be working at the underlying purposes of the entire preschool course: *To guide the children in discovering answers to their three big questions; to surround them with love, understanding, and the good fellowship that is the church so that they may begin to feel themselves part of this fellowship; to help each child grow according to individual capacities and abilities.*

THE ROOM

If you are starting with a new group, reread the letters "Doing Big Things in Little Space" (page 11) and "Company's Coming!" (page 7) as well as suggestions for setting up the room given in Resource Section I (page 57).

Provide more scissors, more difficult puzzles, and some books geared to older children if you have a mixed age group.

Make plans to include water play by putting a dishpan of water in the housekeeping center and a small tub of water for sailing boats in another place.

If part or all of your sessions can be held out-of-doors, buy or borrow a small wagon on which you can load equipment you wish to take outside. This avoids a lot of lugging.

Have pictures representing picnics and other seasonal activities placed about the room.

Add to the book center books related to summer fun, family fun, or other themes you plan to use. These might include several from the Bibliography (page 235–38):

The Carrot Seed
The Indoor Noisy Book
Where Does the Trail Lead?
Wild, Wild Sunflower Child

ACTIVITIES

Adapt these to your situation and use activities from the other resource sections according to the interests and capacities of your children.

Parades, page 208
Rhythm Band, page 208
Treasure Walks, page 208
Making Bouquets, page 208
Making a Garden, page 208
From Bud to Seed, page 209
Outdoor Play, page 209
Outdoor Water Play, page 209
Shadow Play, page 209
Show and Tell, page 209
Visit the Sanctuary, page 209

ART ACTIVITIES

Use any of the art activities suggested on pages 225–28. If you have older children in the group, provide extra scissors. Older children like to do cutting for scrapbooks, posters, or just for fun.

GROUP TIME

This again will vary with your group and situation. If you have a shady place out-of-doors where the children can sit or lie on the grass during group time, wonderful! Provide cool water or juice along with a cracker for refreshments. Have a pan of water and some towels or moistened towelettes for cleaning dirty hands before handling food.

Any of the finger plays, songs, stories, and poems used during the year may be used again during the summer. New materials which may be used to give more meaning to the experiences the children are having are included in this resource section.

Finger plays

Eentsy Weentsy Spider, page 216

Stories

Summer Fun, page 215
Big Tree, page 214

There will be many opportunities to use these stories from other resource sections:

A Looking Walk in Summer, page 151
Fun for Joey, page 86
The Storm, page 154
A Little Boy Wonders, page 156
The Ladybug Helps Kendra, page 155

Song

Looby Loo, page 218
Ring Around a Rosy, page 219
Pop Goes a Weasel, page 222

Poems

At the Seaside, page 216
Thank You, God, page 216

Prayers

You may use some of the sample prayers on page 217, but most of your prayers should grow out of the activities, experiences, and conversations of the morning.

A Sample Teaching Plan for *Summertime*

I hope that the sample teaching plans suggested in these resource sections have been of real help to you in planning your mornings in the preschool. But because each group is different and each of us responds to the needs and interests of the children in a little different way, it is not possible for me to prepare a sample teaching plan that will exactly fit your group. In this last teaching plan, instead of taking a particular group of resources and organizing them around a "kernel" story or activity to fit an average situation, let's plan one of *your* sample summer fun sessions together.

How will you determine your purpose? To do this you will have to think about the children in your group. What summer fun experiences are they having with their families? Do most of the families in your church have gardens? Your purpose might relate to the experiences the children have helping to weed, water or gather flowers or vegetables, and the ways they are learning about their world. Or perhaps yours is a group of city children who have little contact with growing things but whose great joy in the summertime is running through sprinklers, wading in puddles after the rain, splashing in a park wading pool, or visiting the zoo. Then your purpose would relate to the fun children have with water. Know your children and their interests, and plan your purpose to relate these interests to the basic purposes of Christian education for preschool children—love and understanding (see page 37).

PREPARATION

Flexible Plans

It is wise to jot down ideas and make a plan, even though you do not use it at all. The chances are that if you know your children well and have kept them in mind as you planned, you will use most of your plan, adapting it as needed. But if a big storm comes up the night before, you may want to scrap everything and tell the story "The Storm" (page 153) and talk about the fallen branches, the big puddles, and the flowers that were beaten down into the mud.

The Room

- What can you do to make your room a better teacher? Perhaps the best way you can make your room teach about summer fun is to move your room outdoors. This means taking books and appropriate equipment to the church lawn, the park, or a neighbor's lawn.
- If you cannot take the room outdoors, bring the outside in! The "mothers" and "fathers" in your housekeeping center may want to take their babies to the "park" for a picnic. A window box and an open space on a clean floor make a very acceptable park. The window box might also be a place for young gardeners to work. Or your children may be having lots of fun on the beach during summer days. A few shells and pretty stones on the wonder table may remind the children of these experiences.
- In addition to bringing the outdoors in and adding any needed equipment to the interest centers, you will need to select pictures and books to fit your theme. Look through your picture file (page 74), or find summer fun pictures in magazines and mount them for use. Finding pictures would be a good activity for a parents' meeting. Ask the parents to bring stacks of old magazines. Provide scissors, paste,

and mounting paper. Talk about the purposes of the preschool program, and tell how the pictures are used as you work.

- Check the Bibliography (page 235) for possible titles related to your theme. The librarian in your church or public library may be able to suggest other books you can use. Double check each book yourself. What will the pictures say to the children in your group? Are the pictures racially inclusive? Does the text agree with the pictures, and is it a good story for preschool children, or will you have to make your own story to go with the pictures? Are single parent families and families with one child represented?

Special Equipment

- Check the activities you plan to use to help the children have experiences of summer fun. What special equipment will you need for these activities?
- If you are planning a parade, think about what you will need: a record or tape player and marching recording; boxes, bells, and sticks for making rhythm instruments.
- Or perhaps you will plan a "Treasure Walk" (page 208). Do you have a treasure box or bag ready?

SESSION TIME

Greet Children

What plans do you need to make for greeting the children? Will you suggest a special activity or help them find something to do in the interest centers? If you plan to go outside for most of the morning, what can the early arrivals do until you are ready to go out?

Free Play

How can you be available, be helpful, and keep your eyes and ears open to the needs and interests of the children without taking over the free play? You have had a lot of experience with this throughout the year, but it is a good idea to reread the letter "How to Avoid Being in Three Places at Once" (page 17).

Group Time

How can you highlight the experiences of the morning through conversation? What story (or stories) will you be prepared to tell that relates to the particular kind of summer fun you are emphasizing in this session? Always remember, of course, that the story you plan to tell may not be the right one, so that you need to be familiar with many stories to be able to switch to a more appropriate one on a moment's notice. You may plan to tell the story "Summer Fun," but hot weather may suddenly make everyone unhappy. The children may spend the morning quarreling and snatching toys from one another; but by group time they may be feeling sorry about having had bad feelings. You might decide to tell "Tommy's Mistake" instead of "Summer Fun." "Everyone makes mistakes sometimes. . . . The only thing to do is say 'I'm sorry' and then fix up the mistake the best way you can." This comment by Tommy's daddy may help everyone in the group feel better.

Choose the songs you want to sing during group time. Should you make up new words to a familiar song, or do the words fit some of the experiences the children will have?

What finger plays or poems might you plan to use?

Do you have some ideas now of what you might include in a prayer?

Free Play, Going Home Time, Cleanup, Pick up, Saying Good-bye

This part of the session takes planning, too. How will you help the children to keep busy and happy if the parents' class or the church service runs overtime? How will you work with the children to guide them in good habits of picking up and putting away toys they have used? Do some children need special attention during these last few minutes? Many young children find transitions difficult.

AFTER THE SESSION

What can you do to evaluate the morning? What records do you keep on each child to help you know that child better? How can you and the other teachers plan and work more effectively and have summer fun along with the children?

BOOKS

VACATION READING

Suggest to the parents that they take both their children's favorite books and some new books along on family vacation trips. The children will enjoy having old and new stories read over and over.

CARE OF BOOKS

The summer months are a good time to look over all your equipment and supplies. As you sort your books, you may discover that some are worn out and need to be replaced. Others can be made to look fresh and new by adding plastic covers. These covers may be purchased ready-made from bookstores or you can make your own from the clear plastic available in many stores. Use transparent tape to mend any torn pages.

PICTURES

TEACHING PICTURES

The stories included in this resource section could be illustrated by pictures you have found, cut out, and mounted for your picture file. These pictures can be shown to the children while you tell the stories, but they may also be used in other ways. Have them in the interest centers or on the bulletin board or wall for the children to look at during free play time. They could also be placed on the special table.

The children may want to talk to you about the pictures from time to time. After they have heard the story which the picture illustrates, *they* may tell *you* the story in their own words. Or they may make up their own stories about the people or animals in the pictures.

Look through all the pictures in your file. Many of them can also be used during the summertime. For example, if the children talk about planting gardens, show a picture of someone planting, a robin pulling up a worm, or a squirrel with a nut. A picture of a family game might start a conversation about family fun on long summer evenings. Put summer pictures on the bulletin board or on the special table.

ADDITIONAL PICTURES

At a meeting with parents you might involve the parents in finding, cutting, and mounting pictures for use in the preschool. Or have some parents go through your picture file (page 74) to look for pictures that need remounting.

If you cannot get the parents together for a "picture party," you might suggest this as a project for the young people in your church or even as an activity for older children in the vacation church school. You will have to explain to them how to select pictures and how you want them mounted and sorted by subject matter.

ACTIVITIES

Many of the activities suggested in Resource Sections I and II may be used with the themes "Growing" and "Summertime." Some of the most appropriate ones are listed below, along with additional activities for these themes.

Activities Related to Growing

A GROUP PICTURE

Attach a strip of paper eighteen to twenty-four inches in width and eight or ten feet long to the wall or back of a pew. Fasten it with easily removable tape. The bottom edge of the paper should be about two feet from the floor. Stand the children up against the paper one by one and trace around their heads and shoulders. Each child can crayon her or his own picture. Write their names above the pictures. Include every child. When you have finished, you have a class picture. Every one is different, but each one is a member of the preschool group.

SEE HOW I AM GROWING

If you made and saved individual outlines of the children early in the church school year (see page 75 in Resource Section I), bring them out during the unit on "Growing." Trace around each child again, using a different color from the one used for the first outline. Talk with each child about the many ways that child has been growing during this year as the two of you check the difference between the two outlines. When the child walks away from the outline, all the group can see how much that child has grown. The pictures can now be taken home.

VISITORS COME TO THE PRESCHOOL

If you know a good, relaxed parent who could visit the preschool with a little baby, this would be a new experience for many preschoolers. Hopefully, this would be the kind of parent who could answer both the questions and the feelings behind the questions of the children. Perhaps the baby could be fed during the visit.

Be sure all the children in the group are in good health before the parent and baby arrive.

GUESS WHO

(See Resource Section II, page 150.)

MATCH COLORS

(See Resource Section II, page 150.)

Summertime Activities

PARADES

When the group feels in a celebrating mood—or when high spirits need to be channeled into manageable activities—you might have a "parade" in the preschool room. Make flags and banners out of old sheets cut in rectangles or triangles. Color them with crayons and tape or thumbtack them to a dowel rod or smooth stick. Some of the children may help make the flags. Give each child a flag to carry. Play a good march on the piano or borrow a record or tape player and a recording of march music to use on this occasion.

RHYTHM BAND

Young children enjoy using very simple rhythm instruments. Enlist parents to help make drums, rattles, tambourines, horns, sandpaper blocks, cymbals, and rhythm sticks. Instructions for making these instruments are in the Appendix (page 228). Use the rhythm instruments to make your parade a noisy success. Other times, one of the teachers may tap out various rhythms on a drum or with one of the other instruments. The children may walk, run, hop, dance, or respond in other ways to the rhythms.

TREASURE WALKS

A variation of the "Looking Walks" (page 147) would be a treasure walk. Take along a "treasure" box or can or bag. Let the children put whatever they find into the treasure box. They may come back with a pigeon feather, a dandelion, a pretty leaf, a gum wrapper, or a bottle cap.

As you walk along, you will have to help the children "see." Point out the anthills, the spider's web, and the dew on the grass. These, too, are treasures, even though they cannot be put in the treasure box.

MAKING BOUQUETS

If you have cut flowers to arrange for the preschool room, the children will enjoy helping you do it. As you work together you can talk about the beautiful colors, the smell, and the fact that no two flowers in the whole world are exactly alike. How could there be so many different kinds of flowers?

MAKING A GARDEN

God's world is usually orderly and dependable. Preschool children can begin to experience the truth of this statement if you can find a small plot of ground where the children could plant a little garden and care for it all summer. Although radish seeds only produce radishes, not all seeds always grow. Children need to be helped to gain a realistic picture of the world, and part of the mystery of creation is that we don't always know why some seeds do not grow.

FROM BUD TO SEED

Try to visit an outdoor spot in the late summer to learn about growth from bud to seed time. Dandelions show this very well. Even in late summer you will find some tightly closed buds, some blooming gaily, some gone to seed, and some with no flowers at all. This is all part of God's "plan" for life and growth that goes on and on.

OUTDOOR PLAY

Use the out-of-doors as much as possible during the summer. If you have a good lawn or outdoor play yard at the church, use it. Some churches are near small parks where the children can run, play in the sand, rest in the shade, listen to outdoor noises, look at interesting bugs or leaves, and have a quiet time with story, song, prayer, and conversation. These experiences will be more fun if parents know that you will be outdoors most of the morning and dress the children accordingly.

OUTDOOR WATER PLAY

A paint, hardware, or building supply store owner in your church might provide you with several small plastic pails and inexpensive paint brushes ($1\frac{1}{2}$- to 2-inch-wide bristles, short handles). Put water in the pails (less than half full), and let the children "paint" the foundation of the church, the trees, the walk. Try to have enough pails and brushes so that no child has to wait too long to have a turn. Play a song game (pages 218–20) with those who are not painting or let them look for "treasures."

SHADOW PLAY

Playing with their own and one another's shadows is great fun for children in the summer. The children might try to "catch" their shadows or run away from them. Have a child stand very still while you draw the outline of the shadow on a big sheet of paper. The other children may want you to draw their shadows too. A magazine picture of children and their shadows would be good to have in your room for the children to see.

SHOW AND TELL

Summertime is vacation time. You will want to talk, think, and play "vacations." Use poems such as "At the Seaside" (page 216) when you talk about going to the beach or going swimming. Let the children show and tell about things they do in the summer—trips to the beach, the zoo, the band concert, the park, or backyard picnics. Show and tell about trips *you* take too.

VISIT THE SANCTUARY

You may be able to visit the church quite often during the summer services of worship. You may have fewer children, and the church may have more space for you to come and go without distracting the other worshipers. Stay for about ten minutes of the service. See pages 76 and 140 for other suggestions about visiting the sanctuary.

STORIES

Beverly Beaver Grows Big Enough

Growing is a slow process, especially when you want to be able to play the same games as big brothers and sisters, to stay up later at night, to learn to cook or hammer, and do all the things adults do.

This would be a good story to use along with the activity "See How I Am Growing" (see page 208). When the children compare their new outlines with the old ones, they will see how much they have grown physically. They may also talk about other ways they have grown in the things they can do now compared with last fall, such as button their coats, hop, and paint big pictures.

Use any pictures that show children growing as you tell this story.

Once there was a pretty house down the street just around the corner. It had a big green front door, a big shiny brass doorknob, and a little black bell. You could ring the bell if you were big enough. Inside the house lived the Beaver family—Father Beaver, Mother Beaver, and the three little Beavers.

Beverly was the littlest person in the Beaver family, and she wanted very much to be big.

She wanted to be big enough to climb into the tree house the way Brother Bill could. Bill said her legs weren't long enough.

She wanted to be big enough to play cowboys the way Brother Burt did. Burt said that she didn't know how.

She wanted to be big enough to help Mother Beaver cook chocolate pudding without burning herself. Mother Beaver said she wasn't tall enough to cook at the stove.

She wanted to be big enough to visit Father Beaver at his work without getting in his way. Father Beaver said she wasn't old enough.

You see, Beverly Beaver was just three. She thought she would never be big enough.

Mother Beaver said she would soon be big enough if she would eat her vegetables and drink her milk every day.

Father Beaver said she would soon be big enough if she would take a good nap and have a long sleep every night.

Brother Bill said she would soon be able to climb into the tree house if she would practice climbing on the climbing gym at the playground.

Brother Burt said she would soon be able to play cowboys if she would watch him play and would learn how.

All the Beavers said they knew that Beverly would surely grow.

So every day Beverly Beaver ate her vegetables and drank her milk.

Every night she slept a good long sleep.

In between times she practiced climbing on the climbing gym, and she played cowboys the way she had seen Burt play.

But every day she felt the same size and she looked the same size. She was not growing big enough.

Then one day Brother Bill said, "Beverly, I need someone to play with me in the tree; can you climb up there?"

Beverly tried, and her legs were long enough.

Brother Burt wanted her to play cowboys with him. She tried, and she did know how.

Mother Beaver was making chocolate pudding. Beverly stood on her stool in front of the stove. She was tall enough to stir the pudding without getting burned.

When Mother Beaver told Father Beaver about how big Beverly had grown, Father Beaver said she must surely be big enough to visit him at his work.

And she did.

Beverly Beaver was growing big enough, just as she had wanted to do.

Peter's Wonderful Day

The story probably should not be used in connection with a particular child's birthday, because you cannot use it for all children. It could be a kind of celebration of growing, which all children do. In the conversation that follows you might talk about whether toys grow and whether mommies and daddies grow little as their children grow big.

This day was a special day—a very important day. Peter remembered what day it was all day long. Something fun was going to happen, and Peter could hardly wait. He wondered if his friends knew about the special day and the fun that was going to happen. He decided to ask them.

Peter found Ole Holey in his bed. Ole Holey was Peter's teddy bear. He had one eye missing and a hole in his ear, where Peter sometimes carried him. Peter's mother said he was worn out 'cause his stuffing kept coming out, but Peter loved him anyway.

"Ole Holey," Peter whispered in his good ear, "do you know what day this is?"

Ole Holey didn't know.

"Well, pss-s-s-s-s-s-s," whispered Peter. "Will you please come? I want you to come."

Ole Holey looked and looked with his one good eye, and Peter knew that he would come.

In the living room stood Bouncing Horse all alone. Peter climbed on his back and whispered in his ear.

"Bouncing Horse," Peter asked, "do you know what day this is?"

Bouncing Horse didn't know.

"Well, pss-s-s-s-s-s-s," Peter whispered. "Will you please come? I want you to come."

Bouncing Horse bounced and bounced, and Peter knew that he would come.

Halfway under the chair in the living room—*somebody* had not taken very good care of him—was Big Gray Uffant. (It's really Big Gray *Elephant*, but Peter couldn't say that word very well yet.) Peter liked Big Gray Uffant because he had huge floppy ears and he made a loud squeak when Peter squeezed his trunk.

"Big Gray Uffant," Peter asked, "do you know what day this is?"

Big Gray Uffant didn't know.

"Well, pss-s-s-s-s-s-s," Peter whispered in his ear. "Will you please come? I want you to come."

Big Gray Uffant gave one loud squeak with his trunk, and Peter knew he would come.

There was one more friend to ask, Cowboy Slim. Cowboy Slim was Peter's cowboy doll. He was a rag doll with real cowboy clothes. Peter took him to bed every night. But where was Cowboy Slim? Peter looked and looked. Peter looked under his bed. Cowboy Slim wasn't there.

Peter looked in his green toy box. Cowboy Slim wasn't there. Peter looked in his moving van truck. Cowboy Slim wasn't there.

And then he found him! Do you know where? Right on the floor under the coat hook where Peter had dropped him when he came in from playing. He looked pretty dirty, but Peter didn't mind.

"Cowboy Slim, do you know what day this is?" Peter asked.

Cowboy Slim didn't know.

"Well, pss-s-s-s-s-s-s," Peter whispered in his ear. "Will you please come? I want you to come."

Cowboy Slim didn't answer, so Peter just picked him up and took him along.

"We're ready, Mother," said Peter.

"Fine, Peter," said Mother. "Go right in."

Peter and Cowboy Slim went into the dining room, and there was the special, important, fun thing that Peter knew about. It was a birthday party at Peter's own table, with balloons and paper hats and a pink birthday cake with four candles! Peter was four years old.

Ole Holey and Bouncing Horse and Big Gray Uffant were there too.

"Happy Birthday, Peter," cried Mother and Father. They sang the happy birthday song to Peter.

> Happy Birthday to you,
> Happy Birthday to you,
> Happy Birthday, dear Peter,
> Happy Birthday to you.

Peter felt so happy, he squeezed and squeezed Cowboy Slim.

Then Peter sat down at his table and blew a great big blow—*Poof!* Out went all four candles at once. Peter's mother helped him cut his own piece of birthday cake. It was big and pink because Peter just loved pink birthday cake. Peter and his mother and his father and his toy friends all had a happy time at Peter's birthday party.

The Five Toots

Through feeling the same way as the main character of the story, a child may discover a new significance, a new way of understanding self and family. "What is the world like?" The child needs to know. Some children do not like to go to bed; some do like to eat more candy. Parents make them go to bed and will not allow them more candy. Children need to discover that other people have the same kinds of problems and that it is quite all right to make fun of the whole thing. This is a part of growing up.

Once upon a time there was a family named Toots. Toots was their last name. They had first names, too, just like your family.

The father was Tuba Toots.

The mother was Sweet Potato Toots.

The three children were named Rootie Toots, Tootie Toots, and Handy Andy Toots.

The Toots family was the funniest family you ever saw. They did things backward.

At night the children, Rootie Toots, Tootie Toots, and Handy Andy Toots, put Mother Sweet Potato and Father Tuba to bed.

Rootie washed their ears.

Tootie told them to brush their teeth.

Handy Andy tucked them in.

Sometimes, if he wasn't too tired, Handy Andy brought Father Tuba and Mother Sweet Potato each *one* drink of water, but just one. Then he said, "Time to go to sleep," and turned out the light.

Then all the little Toots went down to the kitchen to talk and to drink coffee.

Does your family do it that way?

[Allow time for conversation.]

In the Toots family everyone had a job. Handy Andy took charge of the candy. He and Rootie and Tootie ate as much as they liked, but Father Tuba and Mother Sweet Potato could have only one piece a day. It was not good for their teeth, you know.

Does your family do it that way?

[Allow time for conversation.]

Tootie Toots' job was to make people behave. She meant what she said, and she said what she meant.

She told Mother Sweet Potato to be *sure* to run across the street when she went to play with Sally.

She told Father Tuba that he really *ought* to play cowboys on the furniture. That's what they bought it for.

Does your family do it that way?

[Allow time for conversation.]

Rootie Toots' job was to keep the family clean. Mother Sweet Potato and Father Tuba got covered with dirt every day. They had to have a bath every night. She washed their hair and their faces and cleaned their ears. For some reason they *always* got soap in their eyes. They just wouldn't hold their heads still and keep their eye shut.

The children didn't take baths because they didn't get dirty.

Does your family do it that way?

[Allow time for conversation.]

Rootie Toots, Tootie Toots, and Handy Andy Toots

ate what they wanted,
slept whenever they wanted,
never washed their ears,
and they took good care of Mother Sweet Potato and Father Tuba.

Does your family do it that way?

Anna's Mistake

Growing up is hard. There are so many things we want to do that we are not allowed to do. Sometimes we forget and make mistakes. Children hearing this story might identify themselves with Anna. They might know how bad Anna feels when she realizes she has done something wrong and made her mommy and daddy angry. We hope they know, too, from their own experiences how much better Anna felt when her mother and daddy forgave her and gave her an opportunity to fix up the mistake the best way she could. Love and forgiveness are essential for Christian growth.

A picture of a girl (or several children) looking longingly at a birthday cake would be good to illustrates this story. The children may want to tell you the story whenever they see the picture after you have told the story to them.

Anna liked chocolate cake. She also liked chocolate icing. She liked chocolate cake with chocolate icing best of all.

On Daddy's birthday, Mommy made a chocolate birthday cake with chocolate icing. It was to be a surprise. Anna watched. My, it looked good!

Mommy put it in the cupboard so that Daddy wouldn't see it. Then she went upstairs to get cleaned up.

"Come along, Anna," she called. "Daddy will be home soon, and we want to be ready for his birthday dinner."

Anna went to take one more look at the chocolate cake with the chocolate icing. My! It looked good! She took one little taste with her finger. It was so good!

She took one little taste more. It was better all the time. One more taste, and then another and another. Then she took a big lick with her tongue. Then she broke a piece off with her fingers. Then she—

"Anna!" called her mother. "Come now. What are you doing?"

Anna jumped. She had forgotten about getting cleaned up. In fact, she had forgotten about Daddy's birthday. She had only thought of how good that chocolate cake with the chocolate icing was. Now look at it! The cake was spoiled.

Anna was scared about what she had done. She shut the cupboard door fast and ran upstairs.

She didn't tell her mother. She didn't know how. She knew her mommy would be angry.

Anna didn't feel very good. She didn't eat much of the good birthday dinner.

Then Mommy went for the cake, the surprise birthday cake.

"Oh, my goodness," she cried. "What has happened to the cake? Anna do you know?"

"Yes," said Anna in a little low voice.

"Why did you do this to Daddy's cake? Didn't you understand it was a surprise? Now you've spoiled the whole thing." Mother was angry.

Anna began to cry. "I don't know why I did it. I just got the idea and I did it. I'm sorry, Mommy. I'm sorry, Daddy." Anna felt very sorry for spoiling Daddy's birthday cake.

Mother took Anna in her arms. "I'm sorry too, Anna. I feel very sorry that the cake is ruined. But I'm glad you told me how it happened. It's better that way."

Daddy patted Anna's head. "You made a mistake, Anna, and we are all sorry about that. Everyone makes mistakes sometimes; Mommy and I do too. The only thing to do is to say 'I'm sorry' and then fix up the mistake the best way you can."

Anna felt a little better. Her mommy and daddy were disappointed, but they were no longer angry. They understood how it was.

"I *am* sorry, Daddy. I won't do it again."

"Anna," whispered Mother, "will you help me make a new birthday cake tomorrow for Daddy?"

"Oh, yes," whispered Anna.

So they did. Anna sprinkled little colored candies on the top of the cake and put lots of yellow candles on it. Then she carefully shut the cupboard door herself.

That birthday cake *was* a surprise.

The Little Boy Who Didn't Know Who He Was

Finding answers to the question "Who am I?" is an important part of growing up. Sometimes children feel lonely or rejected and think that everything might be all right if they were someone other than themselves. They need to be reassured that mothers, fathers, and teachers love them "just as they are." It is good to be a preschool boy or girl.

As you tell this story you might pause for conversation between the different parts. "Did you ever pretend to be a puppy? What can boys and girls do that puppies can't do?"

Read the letter "Dealing with Fears and Feelings" (page 123) to help you try to understand what the children are really saying with their questions, comments, and behavior.

Once upon a time there was a Little Boy who didn't know who he was.

He thought it would be fun to be a puppy. So he crawled around on his hands and knees. He barked little puppy barks. He let people rub his ears and pat his head.

But when he tried to eat his peanut butter sandwich from a plate on the floor, the peanut butter got up his nose and in his hair. The Little Boy decided he was not a puppy.

He thought it would be fun to be a kitty. So he curled up to sleep in someone's lap, and he purred whenever anyone stroked his fur.

But when he tried to chase his tail round and round as kittens do, he fell down on the floor in a dizzy heap. Someone stepped on his fingers.

The Little Boy decided he was not a kitty.

He thought it would be fun to be a baby monkey. So he climbed all over people and held onto them tight around their necks or around their waists.

But he was a pretty big little boy and pretty heavy too, so no one could carry him very long. He was always being put down and left alone.

The Little Boy decided he was not a monkey.

He thought it would be fun to be a little boy baby. So he tried to sleep in the baby's bed and to eat his lunch from the baby's bottle.

But his legs felt stiff from sleeping in too small a bed. And warm milk coming from the nipple of a bottle did not taste good.

Besides, he was still hungry.

The Little Boy decided he was not a baby.

He thought it would be fun to be a real big boy. He tried to cross the street all by himself, but a man yelled at him, "Stay out of the street, Little Boy."

He tried to go to school with his big brother, but the teacher said to him, "You're not big enough to be in your brother's school, Little Boy."

He tried to play with the big boys. He said he was "Super Duper." The big boys laughed and said there was no such person as "Super Duper."

The Little Boy sat down and cried. "I'm NOBODY."

The Little Boy's mother came along.

"That's not true. You're my Little Boy and I love you just as you are. It doesn't matter what you can do. All that matters is that you BE YOU."

The Little Boy's daddy came along.

"Yes, that's true. God planned for me to be me and you to be you. We are all different. There is no one just like you—not big brother, not the baby. And I love you very much just as you are."

Then the Little Boy knew who he was. He was himself—not a puppy, not a kitty, not a monkey, not a baby, and not a big boy. He was his mother's and father's Little Boy, and they loved him just the way he was.

Big Tree

Big Tree is a story about the order and dependability of God's world. Every year brings spring, summer, fall, and winter. No season is skipped; never does the order change.

The preschooler experiences these changes in the year's cycle—by planting seeds or going swimming or raking leaves—but does not readily see the seasons as part of a whole pattern of growth. Children do not know that they are growing and changing as surely as Big Tree is.

There is much to wonder about in God's marvelous plan for life and growth. What makes the leaves turn colors and finally drop off? How big will a little child grow? We really don't know all the answers. Like Marc, we wonder.

We hope you will enjoy the delights of each season with your children. They have very little, if any, memory of last spring. Every day the world is fresh and new and exciting. Almost everything is "for the first time."

If you can see it with their eyes, you will find it an exciting place too.

"For now, the winter is past,
the rain is over and gone.
The flowers appear on the earth,
the time of singing has come."
—*Song of Solomon* 2:11–12*a*

"O LORD, our Sovereign,
how majestic is your name in all the earth."
—*Psalm* 8:1

Big Tree stood in Marc's backyard. Big Tree had been there for a long time, longer than Marc could remember.

No one knew how old Big Tree was, not Marc's father, not Marc's mother.

Everyone knew now old Marc was. He was three.

Marc liked Big Tree.

Big Tree was very high. The highest branches stretched way, way high into the sky.

Big Tree was big around. It was so big that Marc could not reach around it, not at all; so big that Marc could hide behind it without one bit of Marc showing.

Big Tree was strong. When the wind blew and the lightning flashed and the thunder crashed, Big Tree's branches tossed and creaked. But its branches did not break, and its roots stayed tight and deep in the ground. In spring, the grass turned green. The tulips bloomed. It was Marc's birthday. Big Tree stretched out its branches and showed some new little leaves in the sun.

Blossoms came. They dropped all over the ground. They even dropped on Marc.

"Stop dropping on me, Big Tree," said Marc. But Big Tree did not stop until all the blossoms were dropped.

In summer, the hot sun shone on Big Tree's leafy green branches. Marc and his mother had a picnic in the cool shade. The ants built little hills at Big Tree's roots. Daddy longlegs climbed up and down Big Tree's cool black trunk.

In fall, Big Tree slowly dropped its leaves. Yellow and brown, down they came, with hundreds of little twigs. Marc raked the leaves into big piles.

Winter came. It began to snow. Marc made a snowperson and stood it beside Big Tree. The ants were gone. The daddy longlegs were gone. The outside was cold, very cold.

One day the snowperson melted. The sun began to feel warm. Marc changed into his spring jacket. The grass turned green again, and the tulips bloomed.

Big Tree stretched out its branches and showed some new little leaves to the sun.

It was spring again. Marc knew it was his birthday time again. Both Marc and Big Tree were one year older.

Still no one knew how old Big Tree was. BUT everyone knew how old Marc was. Do you?

Summer Fun

This story may be adapted to fit the kinds of summer fun the children in your group are experiencing. If few of your children have opportunities to swim in the summer, you might substitute having a little picnic in the park. The important part of this story is the fun of having a friend about your size to do things with you.

Sometimes when you tell the story, you might use paper dolls or hand puppets to represent the child telling the story and his friend Carlos. You might cut out and mount an appropriate picture too.

If you are using this story with a group of older preschoolers, they might enjoy playing the different episodes of the story. They could pretend to bury their feet in sand (cover them with their hands), then wiggle their toes and let their feet pop out. Each part of the story lends itself to pretend play.

It is good to have a friend just your size.

I have a friend. His name is Carlos. He comes to my house to play.

We go to play in the sandbox. Then Carlos gets an idea: "Let's take off our shoes and socks!"

Oh, boy! What a good idea! The sand on top is hot. We dig deep holes and put our feet in and cover them up. It's cool underneath.

"Carlos, my feet are all gone!" I say.

Carlos's feet are all gone too. Then he wiggles his toes and the sand cracks and out pop his feet.

I wiggle my toes and the sand cracks and out pop my feet! Ha, ha, ha! What fun the sand is.

Then Carlos sees an ant, a big black ant, carrying a big crumb.

"Look, look!" Carlos calls to me. "The ant is going on a picnic. He's carrying his food with him."

"Where are you going, little ant?" I ask him politely. Maybe ants can't hear people. He doesn't answer me.

"Carlos, I have an idea. Let's give the ant a tablecloth. Maybe he will crawl onto it and eat his picnic there."

"Good idea!" says Carlos. He takes off his shirt—it is a hot day and he doesn't really need it. He lays his shirt down in front of the ant.

"Here, ant," Carlos calls. "Here's a tablecloth for your picnic."

You know what the ant does? It crawls *underneath* that shirt instead of on top of it. We look and look *and look* for it. The ant must have gotten lost in the grass.

"I'm hungry," says Carlos. "Let's have a picnic right away."

"Yes, let's!" I say. "What shall we eat? Oh, I know! Radishes. I planted some in my garden, right behind my house."

I pull up a radish. It is a BIG, red radish.

Carlos pulls up another radish. It is a VERY BIG, red radish.

"Have a radish," I say.

"Have a radish," Carlos says. He brushes the dirt off, takes a little bite, and says, "Good!"

I brush the dirt off, take a little bite, and say, "Good!"

Then we dig some little holes and put the red radishes back.

Radishes are not *so* good for eating. They *are* good for growing in gardens.

Mother comes to the door. "Children, it's such a hot day, how would you like to go for a swim?"

"Hot dog!" says Carlos.

"Goody!" I say.

Carlos goes home to ask his mother and to put on his swim suit. Mother helps me put on mine.

We get into the car and off we go.

Carlos is my friend and we have fun together.

FINGER PLAYS

Eentsy Weentsy Spider

Eentsy weentsy spider went up the water spout,
(Run thumb and index finger up imaginary spout)
Down came the rain and washed the spider out.
(Arms and hands high, fall down; repeat several times)
Out came the sun and dried up all the rain,
(Make large circle with arms—the sun)
Now eentsy weentsy spider went up the spout again.
(Run thumb and index finger up imaginary spout)

Folk Song from North Carolina

POEMS

At the Seaside

When I was down beside the sea,
A wooden spade they gave to me
To dig the sandy shore.
My holes were empty like a cup.
In every hole the sea came up,
Till it could come no more.
—Robert Louis Stevenson

From *A Child's Garden of Verses*, by Robert Louis Stevenson. New York: Charles Scribner's Sons, 1910.

Thank You, God

Thank you, God,
For many things:
The blue, blue sky,
The bird that sings,
The tickly grass,
The blowy breeze,
And all the cool,
green, shady trees.
Thank you, God.
—Florence Schulz

From *Summer With Nursery Children*, by Florence Schulz. Boston: Pilgrim Press, 1958. Used by permission.

PRAYERS

The following prayers are only examples. You may or may not choose to use them. They will, however, give you some clues for making your own "on the spot" prayers.

O God, sometimes it seemed as if we would never grow big enough to do careful things—helping our parents make chocolate pudding and watering the flowers. Now we are big enough and we are glad. Thank you, God, for growing. Amen.

We are glad for the rain, which gives the world a big drink. We like to watch the birds take baths in the puddles. Thank you, God, for rain. Amen.

Dear God, we wonder where our shadows come from and where they go. We had lots of fun trying to catch our shadows this morning. There are so many things about the world we do not understand, but we are glad we can learn about each wonderful thing. Amen.

We ran and ran this morning. Then we got hot and sat down in the cool shade of the tree. Oh, we like the cool shade and the green grass to sit on, God. Amen.

Sometimes we get cross and unhappy, God. We are sorry when we get very angry and make our friends unhappy. We are glad when we find ways to be happy again. Thank you, God, for happy times. Amen.

SONGS

This is fun for young children if you pick and choose the verses. Do not try for perfection, and take it rather slowly. You will sing about right hands or left hands, but don't try to get the children to be correct about it. That will spoil the fun. Try doing one hand, one foot, and my little head to begin with. Later in the year, some children may be eager to play longer, so you can add another verse.

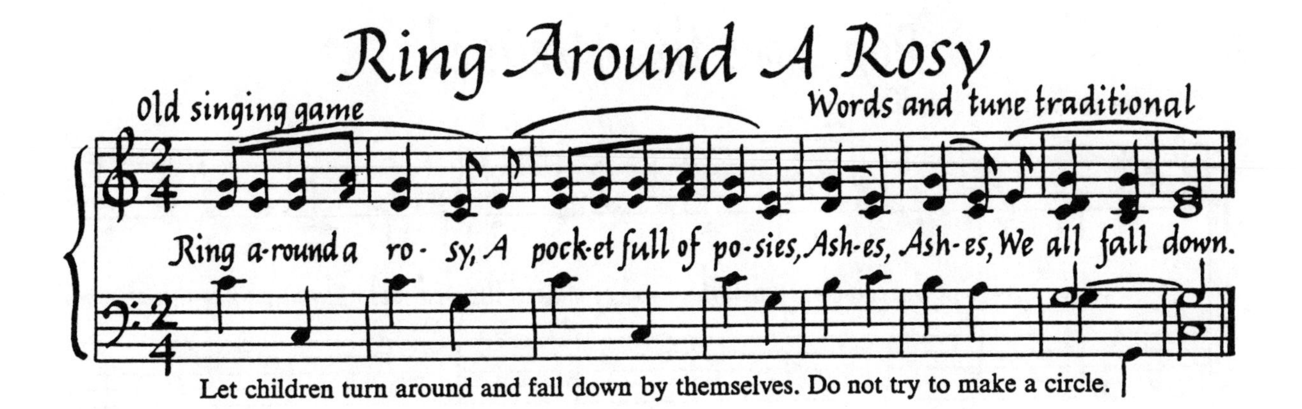
Ring Around A Rosy
Old singing game
Words and tune traditional
Ring a-round a ro - sy, A pock-et full of po-sies, Ash-es, Ash-es, We all fall down.
Let children turn around and fall down by themselves. Do not try to make a circle.

Pop Goes the Weasel

Words and tune traditional

Go round and round, singing the song. On "Pop!" all jump up and fall down, just as in "Ring Around a Rosy."

Appendix

ART ACTIVITIES

Finger Painting

MATERIALS YOU NEED

Finger paint
Glazed paper, 12 x 18 inches or larger (freezer paper, glazed butcher paper, or heavy shelf paper may be used)
Water and sponges
Table with a washable surface
Coverall smocks for the painters
Newspaper to place finished paintings on

FINGER PAINT

Mix powdered tempera with a combination of liquid starch and liquid soap or use the following recipe. Mix one cup of starch (either cornstarch or laundry) with cold water to make a thin paste. Add one cup of mild soap flakes (not detergent) and one half cup salt. Put the mixture in a double boiler and add one quart of water. Cook until thick. Use more water if necessary. Beat the mixture with an egg beater. You may want to add a teaspoon of glycerin to make it more pliable and a cup of talcum powder to give it a pleasant smell and a better texture. Put the mixture into small jars (such as baby-food jars), and then mix in the powder paint. The salt acts as a preservative.

You can, of course, buy finger paint and the paper for it from supply houses, local hobby or art stores, and many discount stores.

At the beginning of the church school year one color is sufficient. It may be red or blue or green. Change it from time to time as you make new batches of paint. In the spring, when the children are older and more experienced, you might let them use two or three colors.

APRONS

Cheap and useful smocks can be made from men's shirts. Remove the collars. Cut off the sleeves about halfway. Put the smock on the child backward and fasten it in the back. If the child is wearing a dress or shirt with long sleeves, roll these up before the child puts on the smock.

You can also make adequate, child-size aprons out of sheets of plastic, discarded plastic curtains, or shower curtains. Bind the edges with bias tape. These aprons have the advantage of being waterproof, but they do not protect the sleeves. They are more appropriate for easel painting.

HOW TO FINGER PAINT

Write each child's name and the date on the unglazed side of the paper before wetting it. Slip the sheet of paper through tepid water, and place it glazed side up on the table before the children, or use a sponge to wet the glazed side of the paper. Use a spoon or a tongue depressor to place a large glob of finger paint on the paper. Let the child spread it around as each wishes. Letting them stand to finger paint gives more freedom of arm movement. If the paper becomes too dry for the paint to spread easily, sprinkle a few drops of water on the paper. When a child is finished, pick up the wet painting carefully and lay it on a newspaper or a clothes rack to dry. It takes at least an hour for the paintings to dry. The children should take turns at painting, two or three at a time.

If the children's washing facilities are some distance from the preschool room, it may save the walls to have a pan of water and a stack of paper towels available in the room so that each child can wash the paint off right there before going on to another activity. If you are wearing your smock and have a large sponge and a few clean rags or paper towels available, you will find finger painting is as much fun for you as it is for the children in your group.

Because finger painting takes careful supervision and quite a lot of teacher assistance with smocks and washing up, it is better not to plan to use easel painting or clay the same day. Children may, however, use crayons or may paste at another table.

Soap Painting

Add a little warm water (about one fourth cup) to one cup mild soap flakes (not detergent) in a large mixing bowl. Beat with a rotary beater until the mixture stands in soft peaks. There should be no liquid in the bottom of the bowl if your proportions are right. Use a table that will not be harmed by soap and water, or cover one with plastic. Give each child several large spoonfuls of "paint" and let the children use the whole table.

The children love to help wipe up the soapsuds with small sponges they can rinse and squeeze dry.

Easel Painting

MATERIALS YOU NEED

Tempera paint, liquid or powder form
Large sheets (18 x 24 inches, if possible) of newsprint
Long-handled brushes
Easels or good substitutes
Smocks or large, coverall aprons for the painters

Any art supply store and many discount stores can provide you with tempera paint, newsprint, and brushes. If it is not convenient or possible to get to an art supply store, order from a catalog (see address list).

PAINT

The powder form of tempera paints is not difficult to use, is less expensive, and more easily stored than the liquid form. Fill the paint jar about one-third full of water. Add paint, stirring constantly, until you get a full, rich color. This paint can be kept for several weeks if you use jars with screw-top covers so that the paint does not dry out. (Small jars, four or five inches high, such as those peanut butter or junior baby food comes in make good paint jars.) To begin with, one color per easel is enough. Later in the year the children will be able to handle three or four colors and keep the brushes in the proper jars (one brush for each color). If you add a small amount of liquid detergent to each jar, any spilled paint washes out more easily.

BRUSHES

The brushes should be about one inch wide and the handles twelve inches long. Wash, press dry, and lay out on a paper after each session.

EASELS

Easels can be purchased from any educational equipment supply house (see address list) or a discount toy store. Or they can be made (page 228) or improvised. Usable easels can be improvised from cardboard cartons. Cut two adjoining sides from a large carton. The fold becomes the top hinge, giving you a double-faced easel. Keep the lower parts from separating by inserting two short strings, knotted at each end, into half-inch slits three or four inches up from the bottom on each side. Make shelves to hold the paint jars by turning up the bottom edges on each side. Place this on a low, narrow table. I have used a stool instead of a table sometimes so that the children would not have to stretch their arms too far when painting. Paper can be thumbtacked to the easel or attached by means of spring clothespins on the sides.

PAPER

Newsprint is the most inexpensive paper for easel painting. The want-ad sections of large Sunday newspapers make quite acceptable paper for painting. There are usually no pictures, no big black type, no heavy lines to introduce pattern. Three year olds usually accept this as unblemished paper; fours and fives may not.

READY TO PAINT

Don't forget the smocks or coverall aprons. Protect the floor with newspapers or plastic. Children should stand to paint.

Be sure to put the names and the date on the papers before they begin to paint. Show them how to tap the brush gently on the edge of the paint jar to eliminate excess paint. Hang the finished painting on a clothes line or rack to dry.

TO MAKE PAINTS GO FURTHER

Make a thick gravy of cornstarch and water by dissolving one tablespoon of cornstarch in a cup of cold water. Bring to a boil, stirring frequently to prevent lumps. Boil three or four minutes and let cool. Add two tablespoons of this mixture to each jar of paint to extend and thicken it.

Clay

Many teachers now use Play-Doh or Kleen Klay. There are also many kinds of modeling material that are satisfactory, clean, and inexpensive for children to use. Plasticine is least satisfactory. It is not easily pliable and therefore not interesting.

Regular clay can be purchased from art supply stores. Five pounds is enough clay for ten children. If your church school is large, it would probably be less expensive to purchase clay in fifty-pound drums. Each teacher or department could have a supply stored in a plastic bag. The bag should be covered with a wet towel and placed in an airtight container. Taking care of clay is not difficult, but it must be kept moist to be usable.

Cleaning clay off table tops takes some minutes each week. Some churches provide thin smooth boards sixteen inches square for each child to use. This makes cleaning up afterwards much easier.

By all means try the homemade modeling materials, even if you also have regular clay. Homemade dough clay is cheap, easy to make, and clean to use. It can be stored several weeks if kept moist. Also it can easily be colored with vegetable coloring or tempera paint. This colored dough clay appeals to some children who would not be at all interested in the regular gray clay.

To play with clay, children need only the clay and a place to work comfortably. They will be more creative with the material if they do not have such things as doll dishes, cookie cutters, rolling pins, and tongue depressors. If they have dishes, they will fill them with clay. If they have rolling and cutting equipment, they will roll and cut. They will not push, squeeze, pat, slap, stick together, or knock apart, perhaps while singing or imagining a story or expressing a strong feeling. Children are not expressive with clay when they have equipment or suggestions for how to use it.

Often a young child has no idea of wanting to save a clay creation to take home. However, if the child wants to save it, any object can be put aside to dry and then painted with thick tempera paint before being taken home. Regular clay cracks easily after it is dry, but the salt and flour dough clay and the cornstarch dough clay are quite strong.

Cornstarch Dough Clay

Mix one cup of salt, one-half cup cornstarch, and one-half cup water in pan. Add vegetable color or dry tempera paint if you care to. Cook over low fire, stirring constantly, until too stiff to stir. When cool, knead until smooth.

SALT AND FLOUR DOUGH CLAY

Proportions of salt to flour can be varied. Some recipes say twice as much salt as flour; others say equal amounts. I find one third cup salt to one cup flour a very satisfactory proportion. Add color, if you wish, and enough water (about four tablespoons) to form an easily handled dough clay. If you get it too sticky, add more flour and keep kneading it in. If you wrap this material in aluminum foil, slip it in a plastic bag, and put it in the refrigerator, it will keep indefinitely. Remember to take it out an hour or two before session time so that the dough clay will warm up and become pliable. If the edges dry and harden, trim them off.

CRAYONING

Use the large, thick crayons of strong, clear colors for preschoolers. Eight colors are probably enough variety. To practice sharing, two children could use one box. Provide manila construction paper, twelve by eighteen inches, for crayon work. You don't need the heaviest paper, but avoid buying paper so thin that it wrinkles or tears in use.

Here, too, children are at their creative best if they do not have an outline or picture to color. Many preschoolers cannot color within the lines of a picture. Their small-muscle development is not up to that, and the effort is frustrating. The children, however, enjoy making large, free, vigorous strokes on tempting blank sheets of paper.

Cutting and Pasting

MATERIALS YOU NEED

Blunt-nosed, easily operated children's scissors
Construction paper in a variety of colors, 9 x 12 inches
Glue sticks

CUTTING

Some preschoolers can operate scissors and like to cut and snip for the sheer fun of being able to do it. Others are not interested at all and do not even hold the scissors correctly. Do not try to teach preschool children to cut. It is a rather precise, small-muscle activity, and most children are not ready to do anything but snip away. At the beginning of the year, cutting and pasting will be two separate activities for most of the children. At the end of the year there may be some who will cut something, lay down the scissors, and proceed to paste what they have cut.

The cutting preschoolers I know like to cut something with pictures on it as well as plain sheets of construction paper. Discarded toy catalogs are tops on the list. (My daughter searched through the pages of toys until she came to her favorites, the "giddy-ups," and she spent fifteen minutes at a time slashing them to bits.) Preschoolers do not understand cutting out as opposed to cutting up. The way they do it makes no difference to them, so it shouldn't to you. If you furnish old magazines for cutting, be sure to talk about the fact that they are *old* magazines that their parents do not want anymore.

PASTING

A scrap box of colored scraps of construction paper makes a fine source of pasting material. Since there is no picture on either side, the child can glue whichever side comes up, turn it over, and have the same shape and color he started with. Happy preschoolers do not comprehend turning the pasted side over. They plaster another piece of paper on top. That's all right. The reason for this activity—as for all the others in the preschool—is not to have the child create something, but to provide an opportunity for fun exploring and experimenting with the material. If you provide recognizable triangles, squares, rectangles, and circles (none smaller than two inches) in the scrap box, these shapes may be very suggestive to some children.

MAKING EQUIPMENT

Church preschool equipment should be simple and sturdily constructed. Good equipment can be purchased from any of the companies listed on page 239. You will want to send for their catalogs. Most of the equipment, however, can be constructed by members of your own congregation at a fraction of the cost of commercial products. The following pages give instructions for making some of the basic items you will need.

Block Center

First, provide a place to store the blocks and cars, trucks, tractors, and other toys used with the blocks. Open shelves on which the blocks can be neatly stacked are probably best. One ingenious teacher made temporary storage space by setting two boxes on their sides a few feet apart and placing a long board across the top to form a shelf for the toys. The blocks were stored in the boxes and on the floor under the shelf.

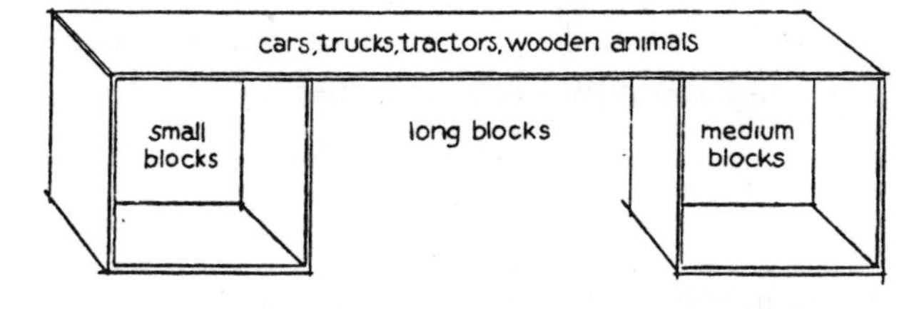

UNIT BLOCKS

Unit blocks are most satisfying to young builders. This means that blocks should be multiples of a basic size. For instance, if you use approximately brick size as your basic unit, your block dimensions would be as follows:

one unit:	$5\frac{1}{2} \times 2\frac{3}{4} \times 1\frac{3}{8}$ inches
half unit:	$2\frac{3}{4} \times 2\frac{3}{4} \times 1\frac{3}{8}$ inches
double unit:	$11 \times 2\frac{3}{4} \times 1\frac{3}{8}$ inches
quadruple unit:	$22 \times 2\frac{3}{4} \times 1\frac{3}{8}$ inches

To make unit blocks, cut hard wood according to the above dimensions. Sandpaper and smooth the corners. The units should be cut carefully so that children can have satisfying building experiences.

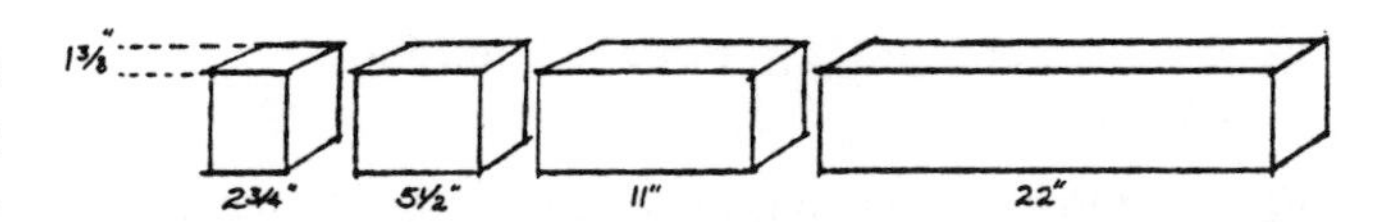

HOLLOW BLOCKS

Young children like to make steps and other structures using large hollow blocks. These are available commercially constructed of lightweight materials that are easy to lift and are quieter to use than wooden blocks. However, the wooden ones are not difficult to make and are less expensive. Like the smaller building blocks, these should be constructed in multiples of one unit.

one unit	6 × 6 × 12 inches
half unit	6 × 6 × 6 inches or 6 × 3 × 12 inches
double unit	6 × 6 × 24 inches or 6 × 12 × 12 inches

Some church schools use the large hollow blocks as chairs.

one unit	8 × 8 × 8 inches
half unit	8 × 4 × 8 inches
double unit	8 × 8 × 16 inches

These blocks are more convenient to use if a groove is cut in one end for lifting. Use hardwood or plywood. Sand and varnish or paint with a nontoxic paint.

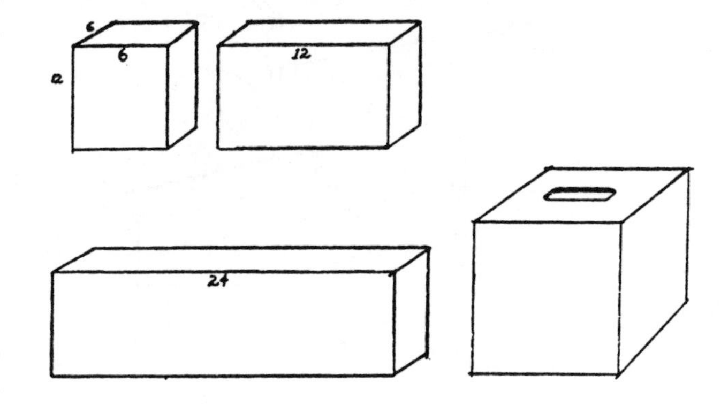

HOUSEKEEPING CENTER

This interest center may be as simple or elaborate as your space and ingenuity allow. Minimum equipment should be a doll bed, large enough for a preschooler to curl up in it, and a small, low table and two chairs. A cupboard to hold the dishes, a stove, and a sink will add to the possibilities for dramatic play. If you have room, add a refrigerator, an ironing board, a doll high chair, and a rocking chair. The equipment catalogs will suggest other items you may want to add. Be sure to have a box for dress-up clothes. Suggestions for making basic equipment are given below.

DOLL BED

The most important thing about the doll bed is that it be at least eighteen inches wide and thirty-two to thirty-six inches long so that the children can lie down on it as well as put their dolls to bed. This also means it should be sturdily constructed and braced. Three ways to make beds are shown here. Your do-it-yourself carpenters may have other suggestions.

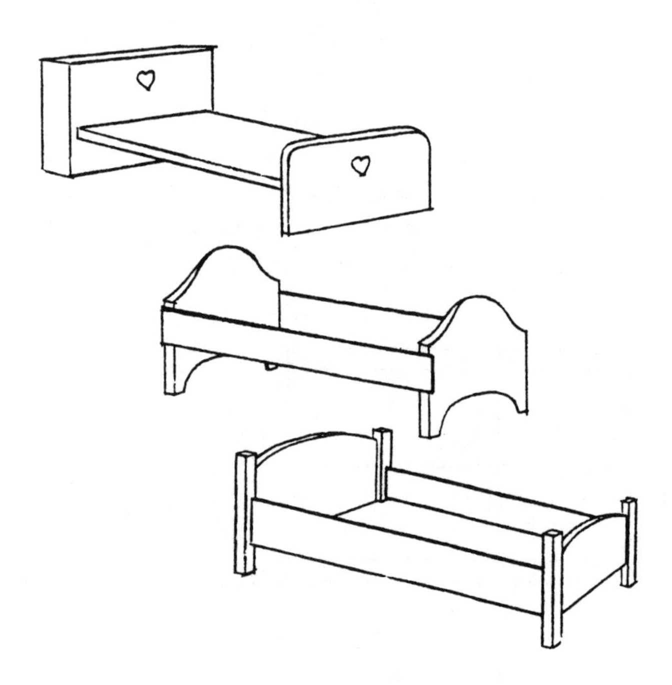

DISH CUPBOARD

Colored plastic crates stack easily to make cupboards. Cloth curtains can be hung across the front if you want to hide the contents.

STOVE

A stout wooden box stood on end can be made into a very acceptable stove. It should stand sixteen to twenty inches high. Sand and paint with white or pastel enamel. Paint black rings on the top to represent burners. Attach knobs across the front. Be sure the knobs can be turned! If your carpenter wants to add to the dramatic possibilities of the stove, he or she could turn the box around, nail a strip of wood across the front on which to fasten the knobs, and hinge on a piece of wood to make an oven door.

If your carpenters are using lumber to construct a stove, they will be able to use larger dimensions than those suggested for a box stove. A good size would be twelve inches deep, sixteen to eighteen inches wide, and about twenty-four inches high.

SINK

A sink in your housekeeping center can provide safe, relaxing water play. There are always doll clothes and dishes that preschoolers can wash and wash and wash. They may even give the baby a bath in the sink. A wooden cupboard arrangement, as pictured on page 227, can be made easily. Use a removable plastic pan to hold the water. A deep pan about half full of water is more satisfactory than a shallow pan and will cause less splashing. A sink with a counter is as much appreciated by preschoolers as busy parents. However, the simple construction is very acceptable. Sinks should be about twenty-four inches high, eighteen to twenty-four inches wide (depending upon type of cabinet), and about twelve inches deep.

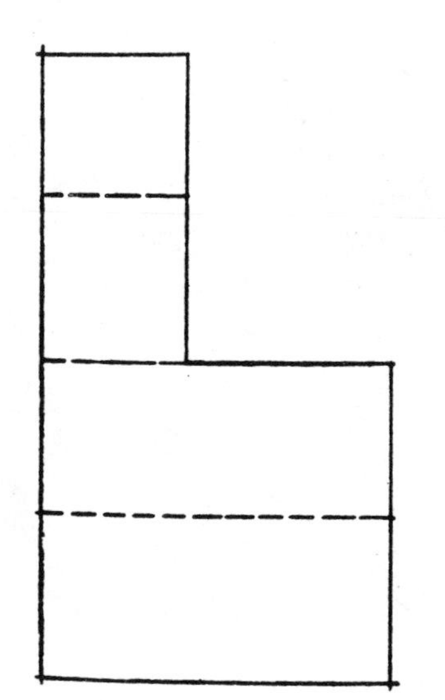

Art Activities Equipment

TABLES AND CHAIRS

Good, sturdy chairs designed for correct posture are important equipment for the preschool. It is better to use no chairs than chairs the wrong height, folding chairs that may pinch fingers, or chairs that encourage poor posture. Seats should be eight or ten inches from the floor. You need only enough chairs to seat about one third of your group.

Tables for art work should be ten inches higher than the chair seats, forty-eight inches long, and thirty inches wide. This allows space for four children to work on sheets of twelve-by-eighteen-inch paper at each table. Table tops should be finished for easy cleaning.

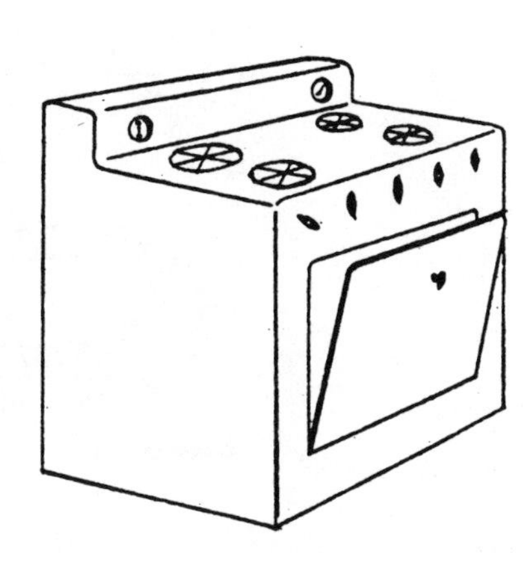

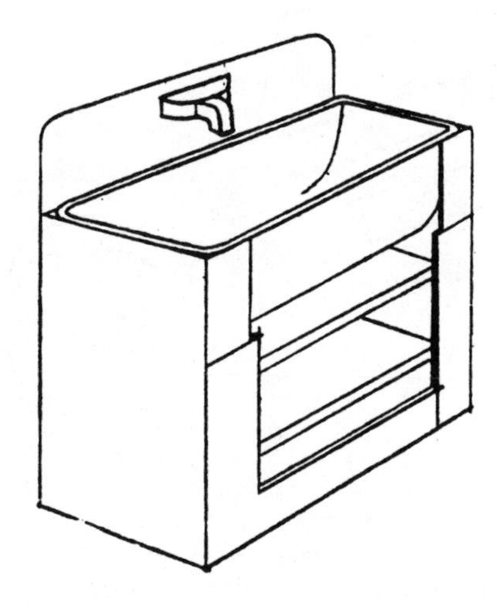

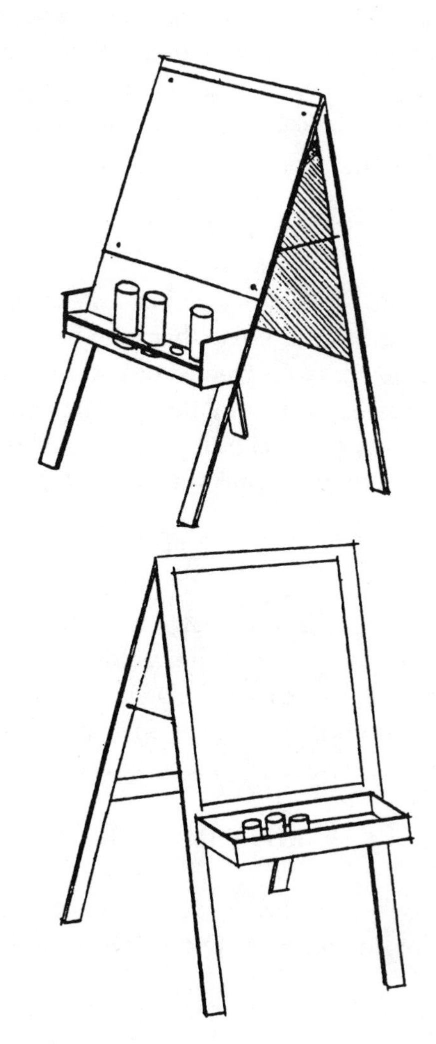

EASELS

Lightweight easels (page 227) can be constructed locally. They should be forty inches high with twenty-four-inch-square working surfaces. The shelf across the bottom should be three or four inches wide, depending upon the size of the paint jars you use, and deep enough to hold the jars safely in place.

Rhythm Instruments

DRUM

Remove the top and bottom from a large can. Cut out two round pieces of rubber (from old inner tubes or other sources of heavy rubber) and punch holes around their edges. Stretch these pieces over the top and bottom of the can and lace back forth as shown. An empty oatmeal box with the cover taped down or a coffee can with a plastic top make acceptable drums. Sticks or wooden spoons make good drumsticks.

RATTLES

Place some pebbles, rice, or beans in small boxes or cans. Empty spice boxes, bandage boxes, or small baking powder cans painted or covered with bright paper may be used. For different sound effects, try a few tacks or paper clips in some of the boxes. Tape the covers onto the cans with sticky tape.

BELLS

Sew small bells (especially plentiful during the Christmas season) to brightly colored strips of cloth, heavy ribbon, or half-inch elastic. The strips may be sewed together at the ends to make bracelets for children to wear around their wrists.

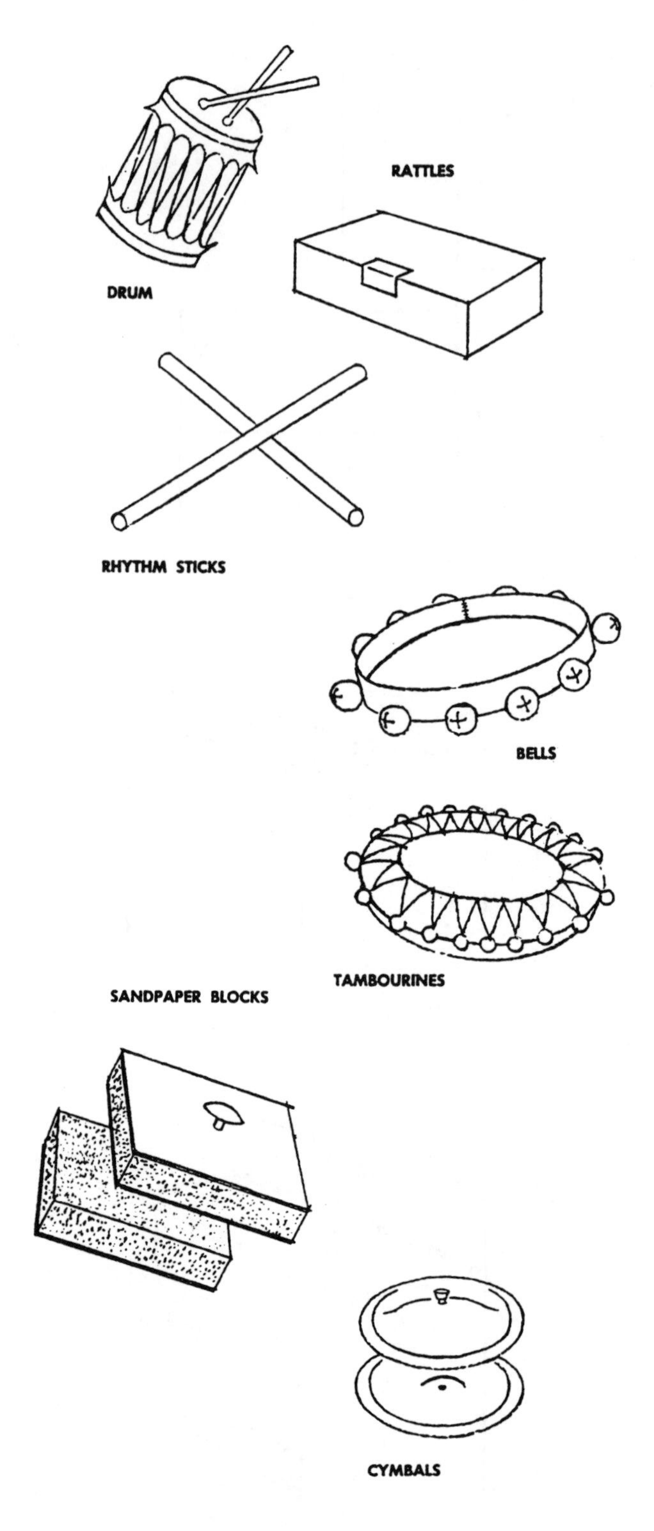

RHYTHM STICKS

Purchase $\frac{3}{8}$-inch dowel sticks from your hardware store or lumberyard. Cut in twelve-inch lengths. Make several pairs of these. Children tap the sticks together to make the sound.

TAMBOURINES

Lace together two small paper plates. Plastic craft strips, yarn, or string may be used for lacing. Attach small bells to the plastic, yarn, or string. Children hold the tambourine in one hand and shake it or strike it gently against the other hand.

SANDPAPER BLOCKS

Nail or glue sandpaper to one side of a flat wooden block (about 4 x 5 x 1 inch). Attach a spool or cupboard doorknob to the opposite side to make a handle. Rub the sandpaper surfaces together to produce an interesting sound.

CYMBALS

Obtain two flat pan lids that have knobs. Show the child using these how to brush them together to make one sound and clap them together to make another.

HORNS

Take a cylinder from a roll of paper towels, plastic wrap, wax paper, or foil. Cover the roll with foil and let the children toot through the cylinder.

Room Dividers

ONE-PANEL SCREENS

Low, single-panel screens can be used to separate the preschool from other groups meeting in the same room or serve as walls dividing different activities in the preschool room. Screens should be thirty-two to thirty-four inches high and forty-eight to fifty inches long. A wallboard panel in a wooden frame serves as a sound deadener and is a good surface for thumbtacking pictures. Pegboard panels may also be used for mounting pictures and can have shelves attached to hold books and wonder objects. Plywood or Masonite panels may also be used.

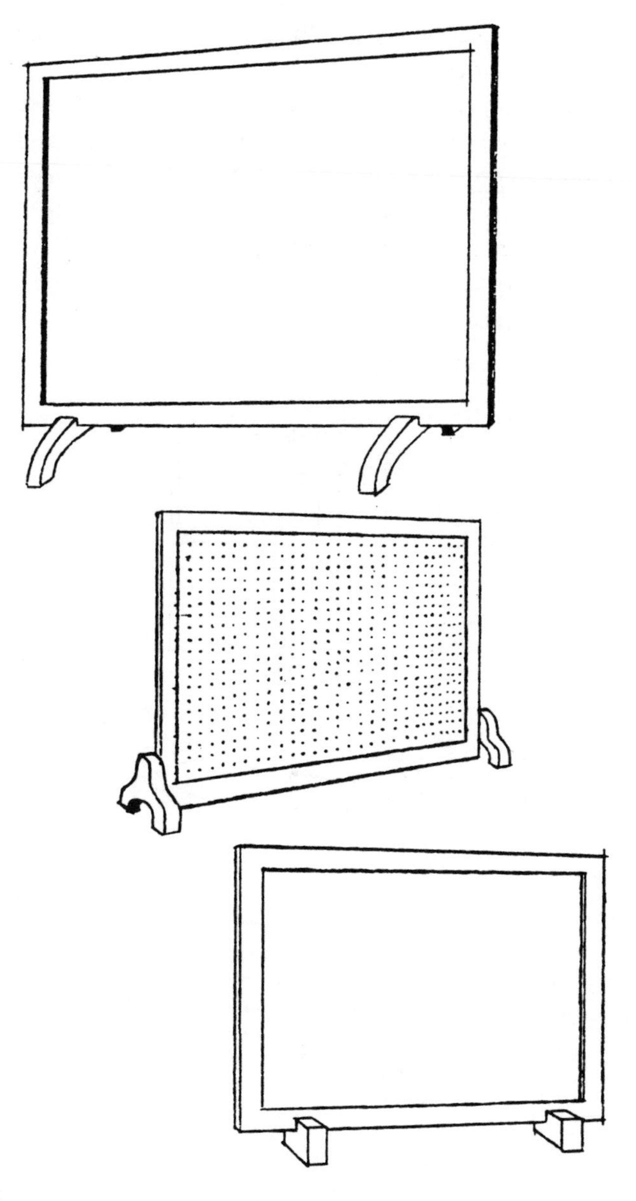

OPEN-SHELF CABINETS

Open storage cabinets for blocks, art materials, puzzles, small toys, and books can double as room dividers. The dimensions of the cabinets will depend upon the space you have. Thirty-six to forty inches is a good height. To store art materials and blocks, you need shelves at least twelve inches deep. If the cabinets are used in the preschool room to serve as walls for the housekeeping and other interest centers, the backs of the cabinets may be made from wallboard or pegboard and used to display pictures.

Mount the cabinets on casters if they are to be moved frequently.

For churches with limited space and multiple-use rooms, two cabinets hinged together at one end and mounted on casters provide good through-the-week storage space for preschool equipment and materials. When needed the cabinets can be rolled into place and opened to form two walls for the preschool space or room.

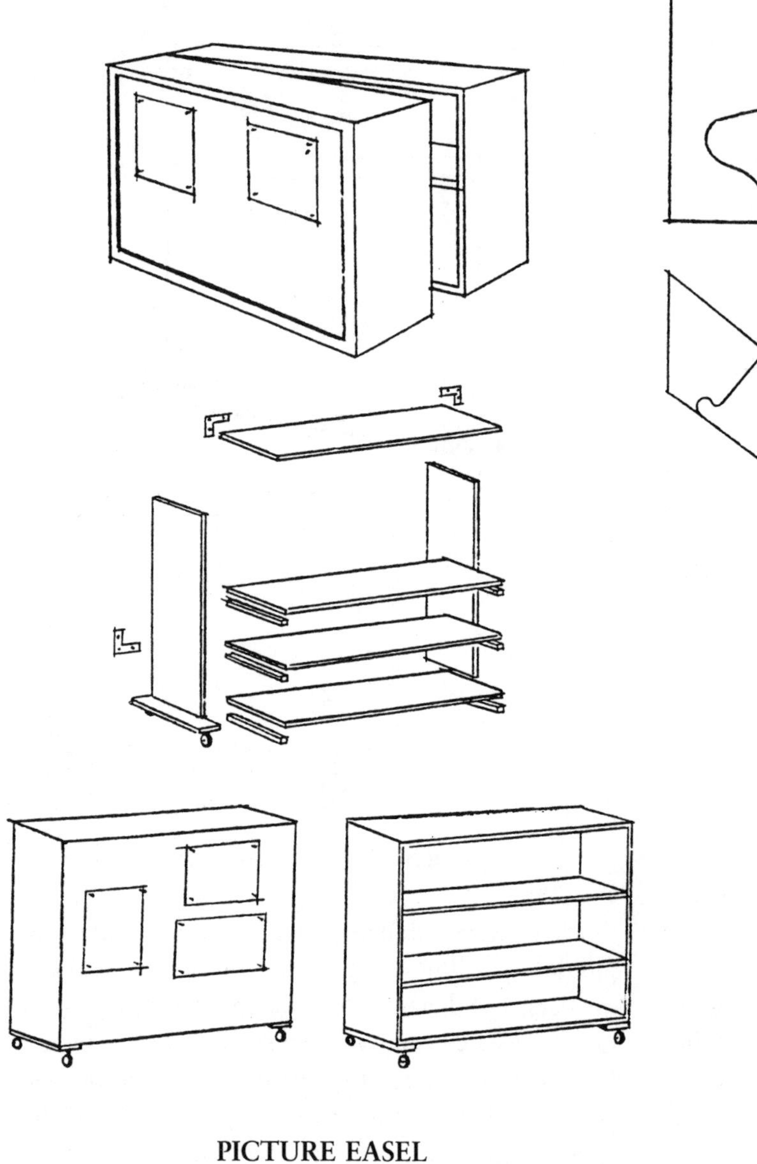

PICTURE EASEL

A temporary easel can be made by folding a piece of lightweight cardboard in half and cutting as shown below. A permanent wooden easel is more satisfactory and easy to make. An easel ten inches wide and twelve inches high is needed for large pictures, eight by ten inches for smaller pictures. Cut out the side pieces with a jigsaw and brace with straight strips or dowel rods.

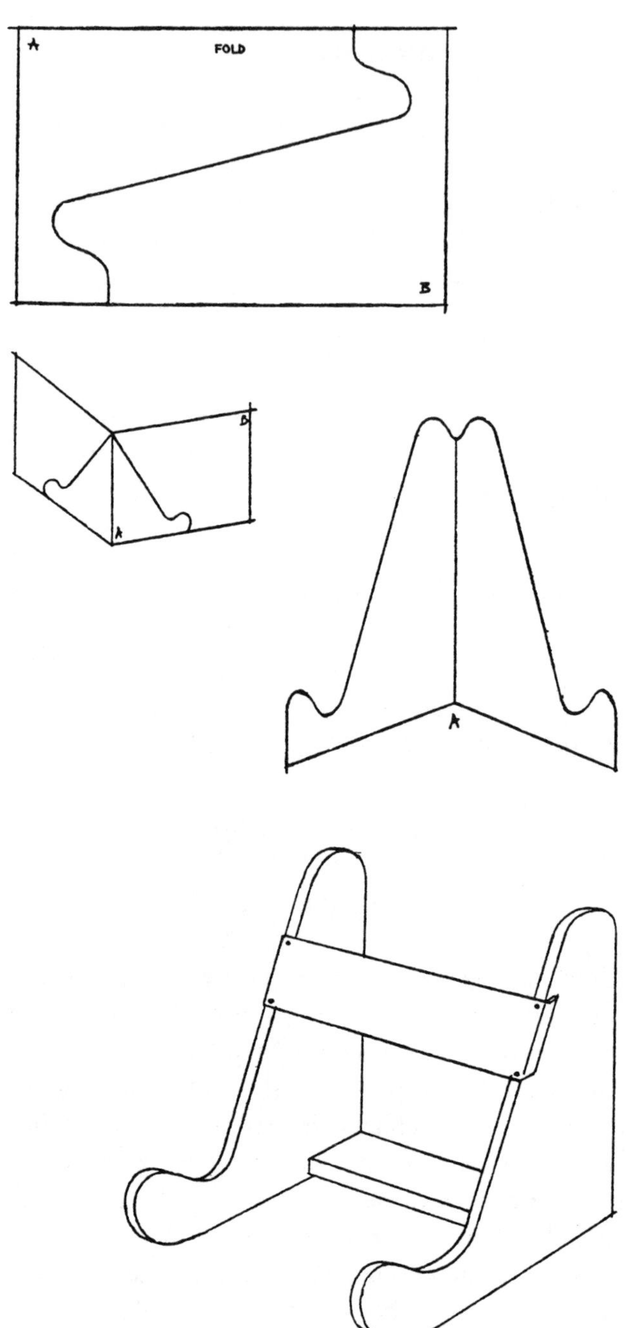

SUPPLIES

(Quantities suggested are for a group of fifteen children. This is a suggested listing. You will want to add other supplies and equipment to meet the needs of your children.)

Art Activity Center

BASIC EQUIPMENT

Crayons (a box of 8 for every 2 children) and manila paper
Clay or other molding material
Glue sticks, pictures or shapes for pasting, construction paper

OTHER

Finger paint, shelf paper, and sponges
Smocks or aprons
Tempera paint, brushes, newsprint, and easels

Block Center

BASIC EQUIPMENT

Unit dimensional blocks
Well-constructed cars and trucks, all sizes

OTHER

Tractors
Trains (interlocking, wheeled or flat-bottomed)
Boats
Wooden animals
Wooden people
Pull toys

Book and Puzzle Center

BASIC EQUIPMENT

8 to 10 picture story books
4 to 6 puzzles (limited pieces)

OTHER

2 stacks of blocks
Wooden beads to string
Mounted pictures (a year's supply, not to be used all at one time)

Housekeeping Center

BASIC EQUIPMENT

3 dolls and doll clothes
Doll bed or cradle; baskets, bassinets, buggies
Table, 2 chairs
Cupboard; soft plastic plates, cups, saucers (not too small), coffee or teapot, sturdy pots and pans

OTHER

Chest for doll clothes
Dress-up clothes
Dustpan, broom, sweeper, ironing board, Iron
Toy stove
Toy refrigerator

Supplies for Larger Areas

Climbing equipment
Doll buggies or strollers
Train or truck to ride on
Rocking boat
Slide
Bouncing horse
Pounding toys

Teacher's Supply Cupboard

First-aid kit
Picture file
Ball of string
Scissors
Sticky tape, markers, pencils
Rubber bands
Paper clips
Paper punch
Push pins
Small paper bags
Rags and sponges
Newspapers
Paper towels
Tissues
Basket (with handle) for cookies
Napkins
Picture stand, cloth, vases for special table
Reserve activity toys:
  rhythm instruments
  large balls
  Nerf balls

ROOM DESIGNS

Shared Space for Preschoolers

This is one end of a thirty-by-fifty-foot room shared by four groups on Sunday morning and used as a social hall during the week. The preschool space is approximately ten by twenty feet. It will accommodate six to eight children. Blocks, toys, books, and puzzles are kept in the hinged cupboard during the week. Housekeeping equipment and special table are lined along the wall with the dividing screens in front of them.

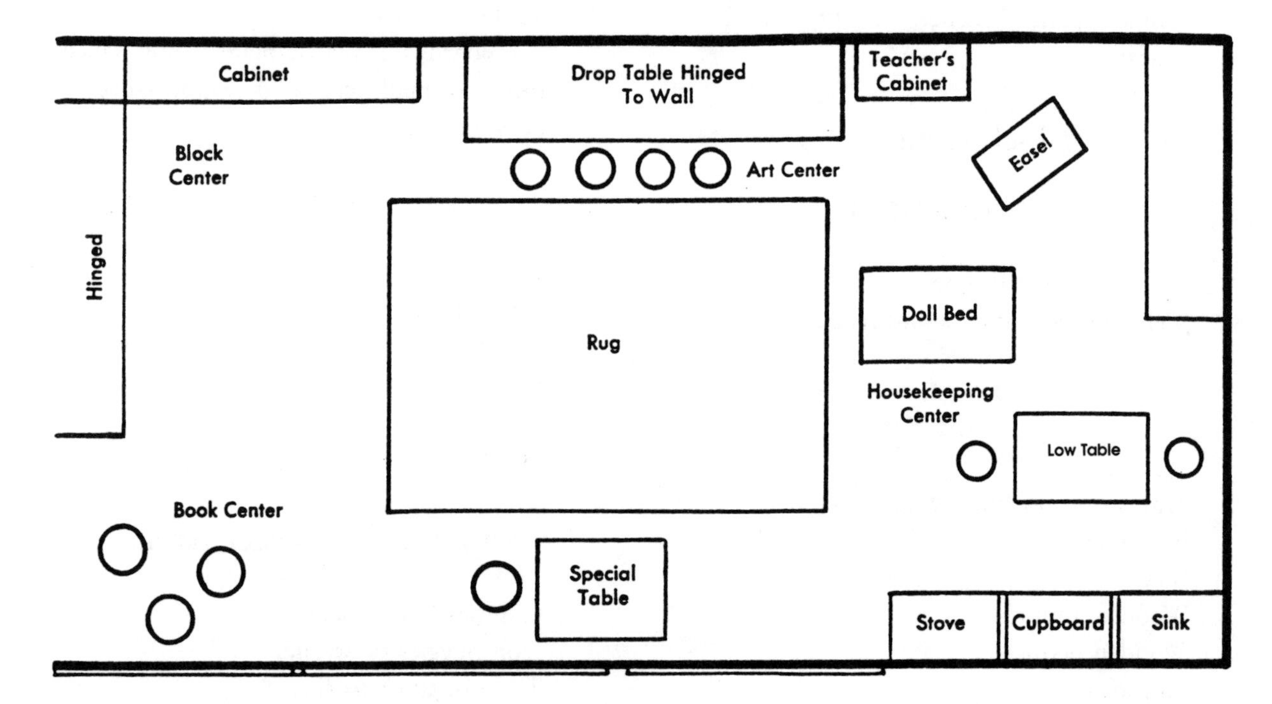

Preschool Space in a One-Room Church

Preschool children need a place of their own, even in a one-room church. This space may be in a corner at the back or front of the church. A pew serves as a table for art work, books, and puzzles. Simple housekeeping equipment and special table are stored under the pew when not in use. An area about eight by fourteen feet (counting some aisle space) can accommodate three or four preschoolers.

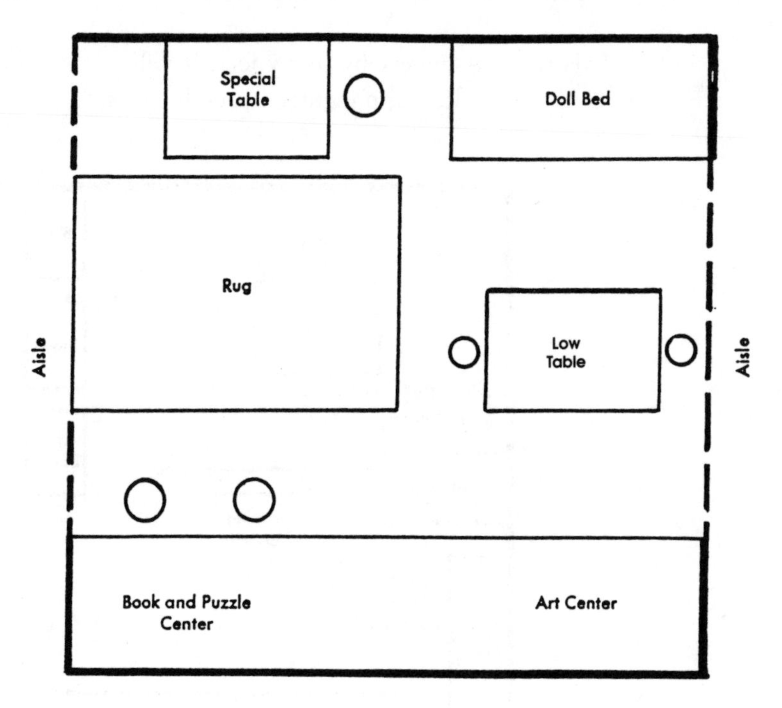

Separate Room for Preschoolers

This room is twenty by thirty feet. It will accommodate fifteen to eighteen preschoolers.

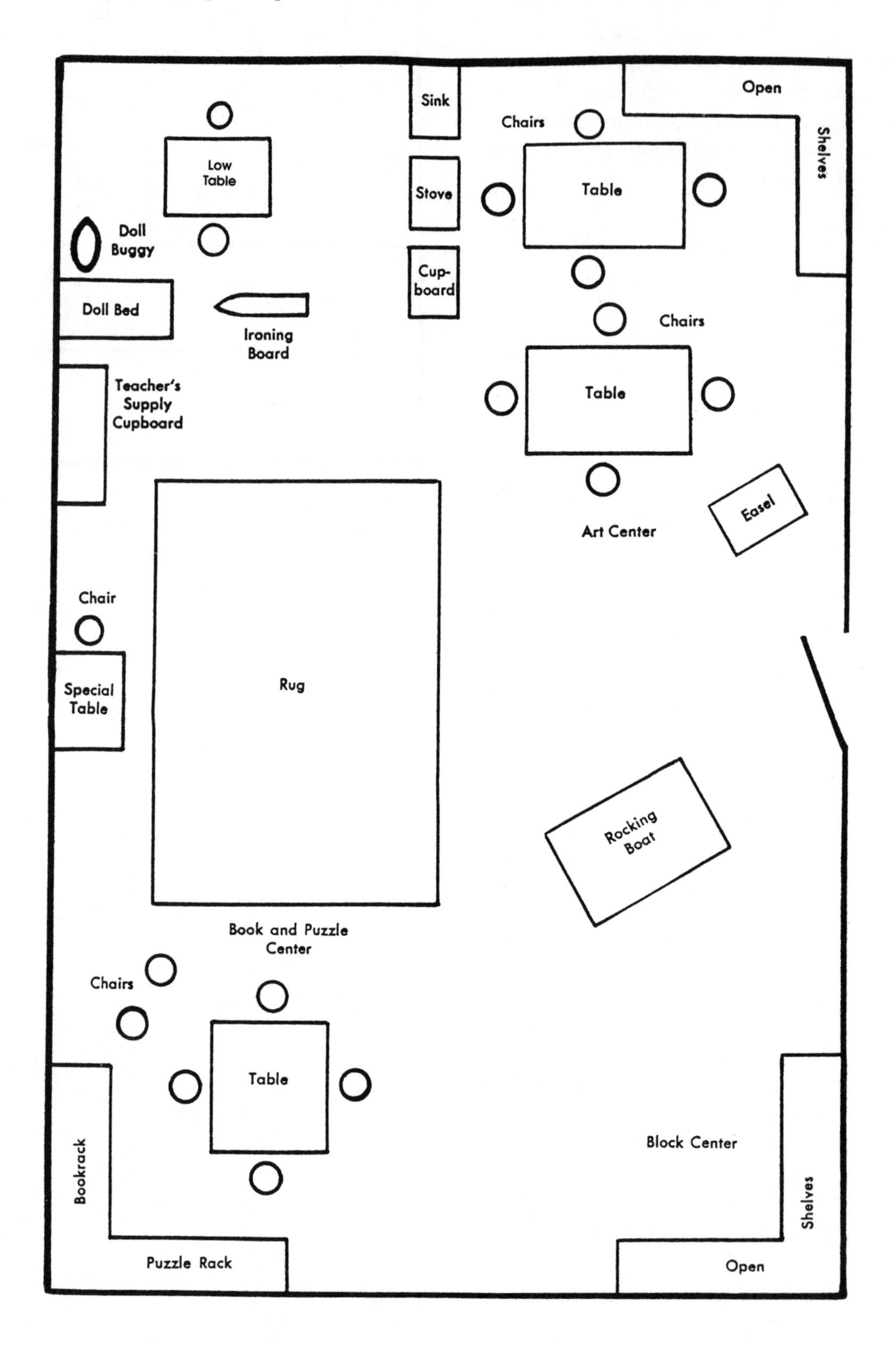

Bibliography

Books for Teachers

CHILD DEVELOPMENT AND EDUCATIONAL ISSUES

Ames, Louise Bates, and Frances L. Ilg. *Your Three-Year-Old: Friend or Enemy*. New York: Dell Publishing Co., 1980.

_____. *Your Four-Year-Old: Wild and Wonderful*. New York: Dell Publishing Co., 1980.

_____. *Your Five-Year-Old: Sunny and Serene*. New York: Dell Publishing Co., 1980.

Ayers, William. *The Good Preschool Teacher: Six Teachers Reflect on Their Lives*. New York: Teachers College, 1980.

Beaty, Janice J. *Observing Development of the Young Child in an Early Childhood Classroom Setting*. 2d ed. New York: Merill, Macmillan Publishing Co., 1990.

Elkind, David. *Miseducation: Preschoolers at Risk*. New York: Alfred A. Knopf, 1987.

Frailberg, Selma. *The Magic Years: Understanding and Handling the Problems of Early Childhood*. New York: Charles Scribner's Sons, 1959.

Garvey, Catherine. *Play*. Cambridge, Mass.: Harvard University Press, 1990.

McKay, Bobbie. *What Ever Happened to the Family? A Psychologist Looks at Sixty Years of Change*. Cleveland, Ohio: United Church Press, 1991.

Paley, Vivian. *Mallie Is Three: Growing Up in School*. Chicago: University of Chicago Press, 1986.

Snyder, Martha. *The Young Child as Person: Toward the Development of Healthy Conscience*. New York: Human Sciences Press, 1980.

RESOURCES

Alberswerth, Roy F., and Deborah Alberswerth Payden. *Talking With Your Child About the Church Year.* Growing Together Series (booklets). Cleveland, Ohio: United Church Press, 1992.

Anderson, Craig V. *Talking With Your Child About the Bible*. Growing Together Series (booklets). Cleveland, Ohio: United Church Press, 1992.

Cole, Joanna, and Stephanie Calmenson. *The Eentsy, Weentsy Spider: Fingerplays and Action Rhymes*. New York: Morrow Junior Books, 1991.

Day, Barbara. *Early Childhood Education: Creative Learning Activities*. 3d ed. New York: Macmillan Publishing Co., 1988.

Dowell, Ruth D. *Move Over Mother Goose: Fingerplays, Action Verses & Funny Rhymes*. Mt. Rainer, Md.: Gryphar House, 1987.

Edwards, Sandra Vasel. *Talking With Your Child About Worship*. Growing Together Series (booklets). Cleveland, Ohio: United Church Press, 1991.

Griggs, Patricia. *Using Storytelling in Christian Education*. Nashville, Tenn.: Abingdon Press, 1981.

Harle-Mould, Linda and Hope. *Talking With Your Child About God's Story.* Growing Together Series (booklets). Cleveland, Ohio: United Church Press, 1993.

Hawkes, Mary, and Paul Hamill, eds. *Sing to God: Songs and Hymns for Christian Education*. Cleveland, Ohio: United Church Press, 1984. [Try #s 5, 22, 24, 25, 28,

42, 50, 55, 65, 74, 77, 78, 120, and 125 with preschool children.]

MacCarteney, Laura Pendleton. *Songs for the Nursery School.* Florence, Ky.: The Willis Music Company, 1937. [Still in print.]

Myers, Barbara Kimes and William R. *Engaging in Transcendence: The Church's Ministry and Covenant with Young Children.* Cleveland, Ohio: Pilgrim Press, 1992.

Nagel, Myra B. *Talking With Your Child About Prayer.* Growing Together Series (booklets). Cleveland, Ohio: United Church Press, 1991.

Ostermiller, R. Kenneth. *Talking With Your Child About Sexuality.* Growing Together Series (booklets). Cleveland, Ohio: United Church Press, 1991.

Paley, Vivian. *The Boy Would be a Helicopter.* Cambridge, Mass.: Harvard University Press, 1990. [Storytelling]

Parker, Kathryn Elmes. *Talking With Your Child About Feelings.* Growing Together Series (booklets). Cleveland, Ohio: United Church Press, 1991.

Prince, Barbara. *Talking With Your Child About AIDS.* Growing Together Series (booklets). Cleveland, Ohio: United Church Press, 1993.

Rosner, Patrice. *Consider the Children: Planning for Young Children During Worship.* St. Louis, Mo.: Christian Board of Publication, 1990.

Schroer, Ann. *Guide for Ministry with Young Children.* Memphis, Tenn.: Board of Christian Education, Cumberland Presbyterian Church, 1988. [24 pages. Also available from United Church Press, Cleveland, Ohio.]

Smith, Judy Gattis. *Teaching to Wonder.* Nashville, Tenn.: Abingdon Press, 1989.

———. *Teaching with Music Through the Church Year.* Nashville, Tenn.: Abingdon Press, 1979.

Smith, Nancy. *Experience and Art: Teaching Children to Paint.* New York: Teachers College Press, 1983.

Wichert, Susanne. *Keeping the Peace: Practicing Cooperation and Conflict Resolution with Preschoolers.* Philadelphia: New Society Publishers, 1989.

An excellent monthly magazine for children, ages 2–7, is *Ladybug* by the publishers of *Cricket* magazine. It is filled with stories, poems, songs, puzzles, and activities that are good for both groups and individuals. Each issue is centered on an appropriate theme. For information write: Ladybug, P.O. Box 50284, Boulder, CO 80321-0284. Phone 1-800-284-7257.

The National Association for the Education of Young Children (NAEYC) publishes a Beginners Bibliography as well as paperback books such as *Discipline* and *Caring.* Write or call for the bibliography and an early childhood education resources catalog. For information write: NAEYC, 1834 Connecticut Avenue N.W., Washington, D.C. 20009. Phone 1-800-424-2460 or 1-202-232-8777.

Books for Children

This list contains both classic and new titles. Your church and local library may have these, as well as other fine new books and books that are out of print. Librarians, bookstore personnel, and teachers can all be helpful resources for your particular needs. This list is one place to start. The thematic groupings are suggestions for use. The reference in brackets indicates the racial/ethnic group of that book's characters and is listed to help you be inclusive in the books you select. These books are for all of God's children, and each book can be used to illustrate a number of themes. Enjoy them!

ANIMALS AND PETS

Brown, Margaret Wise. *Baby Animals.* New York: Random House, 1989.

———. *Big Red Barn.* New York: Harper & Row, 1990.

———. *The Runaway Bunny.* New York: Harper & Bros., 1941.

Carle, Eric. *Animals Animals.* New York: Philomel Books, 1989.

———. *Very Busy Spider.* New York: Philomel Books, 1984.

———. *The Very Hungry Caterpillar.* New York: Philomel Books, 1987.

Flack, Marjorie. *Ask Mr. Bear.* New York: Macmillan, 1958.

Keats, Ezra Jack. *Pet Show!* New York: Macmillan, 1972.

CHRISTMAS

Brown, Margaret Wise. *Christmas in the Barn.* New York: Harper & Row, 1985.

Clifton, Lucille. *Everett Anderson's Christmas.* New York: Henry Holt, 1991. [African American]

The Friendly Beasts: An Old English Christmas Carol. Illustrated by Tomie de Paola. New York: Putnam, 1981.

The Friendly Beasts: A Traditional Christmas Carol. Illustrated by Sarah Chamberlain. New York: Dutton Children's Books, 1991.

Wildsmith, Brian. *A Christmas Story*. New York: Knopf, 1989.

THE FAMILY AND BIRTH

Anglund, Joan W. *All About My Family*. New York: Scholastic, 1987.
Brown, Margaret Wise. *A Child's Good Night Book*. New York: Harper & Row, 1992.
_____. *Goodnight Moon*. New York: Harper & Row, 1975.
Clark, Ann Nolan. *In My Mother's House*. New York: Viking Press, 1991. [Tewa Native Americans]
Cole, Joanna. *How You Were Born*. New York: Morrow, 1984.
_____. *The New Baby at Your House*. New York: Morrow, 1985.
Dorros, Arthur. *Abuela*. New York: Dutton Children's Books, 1991. [Hispanic]
Kraus, Ruth. *The Bundle Book*. New York: Harper & Bros. 1951. [Out of print; may be found in libraries.]
McCloskey, Robert. *Make Way for Ducklings*. New York: Viking/Penguin, 1969.
Margolies, Barbara. *Rehoema's Journey*. New York: Scholastic, 1990. [African: Tanzania]
Roe, Eileen. *With My Brother/Con Mi Hermano*. New York: Bradbury Press, 1991. [English/Spanish]
Rogers, Fred. *The New Baby*. New York: Putnam, 1985.
Rylant, Cynthia. *When I Was Young in the Mountain*. Boston: Dutton, 1982.
Scott, Ann Herbert. *On Mother's Lap*. New York: McGraw Hill, 1972. [Native American]
_____. *Sam*. New York: McGraw Hill, 1967. [African American]
Sendak, Maurice. *Where the Wild Things Are*. New York: Harper & Row, 1963.
Sonnenborn, Ruth. *Friday Night Is Papa Night*. New York: Penguin, 1987. [Hispanic]
Zolotow, Charlotte. *A Father Like That*. New York: Harper & Row, 1971. [on not having a father]

FRIENDS AND HELPERS

Barrett, John M. *Oscar the Selfish Octopus*. New York: Human Sciences Press, 1978.
Brown, Margaret Wise. *Little Children*. New York: Harper & Row, 1971.
Dooley, Norah. *Everybody Cooks Rice*. Minneapolis, Minn.: Carolrhoda Books, Inc., 1991.
Freeman, Don. *Corduroy*. New York: Viking/Penguin, 1968.
Henkes, Kevin. *Chester's Way*. New York: Greenwillow Books, 1988.
Keats, Ezra Jack. *Louie*. New York: Greenwillow, 1983.
Lionni, Leo. *It's Mine*. New York: Knopf, 1986.
Morris, Ann. *Bread, Bread, Bread*. New York: Lothrop, Lee & Shepard (Morrow), 1989. [Multicultural]
Poling, Nancy Werking. *Most Ministers Wear Sneakers*. New York: The Pilgrim Press, 1991.
Rey, H. A. *Curious George*. Boston: Houghton Mifflin, 1988.
Rey, H. A. *Curious George Takes a Job*. Boston: Houghton Mifflin, 1975.
Spier, Peter. *People*. New York: Doubleday, 1980.
Ward, Lelia. *I Am Eyes—Ni Macho*. New York: Scholastic, 1987. [African: Swahili]
Yashima, Taro. *Crow Boy*. New York: Viking Press, 1955. [Japanese]

GROWING

Anhot, Catherine, and Laurence Anhot. *What I Like*. New York: G. P. Putman's Sons, 1991.
Kraus, Ruth. *The Carrot Seed*. New York: Harper & Bros., 1945.
Pearse, Patricia. *See How You Grow*. Hauppauge, N.Y.: Barron's Educational Series, 1988.
Ward, Lelia. *I Am Eyes—Ni Macho*. New York: Scholastic, 1987. [Hispanic]
Zolotow, Charlotte. *I Like to Be Little*. New York: HarperCollins, 1987.

SEASONS: FALL

Dalgliesh, Alice. *The Thanksgiving Story*. New York: Scribner's, 1954.
Ets, Marie Hall. *Gilberto and the Wind*. New York: Viking/Penguin, 1963.
Maas, Robert. *When Autumn Comes*. New York: Henry Holt, 1990.
Spier, Peter. *Rain*. New York: Doubleday, 1982.
Yashima, Taro. *Umbrella*. New York: Viking/Penguin, 1958. [Japanese]
Zolotow, Charlotte. *Over and Over*. New York: Harper & Bros., 1957. [all seasons]

SEASONS: WINTER

Keats, Ezra Jack. *The Snowy Day*. New York: Viking/Penguin, 1962. [African American]

Tresselt, Alvin. *White Snow, Bright Snow*. New York: Lothrop, Lee & Shepard, Morrow, 1988.

SEASONS: SPRING

Brown, Margaret Wise. *Home for a Bunny*. New York: Golden Books, 1956.

Brown, Ruth. *Ladybug, Ladybug*. New York: Dutton, 1988.

Ehlert, Lois. *Planting a Rainbow*. New York: Harcourt Brace Jovanovich, 1988.

Johnson, Crockett. *Will Spring Be Early or Will Spring Be Late*. New York: Crowell, 1959.

SEASONS: SUMMER

Albert, Burton. *Where Does the Trail Lead?* New York: Simon & Schuster, 1991.

Carlstrom, Nancy White. *Wild Wild Sunflower Child*. New York: Macmillan, 1987.

Zolotow, Charlotte. *The Summer Night*. New York: Harper Collins, 1991.

For assistance in developing this bibliography, John Barrett would like to thank Barbara Kimes Myers, Karen V. Mauer, and the staffs of the Bank Street College Bookstore and Books of Wonder, New York, New York.

ADDRESSES

Books

Bank Street College Bookstore
2875 Broadway
New York, NY 10025
(212) 678-1654
(Books for teachers and for children)

Books of Wonder
132 Seventh Avenue
New York, NY 10011
(800) 835-4315
(Books for children)

Cokesbury (United Methodist Publishing House)
201 Eighth Avenue South
P.O. Box 801
Nashville, TN 37202
(800) 672-1789

National Association for the Education of Young Children
1834 Connecticut Avenue, NW
Washington, DC 20009
(800) 424-2460

United Church Press/Pilgrim Press
700 Prospect Avenue East
Cleveland, OH 44115-1100
(800) 537-3394

Music Resources

Suzuki Corporation
P.O. Box 261030
San Diego, CA 92196-9877
(800) 854-1994

West Music Company
P.O. Box 5521
Coralville, IA 52241
(800) 397-9378

The Willis Music Company
7380 Industrial Road
Florence, KY 41042
(800) 354-9799

Equipment and Supplies

Chasdells, Inc.
9645 Gerwing Lane
Columbia, MD 21046
(301) 381-9611
(800) 242-7355

Childcraft
P.O. Box 3081
Edison, NJ 08810-3081
(800) 631-5682

Community Playthings
Route 215
Rifton, NY 12471
(914) 658–3141
(Maple unit blocks and other play equipment, made by Hutterian Brothers and Sisters)

Constructive Playthings
2008 West 103 Street
Leawood, KS 66206
(800) 255–6124

J. S. Hammett Co.
Five regional centers. Call for directory assistance, (800) 555–1212, for the center for your region. Ask for the Early Learning catalog.

New England School Supply
609 Silver Street
Agawam, MA 01101
(413) 786–9800
(800) 628–8608

Pictures and Posters

Check with your library or resource center to see if there are pictures and posters for loan. Art museums are another possible source. Many have catalogs.

National Association for the Education of Young Children
1834 Connecticut Avenue, NW
Washington, DC 20009
(800) 424–2460
(Multicultural, photo posters of young children)

Magazine for Children

Ladybug Magazine
Cricket Country Lane
Box 50284
Boulder, CO 80321–0284
(800) 284–7257
(Monthly magazine, ages 2–7)

Association

National Association for the Education of Young Children
1834 Connecticut Avenue, NW
Washington, DC 20009
(800) 424–2460
("For professionals and others dedicated to improving the quality of services for young children and their families")